Reproductive Rights in the Age of Human Rights

Alisa Von Hagel • Daniela Mansbach

Reproductive Rights in the Age of Human Rights

Pro-life Politics from Roe to Hobby Lobby

palgrave
macmillan

Alisa Von Hagel
University of Wisconsin
Superior, WI, USA

Daniela Mansbach
University of Wisconsin
Superior, WI, USA

ISBN 978-1-137-53951-9   ISBN 978-1-137-53952-6   (eBook)
DOI 10.1057/978-1-137-53952-6

Library of Congress Control Number: 2016937740

Cover design by Emma J Hardy

Printed on acid-free paper

This Palgrave Macmillan imprint is published by Springer Nature
The registered company is Nature America Inc. New York

CONTENTS

List of Figures

LIST OF TABLES

CHAPTER 1

The Reproductive Rights Debate in the Age of Human Rights

1 Introduction

In June 2014, the Supreme Court handed down their ruling in *Burwell v. Hobby Lobby*, a case involving a challenge to the 2010 law, the Patient Protection and Affordable Care Act (PPACA, which will here-in after be referred to as ACA). For-profit corporations challenged the requirement that health insurance plans with prescription coverage include all Food and Drug Administration (FDA)-approved forms of contraception. These corporations argued that this mandate violates the protections of religious liberty established in the free exercise clause of the First Amendment and the Religious Freedom Restoration Act (RFRA). The court ruled in favor of the plaintiffs, finding the requirement was a violation of federal law, because it created a substantial burden on the religious beliefs of the corporate entities in question. The ruling opens the possibility for further restrictions on abortion that are based on the protection of individuals' right to religious liberty. Thus, although the case focused specifically on the employer mandate, many in the pro-life movement view this ruling as a victory in their struggle to limit—and eventually eliminate—the right to abortion.

The debate over abortion has always included discussion of the rights of third-party actors who are secondary in the procedure itself; the right of medical professionals to refuse to participate in abortion or abortion-related services had been established since the 1970s. Specifically, the Church Amendment was adopted in 1973, prohibiting government

© The Editor(s) (if applicable) and The Author(s) 2016
A. Von Hagel, D. Mansbach, *Reproductive Rights in the Age of Human Rights*, DOI 10.1057/978-1-137-53952-6_1

officials from requiring physicians to perform abortion or sterilization based upon moral or religious objections to the practice. Further, restrictions on public funding for abortion were also first enacted during the 1970s, with the first prohibition on government funding for abortion passed in 1976. The Hyde Amendment, attached to the 1976 spending bill for the Departments of Labor, Health and Human Services, and Education, prohibited funding for abortion, primarily affecting Medicaid programming. Both conscience clauses and funding restrictions on abortion continue to be enacted at both the federal and state levels. Furthermore, both types of policies have greatly expanded over time in terms of the effect and breadth of the protections and restrictions imposed.

These two types of public policies have proven to be the most effective means for restricting or limiting access to abortion, particularly at the federal level. Nevertheless, until the case of *Hobby Lobby*, the pro-life strategy rarely focused on the rights of third-party actors. Prior to the *Hobby Lobby* case, the pro-life movement centered its attention on the rights of the fetus and the rights of women, the two subjects involved in the abortion procedure. In advocating for fetal rights, the primary focus and intent of the pro-life movement has been to eliminate access to abortion and secure the overturning of the decision in *Roe v. Wade*. This strategy, based upon the belief in the sanctity of life and the assumption that life begins at the moment of fertilization, represented the central focus of the movement until the mid-1990s. The failure to secure this goal—the complete elimination of the right to abortion—as well as the inability to produce any substantial change in public opinion regarding abortion led to the adoption of a new strategy. This new strategy focuses on women's rights and well-being, arguing that abortion physically and emotionally harms women. As a result, this strategy focuses on limiting access to abortion rather than eliminating it altogether. The development of the women-centered strategy has demonstrated that the pro-life movement is adaptable to changing circumstances and contexts, using new arguments and strategies to promote their cause.

The passage of the ACA in 2010, and the *Hobby Lobby* ruling in 2014, led to the adoption of new strategy by the pro-life movement, which complements the fetus-centered and women-centered strategies. This latest strategy advocates for the rights of third-party actors such as employers, with a special focus on the argument of religious liberty. As such, the ruling in *Hobby Lobby* introduces two main changes into the earlier pro-life discourse and its related public policy. First, the ruling shifted attention from rights that were traditionally at the heart of the debate over reproductive choices—such as the right to life, women's liberty and autonomy, and reproductive rights—to religious liberty. Specifically, both the fetus-centered and women-centered discourses aimed to change people's opinion on abortion through emphasis on the sanctity of life as well as the harm abortion causes women. The focus on freedom of religion, however, shifts the argument away from the debate over the meaning and implications of abortion; in this case, supporting the pro-life movement does not require people to oppose abortion, only to agree that individuals have the right to freedom of religion, or, more generally, freedom from government control. In addition to the changing argument, the focus on religious liberty also represents a shift in pro-life strategy; while the movement has historically been driven by religious adherents who believe in the sanctity of life because of biblical dictates, the movement as a whole has worked to minimize the use of religious arguments, particularly in their public campaigns and fetus-centered discourse. Including religious liberty as a right that is violated during the course of an abortion adds to the issues that are part of the debate over reproductive rights, while also allowing the pro-life movement to further distinguish their work from that of the pro-choice movement.

Second, this ruling introduces a new set of actors in need of protection in the practice of abortion. Initially, the pro-life movement focused solely on the protection of the fetus, placing the movement in opposition to the pro-choice movement, which advocates for women's reproductive choice and autonomy. This fetus-centered discourse often defined women as the source of the threat, situating them in direct conflict with the fetus that needs to be saved. Through subsuming women's rights and health within their discourse in the 1990s, the pro-life movement was able to address the critique of pro-choice activists, as well as others who demanded that women's complex decision-making process is taken seriously. With the *Hobby Lobby* ruling, the pro-life movement expands the participants they will protect, adding employers to the other third party actors they aim to protect. This new group is unique in the subjects it adds to this debate; while the fetus, the mother, as well as health-care professionals are all directly involved or play a role in the procedure in some way or another, employers do not have a direct or active role in the abortion process. Therefore, their inclusion as third-party actors significantly broadens the range of participants whose rights need to be considered in this debate; it now includes persons with religious objection to abortion.

As this account shows, the pro-life movement has expanded the claims made and subjects it protects, creating a complex and broad pro-life strategy that is more inclusive now than ever. These shifts and transitions are quite unusual in the abortion debate as the pro-choice movement is often criticized for its stagnant and unchanging arguments (Calmes 2014; Eckholm 2011; Loonan 2003). At the same time, the pro-life movement has been able to remain relevant, maintaining its support despite the shift within the American public toward greater acceptance of libertarian positions, such as support for same-sex marriage and the legalization of drugs (Leonhardt and Parlapiano 2015). Within this context, this book examines the evolution of the pro-life movement's strategy from the post-*Roe v. Wade* era through the *Burwell v. Hobby Lobby* ruling in 2014, to reveal the ways in which this movement has remained effective. Through analysis of the evolution of the pro-life discourse and public policy outcomes concerning access to abortion, this project provides three main contributions to the existing research on reproductive rights in particular, and right-wing politics in the USA in general.

First, this book traces the development of the pro-life strategy, analyzing its relationship to and use of the human rights framework and arguments. From 1973 to 2015, we argue, the pro-life strategy can be divided into three separate time periods, each with a focus on different subjects in need of protection, either by the state—as in the case of the fetus and women—or from the state, as in the case of medical professionals, taxpayers, or employers. This shift in discourse—from one that focuses on protecting the fetus to one that protects the rights of women, and then employers and their right to religious freedom—represents an expansion of the number of subjects with rights-based claims in the debate over reproductive rights. By using these discourses or rights-based claims to complement—rather than replace—each other, the pro-life movement has increasingly gained public support through representing and advocating for the various participants directly and indirectly involved in the procedure itself. Understanding the development of the pro-life discourse within the framework of the human rights discourse explains both the justification of these arguments and the increasing legitimacy surrounding the claims offered by the pro-life movement.

The second contribution of this project is the analysis of the relationship between this pro-life discourse and public policy outcomes. This examination demonstrates that the shift in discourse has been shaping public policy outcomes, as well as, in some instances, conflicting with existing pro-life policies. The fetal rights discourse, predominant in the 1970s and 1980s, continues to be one of the most commonly used strategies today. However, it has resulted in few political gains for the movement, and has had little effect on public opinion regarding abortion. This failure led to the shift in focus to women's rights and health concerns in the mid-1990s, an approach that resulted in greater political success for the pro-life movement. However, while these victories were manifested in policies that place various barriers or impediments to women's access to abortion, they were neither designed, nor able, to prohibit the practice altogether. This gradual, incrementalist approach created tension within the pro-life movement, corresponding to the conflict and tension present within the conservative movement; the shift toward protecting and promoting women's rights resulted in policies that require greater government intervention and oversight, an approach at odds with the libertarian faction of the GOP. However, while the policy was highly conservative in nature, the public discourse on women-centered issues often combined libertarian and conservative arguments. The final discourse, or the claims raised in *Hobby Lobby*, introduces new actors to the debate, yet a familiar, libertarian discourse remains. These arguments focus on limiting government intervention in reproductive matters, or keeping the government from mandating insurance coverage of contraception. However, while this latest discourse is clearly libertarian, abortion-related public policy during this time period reflects both libertarian and conservative ideals.

The third contribution of this project is the analysis of the current tension within right-wing politics, through an examination of the case of the pro-life movement. We argue that the *Hobby Lobby* case and the discourse and policies that follow from it are representative of the tension—and at times, seemingly a split—within the GOP between the conservative and libertarian bases. The libertarian elements of this most recent pro-life discourse are at odds with the previous legislative developments and general approach to public policy, which follows a more conservative understanding of government intervention and regulation of abortion. As such, this analysis identifies possible directions the GOP may take to resolve this tension. Thus, this examination of the pro-life movement serves as a litmus test for the future direction of right-wing politics in the USA.

2   METHOD

The analysis of the pro-life movement offered in this book is based on two types of data: one focuses on the pro-life discourse, and the second on pro-life public policy. The combination of these two sources allows this research to analyze the type of arguments used by pro-life activists, the legislative focus of pro-life legislators, as well as the relations between the pro-life discourse and legislation in the abortion debate. The use of both qualitative and quantitative methods provides for both descriptive and numerical analyses of discourse and public policy outcomes (King et al. 1994). Through the use of both approaches, this research introduces an in-depth, rich contextual analysis of the pro-life movement as well as a systematic understanding of broader trends and outcomes in the pro-life movement and public policy, more generally.

In this case, the data collected through discourse analysis is used in combination with data on the legislative efforts at the federal and state levels from 1973 to 2015. Each of these types of data was collected separately, highlighting a different aspect in the pro-life strategy. While the definition of discourse analysis changes according to the discipline and question examined (Van Dijk 1985; Schiffrin et al. 2008), the term "discourse analysis" refers to the study of language in use, focusing on the content of the language being used—the themes and issues—rather than an in-depth analysis of the structure and grammar of the language. The use of discourse as a base of evidence introduces data that is complex, and hard to classify, but nevertheless is able to highlight political interaction (Chilton and Schäffner 2002). The aim of this analysis is to reveal the way in which on-the-ground activists as well as leaders of the pro-life movement explain and justify the pro-life position. Therefore, the analysis of different sources focuses on the framing of the issues by the pro-life movement, highlighting especially the type of justifications that are used—and ignored—throughout the decades.

The analysis of the discourse is based on data collected from several different sources. First, the data comprises all newspaper items that include the terms "abortion" and "pro-life," including articles, letters to the editor, and advertisements that were published in *The New York Times* between 1973 and 2015, and in *The Washington Post* between the years 1977 and 2015.[1] Following these criteria, the database contains 1933 articles from

---

[1] The data does not include *The Washington Post* publications between the years 1973 and 1976 due to limited access. The data includes articles published until June 30, 2015.

The New York Times, and 2106 articles from *The Washington Post*.[2] After examining all these items, the researchers identified those articles that contained pro-life discourse: 259 discourse pieces in *The New York Times* (accounting for 13 % of all the pieces found in the newspaper), and 479 in *The Washington Post* (23 %), as seen in Table 1.1. These discourse pieces all include either some statements by pro-life supporters and activists during interviews, demonstrations, and speeches or summaries of such statements by the journalist. In the cases that the piece was written by a pro-life supporter to promote the pro-life mission—either as a letter to the editor or as an opinion piece—the entire piece was analyzed as discursive. The discourse pieces were classified according to two main categories: fetus-centered and women-centered discourse.[3]

The examination of the fetus-centered discourse reveals that the pro-life movement uses four main justifications to argue against abortion. The first two establish the claim regarding the sanctity of the life of the fetus, first using moral arguments—including religious ones—and second, using scientific data as proof that the fetus is a human being. The third fetus-centered argument is that abortion needs to be understood as the Holocaust or an act of genocide, including a comparison between abortion and slavery. This justification emphasizes the extreme and institutionalized nature of abortion, as well as the inability of society to recognize the immoral nature of the practice today, though it will be recognized in the future. The fourth justification frames the rights of the fetus in opposition to the rights of the mother, thus emphasizing the role of pro-life movement in defending the fetus. The second stage of the discourse is the

Table 1.1 Pro-life arguments in *The New York Times* and *Washington Post*

Year	Fetus-centered arguments (%)	Women-centered arguments (%)	Total (%)
1973–1994	263 (79.0)	69 (21.0)	332 (100.0)
1995–2015	326 (68.0)	152 (32.0)	478 (100.0)
Total	589 (73.0)	221 (27.0)	810 (100.0)

[2] In general, *The Washington Post* published more items on this issue, and has a higher percentage of items that include references to the pro-life discourse. However, since the analysis of the newspapers is used to better understand the pro-life discourse as it appears in the mainstream media, the data from both newspapers is often presented together.

[3] During this period, there was very little discourse in the newspapers that focused on the interests of third-party actors. This issue is introduced and examined in Chaps. 4 and 5.

women-centered approach, emphasizing the health and emotional risks for women. The examination of the women-centered discourse reveals the use of three primary arguments against abortion: the inability of women to consent to abortion because of coercion, lack of knowledge, as well as the natural connection between her and her child; the emotional toll of abortion, which causes regret as well as post-abortion syndrome (PAS); and the health risks associated with abortion, such as in the case of breast cancer.[4] While a few discourse pieces do not refer to any of these subcategories, most of them include discussion of more than one subcategory. Therefore, the total of the justifications and subcategories discussed in this book is higher than the number of discourse items that appear in the newspapers.

The second dataset examined in this book is the discourse used in current websites of pro-life organizations. The websites analyzed were identified between January and February 2015, using the search engine Google, and employing the search terms "pro-life" and "organization," as well as snowball sampling, which includes websites referred to by other pro-life organizations' websites. The final dataset includes 152 websites, excluding local organizations as well as regional chapters of larger pro-life organizations. The analysis of these websites is based on the reading of all the webpages—which often include the organization's mission statement, FAQs, fact sheets, and related scientific articles—and classifying the justifications that appear in the websites. All the websites were classified using the following categories: fetus-centered—including the categories of religious argument, references to the Holocaust and genocide, as well as race—and women-centered, including the categories of informed consent, emotional trauma, regret of women and men, and health risks. Other categories include a focus on research, the use of human rights discourse, after-abortion focus, and the use of fetal imagery. In the attempt to map the organizations, the data also includes information about the type of strategy used, the year when the organization was founded, and other issues that the organization focuses on, if any such issues are present. This classification provides the quantitative data, while specific quotes

[4] As will be further discussed in Chap. 3, these scientific claims are often rejected by many in the scientific community, who argue that research finds that abortion rarely leads to feelings of regret and emotional harm (Charles et al. 2008), and that induced abortion does not increase the risk of breast cancer (Collaborative Group on Hormonal Factors in Breast Cancer 2004; Jasen 2005).

and statements provide the qualitative data utilized in this project. Unless directly stated, the quotes that appear in the book, from the websites, newspapers, as well as other primary sources, represent a common claim or argument, rather than unique or rare point.

Unlike the newspaper items, the analysis of the websites introduces the contemporary pro-life discourse, highlighting the most recent developments in the pro-life strategy and its manifestation over the past few years. In addition, since most of these websites are meant to convince pregnant women and the general public to accept and adopt these pro-life sentiments and beliefs, they often contain an elaborate description of their overall claims, and numerous references to research, religion, or any other information that might influence people's opinion on abortion. Further, the intent of these websites—appealing to pro-life supporters as well as those who are still on the fence—results in more developed arguments regarding the pro-life mission. Thus, the websites provide a significant amount of information regarding the pro-life discourse today, which complements the analysis of the newspaper items that shed light on the historical developments of the pro-life strategy.

Out of the 152 websites surveyed, most included some reference to fetus-centered arguments or women-centered arguments against abortion, while almost half addressed both arguments, as seen in Table 1.2. A minority of these websites does not include references to either of these two arguments.

The analysis of pro-life public policy is based on a dataset that includes federal- and state-level public policy, from 1973 to 2015. All federal bills

Table 1.2 Pro-life websites

Pro-life websites	Fetus-centered arguments	Women-centered arguments	Both fetus-centered and women-centered arguments	Neither fetus-centered nor women-centered arguments	Addresses issues other than abortion
152	109 (72 %)	103 (68 %)	71 (47 %)	10 (6.5 %)[a]	21[b]

[a]In most of these cases, the organization's mission is to promote the rights of fathers in the abortion debate

[b]These organizations are divided into two distinct groups. The first are pro-life as part of their "Seamless Garment" approach, which values life and thus also opposes the death penalty as well as calling for human rights protections. The second are organizations that are part of the Christian Right—groups that support traditional family values and oppose gay marriage, the legalization of marijuana, school prayer, and stem cell research

proposed and enacted during this time period were identified through the Library of Congress' website, using the search terms "abortion" and "fetus." All proposed bills, amendments, and resolutions are included in the dataset without distinction according to the format of the proposal, as it is the content of the measure rather than its effect or practical implications that is under review at present. Given the magnitude of policies coming out of state legislatures, only enacted measures are included in the analysis, while at the federal level, all proposed and enacted measures are included. State policies were primarily identified through the reports *Who Decides?* authored by NARAL Pro-Choice America and published on an annual basis. The search engine Westlaw was also utilized to confirm any inconsistencies or missing data in the reports. Finally, the Guttmacher Institute's policy briefings were used to identify the most recent developments in abortion-related state law.[5] Any inconsistencies between the NARAL and the Guttmacher Institute's reports were checked in Westlaw to confirm the accuracy of the data.

Both federal and state legislation have been classified according to the primary party protected or affected by the law, namely the fetus, women, or third-party actors such as health professionals or taxpayers. Although there are numerous policies and laws that invoke more than one constituent or actor with interests in abortion, each is classified based upon the actor that is the primary focus of the legislation. Within each of these three categories, laws are further classified by the issue area or type of policy implemented, as seen in Table 1.3. Finally, each policy is coded as pro-life or pro-choice/neutral. Any measure designed to prohibit, limit, or restrict access to abortion, abortion facilities, or information regarding abortion has been labeled pro-life. This includes, for example, policies that attempt to establish the right to life at the moment of conception as well as those that place medically unnecessary requirements on accessing abortion. Conversely, pro-choice policies include all the measures that seek to maintain women's access to abortion either through legal access to the procedure itself or by providing resources to assist women in procuring abortion when needed.

From 1973 to 2015, 1399 abortion-related measures were proposed in Congress. Congressional activities on abortion measures were highest

[5] The Guttmacher Institute is a nonprofit organization which operates primarily to provide research and public education on reproductive health issues in the USA and abroad (Guttmacher Institute Website 2015).

Table 1.3 Typology for public policy

	Fetus-centered	Women-centered		Third-party actors	
Fetal protections	*Fetal rights*	*Women's health*	*Women's rights*	*Restrictions on funding*	*Rights*
Late-term ban	Personhood/right to life	Wait time/informed consent	Right to abortion	Health exchange restrictions	Right to refuse –Abortion –Birth control –Emergency contraception
Fetal pain (20-week ban) Pre-*Roe* ban/trigger laws	Fetal homicide (criminal sanctions) Fetal tissue –Disposal –Research	Counseling requirements Ultrasound requirements	Right to contraception/prescriptions Clinic access	Private insurance Public employees' insurance	
Partial birth		Crisis Pregnancy Centers (CPCs) Parental notification	Privacy	Medicaid	
Gender/race selection ban		Provider/clinic requirements Medication	Freedom from coercion	Public funding of abortion/related services	

in the first few years following the 1973 ruling in *Roe*, and declined over time. From 1973 to 1994, 794 measures were introduced at the congressional level, 709 (89 %) of which were pro-life. A total of 524 were introduced from 1995 to 2014, of which 401 (77 %) were pro-life. In the year following the decision in *Hobby Lobby*, 48 measures were introduced, with 42 (88 %) pro-life in nature. At the state level, from 1973 to 2015, 1843 abortion-related laws were passed, with 407 laws enacted from 1974 to 1994. Of the 407 laws, 347 (85 %) were pro-life. In the second era examined, 1385 laws were passed at the state level, and 835 (60 %) were pro-life. In the year following *Hobby Lobby*, 51 state abortion-related laws have been passed, all of which were pro-life (Table 1.4).

3   REPRODUCTIVE RIGHTS IN THE AGE OF HUMAN RIGHTS

Pro-life strategy, and its development since *Roe*, has had a role in many of the political and social debates in the past four decades, including, for example, conflict over life and death, the autonomy of women, and the limits of government intervention. While the effects of this strategy have been numerous, this book focuses specifically on three issues: first, the concept of human rights, and especially the types of rights and protections that are included within human rights; second, the changing understanding of reproductive rights, including the approach to women's autonomy and subjectivity; and, finally, the nature of right-wing politics, focusing primarily on the tension between conservatives and libertarians within the GOP. The shifting strategies of the pro-life movement, we argue, have significantly impacted these three issue areas, changing their definition, application, and scope. These three themes are analyzed

Table 1.4 Federal (proposed and enacted) and state (enacted) legislation, including pro-life and pro-choice policy

	Total	*1973–1994*	*1995–2014*	*2014–2015*
Federal-proposed and -enacted laws	1366	794	524	48
–Pro-life	1152	709	401	42
–Pro-choice	214	85	123	6
State-enacted laws	1843	407	1385	51
–Pro-life	1233	347	835	51
–Pro-choice	610	60	550	0

throughout this work, tracing their development in light of the pro-life movement's strategy. The next section introduces these three categories, beginning with an overview of the human rights discourse.

Human Rights

The debate over abortion is, at least partly, a debate about human rights; it is a debate over who counts as human, whose human rights take precedence over another's, and what rights are included under the definition of human rights. In this debate, both the pro-life and pro-choice movements introduce different answers to these questions. On the one side stands the pro-choice movement, which in general does not accept the claim that the fetus is an autonomous and full human being deserving of the same legal protections citizens possess, thus, calling for the prioritization of women's control over their reproductive rights over the rights of the fetus. On the other side stands the pro-life movement, which first and foremost argues that the fetus is a human being, with a significant proportion of the movement claiming that personhood starts from the moment of conception. Thus, society is required to prioritize the fetus' right to life over other rights of mothers, which are less basic and fundamental than the right to life. While this is the classic framing of the abortion debate, the pro-life approach and use of human rights claims are not limited to the argument that the fetus is a human being and, thus, should not be aborted. Instead, as the analyses of the pro-life strategies reveal, the pro-life movement claims to defend also the rights of mothers, as well as the rights of third-party actors. In their arguments, they often emphasize rights-claim discourse in general, and human rights justification in particular. The use of this discourse situates the pro-life argument within a long tradition of protecting human rights, thus increasing the legitimacy and support for its mission.

The idea that human rights need to be protected and respected is widely accepted today. Despite being a modern and abstract concept, "human rights have become 'a fact of the world' with a reach and influence that would astonish framers of the international human rights project" (Beitz 2011: 1). The significant popularity and legitimacy of the concept of human rights has resulted in an increase in the number of transnational institutions focusing on the protection of human rights, as well as cases of international intervention that are meant to stop human rights violations. The "age of human rights," however, is not only influencing the way international and domestic institutions operate or the focus of policy. It is also redefining the human rights discourse as a substitute for all other moral or ethical discourses. Thus, human rights arguments "represent a partial statement of the content of an ideal of global public reason, a broadly shared set of values and norms for assessing political societies both separately and in their relations" (Cohen 2004: 195). Within this context, the argument that an act is a human rights violation may bring broader attention to this event, as well as legitimacy to the fight against this act that is defined as immoral. However, while the concept of human rights is a manifestation of current understanding of "good" and the "good society," rights are specific and detailed, rather than abstract (Henkin 1990). Therefore, instead of being merely a statement of intent or preference, human rights need to be specific enough to provide guidelines for action.

While these traits of the human rights regime—especially the extensive use of human rights discourse around the world, the shared institutions, and the moral dimension of the human rights claims—seem to promote a shared understanding of the concept of human rights, the human rights discourse is used by diverse groups, regimes, and individuals, for making and legitimizing different claims about justice (Donnelly 2007; Douzinas 2000; Haule 2006; Mendus 1995).[6] This fact reflects the wide disagreement about the content, as well as ranking, of different human rights. This disagreement is particularly problematic in the "age of human rights," since the legitimacy that this concept enjoys leads many to use the concepts in innovative—and even contradictory—ways. This kind of use is often done without any attempt to first establish some shared moral values or definitions of what constitutes a human right (Haule 2006). At the heart of the disagreement about the concept of human rights is the question of what rights or acts should be thought of as human rights. Specifically, much of the debate focuses on whether human rights include only what is necessary for a minimum standard of living—such as life, and basic protections to ensure freedom—or do human rights include a broader list of rights, as those that appear in the Universal Declaration of Human Rights (UDHR) and other international and regional conventions (Benhabib 2008). As a result of this disagreement and of the widespread use of human rights claims, many of these human rights claims are

[6]The extensive use of the discourse of human rights does not correlate with less human rights violations. Rather, the twenty-first century has been characterized by more violence, genocides, and human rights violations than any period in history (Douzinas 2000; Haule 2006).

incompatible. The abortion debate is one such example; two opposing groups, which use human rights discourse, fiercely debate the question of whose rights need to be protected, and what rights are included under the human rights concept (Haule 2006).

Another example of a debate between two groups that use the human rights discourse is the tension between universalism and cultural relativism. On the one side of this debate is the argument for the universality of human rights; it reflects the assumption that not only all human beings have equal rights to access human rights, but also these rights need to be the same ones. The universality of rights, some argue, promotes and protects the concept—as well as application—of human rights (Donnelly 2007; Henkin 1990). On the other side is the argument regarding the need to respect cultural relativism within the human rights regime. This respect is especially important in the fight against attempts of some to use the universalistic human rights discourse as means of oppression and imperialism (Cowan et al. 2001; Donnelly 2007; Habermas 1998; Haule 2006; Goodhart 2008). While some argue that the use of the terms "universalism" and "relativism" limit the discussion by framing them as dichotomous, others approach this debate by focusing on the different agents who are the subject of these rights; individuals (Henkin 1990; Mendus 1995), communities, or any combination of the two (Donnelly 2007; Kymlicka 1996). The UDHR, as well as other treaties, does not provide an answer to this debate; while its language promotes a universal understanding of rights, some of the rights that are included—such as dignity, respect, and equality—may have different manifestations in different cultures and contexts, thus making it possible to define them as cultural relativists.

The disagreement regarding the universal nature of human rights is central to the use of the human rights discourse by the pro-life movement. The analysis of the pro-life strategy in this book reveals that in varying forms and constructs, the human rights discourse plays a role in all three pro-life strategies; the fetus-centered strategy utilizes human rights arguments to support the need to protect the fetus as a human being. This strategy is based on universalistic understanding of human rights, defining abortion as an immoral act regardless of the specific context or personal preference. The women-centered discourse—although not necessarily the legislation—is based on a positive concept of human rights. A negative right is often understood as the right to be protected from harm by the government or others, while positive rights are thought of as the right to have something provided to you. This distinction is criticized by some human rights thinkers as theoretical, as well as problematic on normative grounds (Donnelly 2013). At the same time, this distinction is nevertheless often used to distinguish between more inclusive accounts of human rights—for example, the inclusion of social, economic, and cultural rights as human rights—versus more limited accounts, which emphasize mainly the right of people to be free from other's control. The third-party discourse argues for an expansion of the right to religious freedom, as well as the subjects whose human rights are being violated by the performance of abortion. This most recent discourse follows the cultural relativist approach, calling for respect of personal preferences even if it contradicts other's understanding of human rights.

The ability to shift these definitions and targets is a result of one of the main traits of the human rights discourse: the lack of a foundation for the concept of human rights. The question of foundation, or lack of, is one of the most commonly discussed questions within the human rights literature (Donnelly 2007). In general, the debate focuses on whether there is any origin or basis for human rights—such as natural law or positive law (Donnelly 2007; Douzinas 2000; Haule 2006)—or whether the lack of foundation—the fact that there is no shared basis or justification for the concept of human rights—is part of the concept of human rights. Among the justifications for the lack of foundations are the arguments that the concept is validated by its public acceptance (Henkin 1990) or its global appeal (Goodhart 2008) rather than some foundational argument. Another argument is that the attempt to find a foundation is doomed to fail, and we should instead focus on articulating human rights practices (Mendus 1995). This absence, however, leaves us with the unanswered questions of who is in possession of human rights, what rights are human rights, and what constitutes a violation of such rights, thus opening the possibility for conflicting definitions to be introduced and debated. The lack of such foundations is the basis for the debate between universalist and cultural relativist approaches to human rights; in order to provide an answer to the question whether human rights are universal or culturally specific, some argue that there is a need to first agree on the question of foundation (Donnelly 2007, 2013). It is within this context that the pro-life movement uses the human rights discourse in different—and even opposing—ways, expanding and shifting the rights and subjects who are the focus of the rights claims.

The analyses offered in Chaps. 2–4 and 6 examine the implications of the use of human rights discourse by pro-life individuals and organizations.

The different conceptualizations of human rights reveal the ways in which pro-life arguments are promoted and translated into action, as well as the way these discourses challenge and change the nature of human rights claims. In the attempt to highlight the discursive use of these concepts, as well as the multiple claims that are included within the discourse, this account avoids any judgment regarding whether this use of the concept of human rights is "correct," or whether it actually represents a misuse of the concept of human rights (Speed and Collier 2000).

Reproductive Rights

The term "reproductive rights" encompasses a broad range of issues involving reproduction and reproductive health. In the USA, the discussion of rights generally includes the choice to have or not have children, the timing and spacing of childbirth, and the freedom to make these decisions without coercion or threats of violence (Rubin 1994). The primary issues at stake in the discussion of reproductive rights include the right to birth control, abortion, sterilization, and, more recently, the right to obtain fertility treatments. Controversy over the right to birth control, abortion, and sterilization is not new, and the current debates over these issues reflect many of the same themes regarding the right to life, the rights of individuals, and freedom from coercion (Engelman 2011).

The birth control movement of the early 1900s was a culmination of broader social and political changes taking place in the USA at the turn of the century. Increased immigration, the tremendous growth of manufacturing cities on the East Coast, and the absence of social welfare or safety net led to the development of this movement, encouraging smaller families and preventing self-induced abortions. Despite the broader social changes under way in the USA, and the growing acceptance of birth control among some quarters of the population, birth control was illegal under the Comstock Act of 1873. A product of Victorian-era ideals, the Comstock Act promoted purity, self-restraint, and traditional gender norms, criminalizing pornography, erotica, as well as birth control and abortion (Rubin 1994). The birth control movement aimed at ensuring that women were educated and aware of issues surrounding reproductive health and the options available to them. As such, this movement represented one of the first large-scale efforts to promote women's autonomy and choice in the spacing and timing of childbirth (Engelman 2011).

The period after World War I (WWI) was a turning point in the approach to reproductive health and rights by the US government. The use of birth control, common among most Western nations, and the rising rates of venereal disease among soldiers on returning to the USA turned reproduction and sex into a public health issue. By the 1930s and 1940s, birth control had gained greater acceptance among the general public, and despite the continued presence of laws that criminalized its use, it was used among all segments of the population. Religious authorities continued to speak out against its use, declaring that it facilitated immorality and a sexually permissive society. Specifically, Catholic leaders were at the forefront of the religious outcry against the use of birth control, maintaining that its use was unnatural and indecent. In the mid-1900s, despite the significant increase in use of birth control among all segments of the population, its use continued to produce controversy with beliefs of morality and traditional sexual norms (Engelman 2011).

By the 1960s, as part of the broader social changes occurring within the USA, the women's movement had reached full force. Working toward the promotion of women's social, economic, and political equality, access to birth control and legal abortion were seen as critical to achieving these ends. Although contraception was commonly accepted within the USA, it is not until the late 1960s and early 1970s that the Supreme Court overturned the laws prohibiting the distribution of birth control (381 U.S. 479, 1965; 405 U.S. 438, 1972). More critical to increased rates of contraception use was the development and FDA approval of the birth control pill, which has been hailed as the greatest advancement of women's reproductive health and, more generally, their political and social equality. The pill allowed women to take control of reproduction, leading to greater college attendance, delayed marriage and childbirth, and, for some, increased economic opportunities (Carbone and Cahn 2011). Thus, the fight for increased access to reliable forms of birth control has been and continues to be seen as critical to women's autonomy and social equality.

Also occurring at the same time was the fight to reform abortion laws, which in the 1960s was defined by a patchwork of laws that varied significantly by state. Most states (33) prohibited abortion in almost all circumstances, leading many women to attempt a self-induced abortion, obtain an illegal abortion, or travel to another state or country (Benson Gold 2003). Thus, in the 1960s, the drive to legalize abortion came largely from physicians' concern for public health. Based upon this public health approach, the laws that were introduced offered women the opportunity to make a request, to a panel of judges, for an abortion because of health and safety concerns. The mobilization of the women's movement, occurring at the same time, introduced arguments for the legalization of abortion based upon claims of individual rights, and specifically the promotion of women's autonomy and control (Siegel 2012).

Following the ruling in *Roe*, the pro-choice movement continued to advance the right of full access to birth control and affordable abortion, promoted on the basis of individual rights of freedom and autonomy to choose when or if one bears children (Fried 2013). The pro-choice movement, initially composed by many of the same actors in the women's movement, was by default left with defending the court's precedent in *Roe v. Wade*. Thus, the arguments and rhetoric were designed to maintain the status quo, and ensure the rights established by the courts were maintained. The pro-choice movement has consistently maintained this narrative of choice, limiting any references to the fetus (Morgan and Meredith 1999), while utilizing the terminology and messages first employed during the 1960s, including "the right to control your own body, reproductive freedom, and sexual liberation as empowerment" (Stolberg 2009). In fact, the reliance on this narrative of choice has recently prompted efforts to change messaging, particularly as younger women and men are less likely to self-identify as pro-choice or support this political cause, despite polling that demonstrates the same, consistent level of support for abortion among the American people (Calmes 2014; Lauro 1999; Stolberg 2009).

The dynamic nature of the pro-life movement, and their continued efforts to refine their messaging over time, has left the pro-choice movement at a disadvantage at a point in time when claims of individual rights, including female empowerment, liberation, and choice, no longer resonate with younger generations. This has been evident in the public opinion polls during the years, which according to Gallup have shown almost no change in the percentage of people who oppose abortion under all circumstances (19 % in 1973 and 2015), as well as those who support abortion only under certain circumstances (55 % in 1973 and 51 % in 2015). While this consistency may seem like a loss for both sides, the significant increase in the support for other social issues—such as same-sex marriage and the legalization of drugs (Leonhardt and Parlapiano 2015)—defines abortion as an outlier.

The struggle over access to abortion—and more recently, birth control—has remained a contentious issue in the USA, and is still at the center of debates over morality, religion, rights, autonomy, and public health. In the last few decades, a number of other reproductive health issues have also entered into public discussion of reproductive rights. The rise of infertility treatments and assisted reproductive technologies has introduced a new "right" under the umbrella of reproductive rights—the right to have children. While the battle had always centered on the right to not have children, or at least control the timing and spacing of childbirth, the introduction of various forms of fertility intervention has shifted the debate to one in which having one's own genetic or gestational child is considered a right. To exercise this right, most often the focus concerns insurance coverage of fertility treatment and equal access to treatment for same-sex couples and single individuals (Blank 1997).

Right-Wing Politics

The development of the abortion debate goes hand in hand with the ideological shifts that have occurred within the two primary political parties in the USA. These shifts have affected both the discourse surrounding reproductive rights and the public policy dealing with abortion and related issues. The development of the pro-life movement during the late 1970s and 1980s occurred simultaneously with the realignment of the political parties. Both the Republican and the Democratic parties' supporters became more ideologically consistent, and in turn, elected officials and the general public became more polarized. As the Republican Party became much more conservative over time, the two primary factions that serve as the base of the party—conservatives and libertarians—increasingly became at odds with one another, both with respect to their political goals and issue positions. Further, during this process, the pro-life movement became more and more intertwined with the GOP.

Conservatism in the USA prioritizes minimal government involvement in fiscal matters, particularly with respect to regulation and oversight of the private market. This approach is based on the belief in the link between freedom and property, as well as a free market as the best available economic system (Dunn and Woodard 2003). This is the issue that conservatives and libertarians most often agree about, reflecting their shared dislike of government intervention. Conservatives most clearly stand in contrast to libertarians with respect to their stance on social issues; they generally favor tradition, prioritizing family values and religion. While these values call for limited government intervention—especially at the federal level—conservatives do not believe in lack of authority; instead, "freedom lies in the interstices of social and moral authority" (Nisbet 1980), replacing the arbitrary power of the state with decentralized social institutions. The Christian Right is often considered akin to social conservatives, generally opposing abortion, same-sex marriage and the recognition of LGBTQ rights, pornography, and the teaching of evolution in schools. These phenomena, they believe, are a result of big government, which is trying to shape and define morality, thus leading to a breakdown of the social order. Instead, the government should regulate activities that undermine the moral standing and traditional institutions in the USA; prohibiting abortion, requiring school prayer, and encouraging traditional family values and traditional marriage are some of the issues that should be promoted by the state in order to strengthen the nation and social order (Dowland 2009). Thus to preserve this social order, conservatives—and social conservatives in particular—are often in support of government intervention and increased oversight.

For libertarians, the emphasis on deregulation and limited government involvement is based on the belief that individual autonomy and freedom are the highest social values. Since the state was developed to ensure the protection of individual rights, it has no authority to compromise freedom as a means to create social order. In addition, libertarians do not distinguish between moral and immoral authority, instead arguing that all authorities are based on arbitrary power. Therefore, on social issues such as abortion, same-sex marriage, and LGBTQ rights, and the role of church in education or state matters, libertarians stand in stark juxtaposition to conservatives, and in particular, social conservatives. Libertarians prefer limited or no government involvement in these issues, instead calling for individual autonomy, freedom, and privacy (Libertarian Party 2014; Nisbet 1980).

The analysis of the pro-life strategy in this book reveals that the discourse since the 1973 ruling in *Roe v. Wade* reflects both conservative and libertarian ideals, sometimes simultaneously and sometimes separately. The nature of the discourse shifts over time—from the mostly libertarian arguments of the fetus-centered approach, through the more conservative justifications of the women-centered approach, to the almost purely libertarian argument regarding the rights of third-party actors. The pro-life legislation also moves between these two categories, although not necessarily in accordance with the discourse; while both fetal rights and third-party legislation utilize claims that are either libertarian or conservative in nature, the women-centered approach is based on conservative justifications for the protection of women. The changes in the nature of the discourse and legislation reflect the tension between conservatives and libertarians within the GOP, while at the same time also influencing some of these tensions and creating alliances between the factions.

4   ORGANIZATION OF THE BOOK

The book is divided into four main chapters, each examining one type of pro-life strategy, analyzing its discourse and legislation as well as broader implications it carries. Chapter 2 focuses on the development of the fetus-centered strategy between 1973 and 1994, a strategy that is used by the movement to reverse the Supreme Court ruling in *Roe* and remains central to the movement to this day. The chapter analyzes the way in which the fetus-centered argument was used in the pro-life discourse, using religious, universal, and scientific arguments to prove that the fetus is a human being from the moment of conception and thus eligible for the same protections as a human being. Despite many legislative attempts to define the fetus as a human being—manifested mainly in the hundreds of Human Life Amendment proposals—fetus-centered legislation generally failed to reverse the ruling. The chapter concludes with an account of the implications of this strategy on the concepts of human rights, reproductive rights, and right-wing politics, followed by the analysis of the failure of the fetus-centered strategy to change policies, which led to the development of the women-centered strategy of the 1990s.

Chapter 3 examines the development and use of the women-centered strategy of the pro-life movement, which since the mid-1990s has been used together with the fetus-centered strategy. The transition to this strategy was calculated and planned, a result of market surveys and the need to answer the challenges posed by the pro-choice movement. This strategy focuses on the well-being of women, arguing that abortion not only kills the fetus but also harms the mother. Unlike the fetus-centered argument, which focuses mainly on normative arguments, this discourse often includes references to scientific data or language; it uses facts and findings to show that abortion causes emotional and physical damage to women. As a result, the legislative attempts following this strategy are less focused on overturning *Roe*, but rather on increasing the number of limitations and restrictions on abortion. This incremental legislative approach continues to be effective today in restricting access to abortion, especially at the state level. In addition, the women-centered strategy defines women as a vulnerable subject in the abortion debate—rather than an enemy—thus changing the relations between the pro-life and pro-choice movements; the pro-life movement is now framing its mission as protecting both the fetus and the mother from abortion.

The analysis of the pro-life strategy concerning the interests of third-party actors is presented in two chapters. Chapter 4 examines the legislative protections of third-party actors, beginning in 1973 through 2015.[7] The most common legislative protections include conscience clauses and taxpayer restrictions. The first, conscience clauses, were developed primarily as a way to protect health-care providers who have religious objections to participating in the abortion process. The second type of legislative protections limit public funding of abortion, emphasizing the rights of taxpayers not to pay for a service that is personal—as well as controversial—in nature. The passage of the ACA, and especially the opposition to the employer mandate that requires the coverage of all FDA-approved contraceptive devices that was the focus of the *Hobby Lobby* ruling, represents a turning point in the approach of the pro-life movement to third-party issues. However, and despite the increased attentions to this issue, the analysis of legislative proposals surrounding the ruling reveals that the pro-life legislation concerning third-party actors remains focused on taxpayers, on the one hand, and religious liberty of individuals, on the other.

Chapter 5 continues the analysis of the way that the pro-life movement has been utilizing the issue of third-party actors, focusing particularly on the increase in the use of freedom of religion arguments. The case and the ruling were framed by the pro-life movement as a victory for individuals who aim to follow their religious values while being employers. This framing, which is not always closely tied to the legal question examined, is based on libertarian values. The pro-life movement has been utilizing these arguments of religious liberty, thus expanding the topics that are at the center of the pro-life mission; instead of protecting only the life of the fetus, and the well-being of the mother, the pro-life movement now also defends the religious freedom of all individuals who feel forced by the government to act against their values. This framing of the pro-life movement makes its strategy more relevant to other debates over religious freedom—such as same-sex marriage—while also increasing the base of

---

[7] As is shown in the chapter, until the case of *Hobby Lobby*, there was very little pro-life discourse concerning the rights of third-party actors in the abortion debate.

support of the pro-life movement, without the need to change people's opinion on abortion. This new strategy also transforms the concept of religious liberty, and challenges the separation between contraceptive services and abortion.

The concluding chapter of the book discusses possible implications of the third-party pro-life strategy. The application of the concept of religious liberty to closely held corporations, together with the public framing of the *Hobby Lobby* ruling as granting rights to individuals, expands human rights—and not only economic rights—to nonhuman entities. The discourse of religious liberty, and especially the case of *Hobby Lobby*, highlights the centrality of the use of scientific language and data in the pro-life strategy over reproductive rights. The comparison between the abortion debate and the antienvironmentalist movement reveals shared tendencies in the use, misuse, and rejection of science. This is used to highlight future directions in the use of science in the debate over reproductive rights. The use of the religious freedom argument in legislation—especially regarding same-sex marriage and LGBTQ protections—provides a possible answer to the tension between conservative and libertarians within the GOP, with policies designed to restrict rights to the LGBTQ population through limiting interference in religious liberty.

NOTE: Despite the opposition in the medical community, the *Hobby Lobby* case defines the four contraceptive devices in question as abortifacients. This book follows the plaintiffs' definition, thus framing this case as part of the abortion debate. For this book, the medical debate or facts are less relevant than the way in which the activists and supporters understand and construct the discourse. The focus on discourse shapes the terms that are used—and not used—in this project, as well as the discussions and debates that are addressed. In general, we adopt the terms and concepts used by pro-life activists themselves; this, in order to facilitate an analysis of the mechanisms by which the pro-life argument is promoted, but also to avoid changing the discourse by using other terms, that have different—and even opposing—meanings. For example, the book avoids the term "anti-choice" to describe the pro-life movement. One exception is the use of the term "fetus"; while the book does include references to "unborn children," as well as other pro-life terms, the term that is commonly used is "fetus." Although this term may be seen as more neutral, we acknowledge that the pro-life movement sometimes prefers the use of other terms that emphasize the human nature of the unborn child.[8] In addition, because of the focus on the pro-life movement, the book rarely includes references to the pro-choice answer to these claims, unless the pro-life discourse itself makes an argument regarding the pro-choice approach.

REFERENCES

Beitz CR. The idea of human rights. Oxford: Oxford University Press; 2011.

Benhabib S. The legitimacy of human rights. Daedalus. 2008;137(3):94–104.

Benson Gold R. Lessons from before Roe: will past be prologue? Guttmacher Rep Public Policy. 2003;6(1).

Blank RH. Assisted reproduction and reproductive rights: the case of in vitro fertilization. Polit Life Sci. 1997;16(2):279–88.

Calmes J. Advocates shun 'Pro-Choice' to expand message. The New York Times. 2014 July 28.

Carbone J, Cahn N. The power of the pill. Roosevelt Institute. http://www.rooseveltinstitute.org/new-roosevelt/power-pill. 2011.

Charles VE, Polis CB, Sridhara SK, Blum RW. Abortion and long-term mental health outcomes: a systematic review of the evidence. Contraception. 2008;78(6):436–50.

Chilton P, Schäffner C, editors. Politics as text and talk: analytic approaches to political discourse. Vol. 4. John Benjamins Publishing; 2002.

Cohen J. Minimalism about human rights: the most we can hope for? J Polit Philos. 2004;12(2):190–213.

Collaborative Group on Hormonal Factors in Breast Cancer. Breast cancer and abortion: collaborative reanalysis of data from 53 epidemiological studies, including 83,000 women with breast cancer from 16 countries. Lancet. 2004;363(9414):1007–16.

Cowan JK, Dembour MB, Wilson RA. Culture and rights: anthropological perspectives. Cambridge: Cambridge University Press; 2001.

Donnelly J. Universal human rights in theory and practice. Ithaca: Cornell University Press; 2013.

Donnelly J. The relative universality of human rights. Hum Right Q. 2007;29(2):281–306.

---

[8] In her analysis of the pro-life amicus briefs in *Webster*, Woliver (2013) found that the term "fetus" was never used. Instead, the pro-life discourse used more than 40 different terms to describe the unborn child, including "children in the womb," "human life before birth," "minor child," "unborn grandchildren," and "those who will be citizens if their life are not ended in the womb" (7). Instead of woman, the briefs mainly used the word "mother."

Douzinas C. The end of human rights: critical thought at the turn of the century. London: Bloomsbury; 2000.

Dowland S. 'Family values' and the formation of a christian right agenda. Church Hist. 2009;78(3):606–31.

Dunn CW, Woodard JD. The conservative tradition in America. Lanham: Rowman & Littlefield; 2003.

Eckholm E. Anti-abortion groups are split on legal tactics. The New York Times. 2011 December 4.

Engelman P. A history of the birth control movement in America. Santa Barbara: ABC-CLIO; 2011.

Fried MG. Reproductive rights activism in the post-roe era. Am J Public Health. 2013;103(1):10–4.

Goodhart M. Neither relative nor universal: a response to Donnelly. Hum Right Q. 2008;30(1):183–93.

Habermas J. Remarks on legitimation through human rights. The Modern Schoolman. 1998;75(2):87–100.

Haule RR. Some reflections on the foundation of human rights: are human rights an alternative to moral values? Max Planck UNYB. 2006;10(1):367–95.

Henkin L. The age of rights. New York: Columbia University Press; 1990.

Jasen P. Breast cancer and the politics of abortion in the United State. Med Hist. 2005;49(4):423–44.

King G, Keohane R, Verba S. Designing social inquiry: scientific inference in qualitative research. Princeton: Princeton University Press; 1994.

Kymlicka W. The good, the bad and the intolerable: minority group rights. Dissent. 1996:22–30.

Lauro PW. An abortion rights coalition hopes its campaign will get young women to discuss their choices. The New York Times. 1999 Dec 16.

Leonhardt D, Parlapiano A. Why gun control and abortion are different from gay marriage. The New York Times. 2015 Jun 30.

Libertarian Party. What is the libertarian party? http://www.lp.org/introduction/what-is-the-libertarian-party. 2014.

Loonan P. Don't compromise on abortion. The New York Times. 2003 Jan 15.

Mendus S. Human rights in political theory. Polit Stud. 1995;43(1):10–24.

Morgan LM, Meredith WM. Fetal subjects, feminist positions. Philadelphia: University of Pennsylvania Press; 1999.

Nisbet R. Conservatives and libertarians: uneasy cousins. Modern Age. 1980;24(1):2–8.

Rubin ER. The abortion controversy: a documentary history. Westport: Greenwood Press; 1994.

Schiffrin D, Tannen D, Hamilton HE. The handbook of discourse analysis. Oxford: Wiley; 2008.

Siegel R. Dignity and sexuality: claims on dignity in transnational debates over abortion and same-sex marriage. Int J Const Law. 2012;10:335–79.

Speed S, Collier JF. Limiting indigenous autonomy in Chiapas, Mexico: the state government's use of human rights. Hum Right Q. 2000;22(4):877–905.

Stolberg SG. In support of abortion, it's personal vs political. The New York Times. 2009 Nov 28.

The Guttmacher Institute. About the guttmacher institute. http://www.guttmacher.org/about/index.html. 2015.

Van Dijk TA. Introduction: discourse analysis as a new cross-discipline. Handbook of discourse analysis, vol 1; 1985. p. 1–10.

Woliver LR. Rhetoric and symbols in American abortion politics. In: Githens M, Stetson DMB, editors. Abortion politics: public policy in cross-cultural perspective. New York: Routledge; 2013. p. 5–28.

CHAPTER 2

The Fight over Abortion: Fetal Rights in the Post-*Roe* Era

1 INTRODUCTION

The 1973 Supreme Court ruling *Roe v. Wade*, while quite controversial among the general public and policymakers, was initially met with opposition from a small, primarily Catholic, pro-life movement. During this time period, social issues such as abortion were not partisan—or seen as political—issues. The primary divisions between Republicans and Democrats were based upon economic and civil rights issues. As such, conservatives were primarily focused on promoting limited government in the economic sphere and fighting against the civil rights measures pushed by northern liberals. Until the late 1970s and early 1980s, religious issues were largely left outside of the political sphere. Further, the ruling in *Roe* offered a conservative justification for establishing the right to abortion, which is based upon limiting government interference in a private, individual matter (Dowland 2009). As a result, during the early 1970s, Catholics played a central—if not singular—role in leading the fledgling pro-life movement, while Protestants and Evangelicals were unwilling to yet enter this political battle over the right to abortion (Greenhouse and Siegel 2011).

During the next two decades, primarily from the late 1970s on, religious adherents began to come together in their opposition to abortion and different pro-life organizations slowly became more unified, transforming what was until then a "loosely knit coalition" (Isaacson 1981) into an organization that started to resemble the contemporary pro-life movement.

© The Editor(s) (if applicable) and The Author(s) 2016
A. Von Hagel, D. Mansbach, *Reproductive Rights in the Age of Human Rights*, DOI 10.1057/978-1-137-53952-6_2

While the arguments and strategies offered by pro-life activists during these first few years were relatively diverse, one of the unifying principles was the primary focus on the fetus. The primary pro-life strategy of these decades, which was evident in both discourse and public policy, was that abortion kills a preborn human being, and thus it is murder. This focus on the fetus resulted in a discourse that rarely included references to other actors with interests in the debate, particularly women. The only references to women appeared as part of the claim that women are mothers by nature and should be allowed to become such in practice. However, the discourse emphasized the right to life, which was more fundamental or essential than women's right to choose, concluding that the fetus' right to life supersedes any other right.

This chapter examines the development and use of the fetus-centered strategy between 1973 and 1994.[1] While the framework for analysis is based on existing literature (Luker 1985; McBride 2008; Siegel 2007, 2008a, 2012), this investigation employs qualitative and quantitative data to trace the development and use of the public discourse, the resultant legislation, and the interactions between the two. The first section of this chapter introduces the development of the pro-life movement in the years leading to, and following, the ruling of *Roe v. Wade*. It was during these years that different pro-life organizations transformed into the movement we know today, a transformation characterized by, among other things, the growing use of the fetus-centered strategy. The second section of the chapter traces the structure of the fetus-centered argument, analyzing the different claims that together create a comprehensive fetus-centered discourse. This analysis is based on primary sources such as newspaper articles and public speeches, revealing the method by which arguments regarding the sanctity of life were employed by the pro-life movement. The outcome of this strategy is a vague and largely theoretical discourse that was unconvincing among all but the most ardent pro-life supporters. The third section analyzes proposed and enacted laws at the federal and state levels, examining the focus and methods employed to establish

---

[1] While the legalization of abortion in 1973 makes it a clear starting point for the start of this analysis, the decision to end the period in 1994 was based upon the evidence that shows a change in strategy in the mid-1990s, including other scholarly work that uses this timeline (Siegel 2007, 2008a; Siegel and Blustein 2006; Suter 2008). The fetus-centered strategy, however, did not disappear in the mid-1990s. Instead, since the mid-1990s the fetus-centered strategy has been accompanied by an additional strategy, the women-centered strategy, which is the focus of Chap. 3.

limits or restrictions on the practice of abortion, and the success of this particular approach. The final section of this chapter analyzes the implications of the fetus-centered strategy for the understanding of human rights, reproductive rights, and right-wing politics, concluding with a discussion of the failures of this approach and the transition to a new type of discourse by the pro-life movement.

2   THE DEVELOPMENT OF THE PRO-LIFE MOVEMENT IN THE AFTERMATH OF *ROE*

The ruling in *Roe* applied the previously established right to privacy to the practice of abortion, ensuring that women have access to this procedure—without government intervention—during the first and second trimester. The right to privacy, as used in the *Roe* decision, was based upon the legal precedents established in *Griswold v. Connecticut* (381 U.S. 479, 1965) and *Eisenstadt v. Baird* (405 U.S. 438, 1972) cases which established the right to birth control among married persons and nonmarried persons, respectively, through the identification of the penumbra of privacy rights applied through the due process clause of the 14th Amendment (McBride 2008). This case is often viewed as a critical victory of the women's movement; this ruling, on the heels of *Griswold* and *Eisenstadt*, was seen as critical to ensuring women's equality, politically, economically, and socially (Rose 2007).

Specifically, the case of *Roe vs. Wade* concerned a criminal statute in Texas that prohibited the attempt to procure or carry out an abortion, except to save the life of the mother. This statute, together with other such state-level restrictions enacted at the beginning of the twentieth century, led to the criminalization of abortion seekers, those assisting and abetting those obtaining an abortion, and providers. These restrictions facilitated the development of an increasingly unsafe and largely underground network of illegal abortion providers across the country (Benson Gold 2003). For the first half of the twentieth century, abortion laws varied substantially between states; 14 states were explicit in the criminalization of abortion for both providers and seekers, while 7 states only prosecuted abortion providers. The variability in approaches to the regulation of abortion was further complicated by uneven and inconsistent interpretation and enforcement of these laws. Further, the rising number of women harmed and the increased death rate associated with illegal abortions brought increased awareness to the public health dimensions of this issue (Greenhouse and Siegel 2011; McBride 2008).

Within this context, there was a growing call for political change, and by the late 1960s and early 1970s, a reform movement was underway, driven primarily by the American Law Institute (ALI). Prior to the *Roe* case, 17 states had either reformed or repealed their abortion laws. However, the majority of states continued to prohibit the procedure for all cases except when the life of the mother was at risk (Benson Gold 2003). The public health concerns associated with illegal abortions prompted the involvement not only of ALI, but that of physicians as well. As physicians also began to articulate to the general public the need for reform to abortion laws, public support for abortion—particularly therapeutic abortion—began to rise considerably. The changing social norms occurring during this time period made topics such as sex, birth control, and abortion more acceptable topics for discussion. Based upon these broader social changes, increased acceptance and demand for safe and legal contraception and abortion also facilitated increased support for abortion reform. Finally, a significant degree of support for reform to abortion laws came from the women's movement, a movement working toward women's political and social equality. Legal abortion represents one avenue to achieve this goal, in particular through ensuring increased autonomy and control over reproduction (Greenhouse and Siegel 2011; Rose 2007).

While this battle over access to abortion primarily occurred within the states, it is the ruling in *Roe v. Wade* (410 U.S. 113) and its companion case *Doe v. Bolton* (410 U.S. 179, 1973) that represents the most significant turning point in this political struggle, the discourse surrounding abortion, and the practice itself. The court's ruling established a woman's right to an abortion without government intervention prior to viability. Any significant restrictions or barriers to abortion during the first trimester were prohibited, in effect invalidating all state laws governing abortion. Further, any regulation of the practice after the first trimester must align with the framework established in the ruling. The ruling did recognize the state's interest in protecting the fetus, and thus allowed the possibility of restrictions on the procedure after viability. Any restrictions imposed through state or federal law, however, must include an exception for the life and health of the mother (410 U.S. 113, 1973).

The ruling shifted the predominant themes of the larger debate surrounding abortion; prior to the ruling, the health and safety risks associated with illegal abortions were some of the primary themes of the discussion and a central driver of the movement for reforming state abortion laws. In the years following the ruling, however, the medical and public health aspects associated with abortion became less central as questions concerning the start of life and the rights of healthcare professionals to refuse to participate in abortion soon came to dominate the public debate over abortion and reproductive rights (Greenhouse and Siegel 2011).

Prior to *Roe*, support for legislation designed to restrict access to abortion came primarily from Catholics, who opposed abortion based on the belief that personhood—or life—begins at the moment of conception. Following this belief, an unborn child should be granted the same legal protections and status that all individuals possess. This approach, commonly referred to as the fetus-centered strategy, became the central focus of the pro-life movement, gaining increased prominence as the pro-life movement grew in influence and size. The development of this discourse was primarily influenced by Schaeffer and Koop's book *Whatever Happened to the Human Race?* (Harding 2001; Meagher 2008). This book, which was accompanied by a film of the same title, made abortion part of the evangelical mission, convincing religious leaders and organizations that the topic is not merely an issue of Catholic concern (Dowland 2009; Greenhouse and Siegel 2011; Williams 2012). The $1 million film included graphic descriptions and depictions of the process of abortion and euthanasia, and was screened at churches in the attempt to engage evangelical Christians in the fight against abortion. Despite the reluctance of some evangelical churches to become involved in this controversial debate, the movie was successful in attracting evangelical support—as well as some prominent activists such as Jerry Falwell—to the pro-life movement (Williams 2012; Ziegler 2013).

By the 1980s, it was the local preachers and church leaders that served as the key drivers behind the pro-life movement. It was this alliance between Catholics and Evangelicals on the abortion issue that facilitated the creation and increased political influence of the Christian Right coalition. The coalition framed opposition to abortion as protecting the family and "traditional family values." As such, abortion was coupled with other morality issues—including the sexual revolution, homosexuality, feminism, and pornography—which were all understood as attacks on the family (Dowland 2009; Harding 2001). Since the institution of the family is defined as "the fundamental institution of society, an immutable structure established by our Creator," its survival became crucial for the survival of the country (Dowland 2009: 607). By the mid-1980s, however, Evangelicals adopted a more conservative position than Catholics, starting to identify abortion as "a unique evil, far worse than other national sins" (Williams 2012: 207). The centrality of the Christian right coalition within the pro-life movement resulted in an association of the movement with religious institutions, thus limiting the audience it was able to reach. This despite attempts by Catholics, at first and Evangelicals by the 1980s to promote political change through broadening the movement's base and influence (Greenhouse and Siegel 2011; Siegel 2014).

These attempts to broaden the base of support for the pro-life movement, which were unsuccessful, were also meant to broaden the GOP's base of support, primarily through attracting Catholic voters, who had traditionally aligned with the Democratic Party (Siegel 2014). The focus on morality was designed to counter the liberalization of norms and attitudes toward sex, marriage, and the family that transpired during the 1960s. The emphasis on social conservative issues such as abortion, illegal drug use, and amnesty for Vietnam War draft dodgers was successful; for the first time since the pre-Civil War era, the GOP was able to bring a significant new population of voters to the party, mainly white, Southern men (Greenhouse and Siegel 2011; Petrocik 1987). Appeals to this demographic—socially conservative Southerners who identify as pro-life, but are still identifying as Democrats—assisted the GOP in eventually gaining greater political control during the 1980s. It is during these years that the GOP's position on abortion became solidified through its introduction into the national party platform. This addition, represented by the party's inclusion of "family values" as key principles of their agenda, fueled rising support for the pro-life movement as it became part of the broader conservative movement (Freeman 1993; Green et al. 2004; Petrocik 1987; Ziegler 2013).

On the ground, the two decades after *Roe* were dedicated to expanding the support of the pro-life mission. While pro-life organizations still lacked the power and unity that defines the movement today, in the late 1970s and throughout the 1980s, the majority of organizations adopted the fetus-centered strategy, focusing on the argument that the fetus is a human being with essential, fundamental rights in need of protection. The virtually uniform embracing of the fetus-centered strategy was a result of four main factors. First, the fetus-centered argument was understood by activists as the most efficient way to challenge *Roe*; the Supreme Court ruling that established the right to abortion, many pro-life activists argued, resulted from the inability of the court to resolve the question of when life begins (Greenhouse and Siegel 2011; Isaacson 1981; McDonagh 2007; Sanger 2008). Therefore, by solving this question, essentially ending the debate over the start of life, the court will be compelled to reverse *Roe* and ban the practice altogether. President Ronald Reagan agreed with this assumption, arguing that the question of when life begins stands at the heart of the debate, as well as its solution; in a statement from 1981, he claimed "what is necessary in this whole problem, and has been the least talked of, is determining when and what is a human being. Once you have determined this, the Constitution already protects the right of human life" (Isaacson 1981).

Second, convincing the public that the fetus is a human being was understood by pro-life supporters as the most effective way to change public perception on the issue of abortion. Scott Klusendorf, the founder of the Life Training Institute, argued that the pro-life movement should focus on making a convincing "case for life: Babies are dying whose lives could be saved if pro-life advocates were equipped to argue their case persuasively. We can win if we force abortion advocates to defend killing babies. The battle over partial-birth abortion indicates this" (Klusendorf 1999). The decision to focus on the life of the fetus was also influenced by the availability of safe and legal abortion, which substantially diminished the medical risks for women procuring this form of treatment. In light of the sharp decline in injury and death associated with abortion, the stated concern for the life of the fetus slowly became more compelling than arguments regarding the health and well-being of women (Greenhouse and Siegel 2011).

Third, the opposition to feminism influenced the adoption of the fetus-centered argument. Feminism, according to the pro-life approach predominant in the 1970s and 1980s, undermines traditional family values; as Rosemary Thomson, a Republican activist who worked with Phyllis Schlafly, warned in 1978, "the national leaders of the women's movement, who were working so hard to ratify ERA, were the same clique promoting homosexual rights, abortion, and government child rearing" (Siegel 2014: 1373). Connie Marshner, president of the American Catholic Council, further developed this argument, stating

Feminism replaced the saccharine sentimilizations of women and home life and projected instead of new image of women: a drab, macho feminism of hard-faced women who were bound and determined to serve their place in the world, no matter whose bodies they have to climb over to do so.... Macho feminism despises anything which seeks to interfere with the desires of Number One. A relationship which proves burdensome? Drop it! A husband whose needs cannot be conveniently met? Forget him! Children who may wake up in the middle of the night? No way! To this breed of thought, family interferes with self-fulfillment, and given the choice between family and self, the self is going to come out on top in their world (Klatch 1987: 128–129).

The legalization of abortion, therefore, signified the victory of women who prefer to be "free" rather than perform their responsibility as mothers and housewives. This outcome of feminism, however, is often ignored, since "the unending feminist arguments in favor of abortion rarely acknowledge that their primary goal may be the complete liberation of women from children. Hostility to Mother's Day is one thing, a natural aversion to children is quite another" (Fox-Genovese 2002: 13). Therefore, according to Phyllis Schlafly, a social and political conservative primarily known for her fight against the Equal Rights Amendment (ERA), it is crucial to realize "that if we didn't get out and defend our values, this little feminist pressure group was going to end up changing our schools, our laws, our textbooks, our Constitution, our military, everything—and end up taking our husband's job away" (Bennetts 1980: B6). Thus, in the context of a feminist movement that was concerned only about women's personal and absolute freedom and rights, the pro-life movement has the responsibility to defend the life of the fetus, while working to protect traditional family values.

Fourth, politically, the fetus-centered strategy—and especially the focus on the argument that the fetus is a human being—has the potential to secure wider support, beyond social conservatives who are worried about traditional social and family values. The fetus-centered strategy aims to extend rights to the unborn, but avoids arguments for expanding the protection of life after birth. The focus on this relatively limited intervention in private matters, emphasizing merely the right to life, was designed to reach a more libertarian audience, which remains hesitant to increase regulations and government intervention of any sort. As Phyllis Schlafly stated, "the bottom line of the pro-family people is to get the Federal Government off our backs" (Bennetts 1980: B6). This libertarian approach focuses on the application of basic freedoms and rights, which already exist and are protected by the state, to the preborn. Thus, there is no need for further intervention and involvement of the state in private matters.

The fetus-centered strategy is still the main pro-life strategy today. Billboards, slogans, and campaigns all around the USA reflect some aspect of the argument that the fetus is a human being, deserving the same rights and protections as other persons. This strategy has been shaping both the public discourse on the abortion debate and the legislative attempts to limit or restrict access to abortion following the 1973 ruling. The following section traces the different aspects and claims that appear in this discourse, providing an in-depth analysis of both the arguments that constitute this discourse, and the frequency and time period in which each argument was used.

3   THE FETUS-CENTERED DISCOURSE

The fetus-centered strategy was accompanied by a public discourse that centered on arguments regarding the "sanctity of life," with very little attention to the other actors, such as women, also involved in the process. This section analyzes the discourse obtained from multiple sources and publications. First is the analysis of newspaper items from *The New York Times* and *The Washington Post*, the nation's two primary newspapers of record. The data includes 698 articles published in *The New York Times* between the years 1973 and 1994, and the 659 articles published in *The Washington Post* between the years 1977 and 1994. While these numbers comprise all the items—including articles, letters to the editor, and advertisements—that include the terms "abortion" and "pro-life," the analysis in this chapter is based primarily on the items that include pro-life discourse[2]: 135 items from *The New York Times*, which account for 19 % of all *The New York Times* items, and 140 (21 %) from *The Washington Post* include some reference made by pro-life supporters and activists, often as part of an interview, speech, rally, or letter to the editor. In the 275 data points, pro-life arguments were mentioned 332 times. Two hundred and sixty-three (79 %) of these arguments are fetus-centered justifications of the pro-life position,[3] while 69 (21 %) are classified as a women-centered discourse, emphasizing the harm that abortion causes women.

Second, this section analyzes the pro-life discourse as it appears in the websites of pro-life organizations. Out of the 152 pro-life websites surveyed between January and February 2015 (identified through an online search, utilizing the search terms "pro-life" and "organization"), 109 (72 %) websites include fetus-centered claims. Of the 109 websites, 71 include both fetus-centered and women-centered arguments, with 38 websites exclusively employing fetus-centered arguments. To complement this account of the development of the fetus-centered discourse, this section also uses central primary sources written during this time period by prominent pro-life leaders. Among the sources that influenced the strategy and discourse of the pro-life movement are Diamond (1992), Falwell (1981), Koop and Schaeffer (1979), White and Falwell (1986), and Willke (2001).

[2] Discourse items are defined as any item that includes statements made by pro-life activists or leaders, or reports on such statements.
[3] Seventy-six percent of *The Washington Post's* items and 82 % of *The New York Times'* pieces use a fetus-centered approach.

The primary claim or argument of the fetus-centered discourse is that the fetus is a human being, and thus abortion is immoral and considered murder. In the attempt to develop an argument that is convincing to diverse audiences, including nonreligious individuals, this discourse includes four distinct claims, all centering on the need to protect the life of the fetus. The first argument is that the fetus is a human being. This argument sometimes includes explicit references to religion and God, but more often is left vague, without the development of any justification for this claim. The universal and broad nature of this argument is meant to appeal to an audience that is not necessarily religious but, rather, generally values human life. The second claim regarding the sanctity of life focuses on scientific evidence for the claim that human life begins at conception. This claim aims to solve once and for all the question of when life begins, by concluding that it is not a matter of opinion or belief but, rather, of a widely accepted scientific fact. The third claim that constitutes the fetus-centered discourse argues that abortion is an act similar to genocide or the Holocaust. This argument defines abortion not merely as the murder of individuals but also as part of an ideology that is meant to get rid of an entire population, and change social reality altogether. Specifically, this argument sometimes includes a direct reference to African Americans as the population that abortion is meant to eliminate. The fourth claim that makes up the fetus-centered discourse is the argument that since the fight to end abortion is a fight over the right to life, women's right to choose is always secondary. Together, these four arguments convey a comprehensive argument against abortion, presenting it as an individual, as well as institutionalized, act of murder.

The Fetus as a Human Being: The Sanctity of Life

The primary claim of pro-life supporters is that the fetus is a human being, thereby converting abortion—at any stage of development—into murder. This argument plays a central role in the sanctity of life claims, best illustrated by signs used during the March for Life, a pro-life rally held in Washington, DC, every year since 1974. For example, during the 1976 rally, signs targeting President Jimmy Carter declared "Carter Backs Baby Murder," "Governor Carter, We Don't Want an Anti-Life President," and "Carter Favors Supreme Court's Slaughter of the Innocents" (Kihass 1976). The signs from 1977 included slogans such as "Give Life a Chance," "Life Not Death," and "Life Ain't Peanuts, Jimmy." The 1979 March for Life included the sign

"Thank God, Jesus wasn't aborted" (DeWitt 1979). The 1984 rally included the signs "abortion is the ultimate child abuse," "Stop killing babies," and "Before you're born is much too soon to die." In a different demonstration in 1989, pro-life activists created the "Cemetery of the Innocent," with crosses representing the deaths of the preborn where people come and pray (Rosenthal 1989), while another rally in the same year included people marching "through the streets, chanting, 'Choose Life! Choose life! Choose life!' They held a mock funeral service at a local cemetery for aborted fetuses. And their signs were everywhere: 'Stop Baby Butchers,' 'God Above All,' 'Aborted Babies were Given No Choice'" (Schmalz 1989).

This type of argument stands at the center of Schaeffer and Koop's influential book *Whatever Happened to the Human Race?* (1979). In their writing, they identify the development of the "humanistic" approach—one that emphasizes the agency and autonomy of human beings rather than religious or spiritual forces—as the cause for the decay of morals in our society today, and the inability of people to distinguish between right and wrong. The challenge of our time is thus the conflict between "those who regard individuals as expendable raw material—to be molded, exploited, and then discarded"—and "those who see each person as unique and special, worthwhile, and irreplaceable" (Koop and Schaeffer 1979: 16). Since, as they claim, humanism leads people to believe that "only what can be mathematically measured is real and that all reality is like a machine" (21), individuals then reject the idea that there is "anything stable or 'given' about human nature" (27). This is the reason for the decline in the value that we attach to the sanctity of life, a decline that is also responsible for the increase in cases of child abuse and child pornography. Jerry Falwell, the cofounder of Moral Majority who was inspired by this book (Williams 2012), later employs these examples to argue that abortion is a type of child abuse; this argument is most clearly seen in the claim, "Child Abuse: as the child has the right to protection from the moment of conception, through every stage of development, the government, acting for the common good, should take prudent and appropriate action to protect the life and safety of any child threatened" (Falwell 1981: 135–136).

The argument that the humanist approach is the reason for society's moral failure highlights the connection between respect for human life and religious values; "If man is not made in the image of God, nothing then stands in the way of inhumanity" (Koop and Schaeffer 1979: 29). The link between the morality and religion appears also in Falwell, who argues that now, in our society, we are losing respect for the sanctity of human life. America has allowed more lives to be killed through abortion than in all our wars and traffic accidents. Only a perverted society would make laws protecting wolves and eagles' eggs, and yet have no protection for precious unborn human life (1981: 166).

This link is problematic since it defines the debate over abortion as a debate over religion, thus limiting the support for the pro-life mission. Schaeffer and Koop themselves reject this link when they argue that abortion "is not a religious issue. It is a human issue!" (53).

The pro-life movement recognized that avoiding the use of religious justifications as the basis for the claim of sanctity of the life of the fetus, instead structuring it purely as a moral argument was essential for its success. For example, as Father Driscoll argued, "I make a distinction between religious and moral beliefs.... The church should not try to force its religious beliefs on others, but I believe this is a moral issue, just like Vietnam. The issue then as now, was: is this the right way to treat our fellow man?" (Klemesurd 1978). In his response to the claim that the church's position on abortion threatens women's rights, a Catholic Bishop answers: "We... stand with the child who has no voice of his or her own, and we also stand with the woman facing problems in pregnancy, doing all we can to provide her with effective, morally acceptable assistance" (Hyer 1985). This point, pro-life activists argue, explains why "there are countless people in our country who uphold protection of the human fetus and do not base their position on 'religious doctrine'" (Ahern 1982).

Instead of religious references, pro-life supporters used arguments regarding the essential value of human life. These arguments, however, are often vague; even in the few cases that employ the human rights discourse, there is no explicit justification for the claim of sanctity of life. For example, in his 1974 appearance in front of the Senate Committee on the Judiciary's Subcommittee on Constitutional Amendments, John Cardinal Krol, the Archbishop of Philadelphia, stated that "we do not propose to advocate sectarian doctrine but to defend human rights, and specifically, the most fundamental of all rights, the right to life itself" (Rubin 1994: 192). One example of such a general claim appeared in the letter to the editor published in *The New York Times* in 1976; "The right to life must be the founding right if our nation is to remain a nation of freedom and equality for all." A similar statement was made by the Rev. James Brix, stating that the reason for activism in the pro-life movement is "So that the babies in their mommies' stomachs won't be killed" (Ziebart 1985).

The analysis of newspaper items also reveals this tendency to focus on nonreligious, moral arguments to justify the claim to prohibit abortion. Between 1973 and 1994, the argument that the fetus is a human being and, thus, should not be aborted appeared 185 times (70 % of all fetus-centered references). In 141 of these cases, however, this argument remained general—and even vague—with no explicit justification, religious or otherwise.[4] The lack of any justification is manifested in statements such as "It's a constant awareness of how precious life is and how it's really being destroyed. We're just totally involved in the helpless unborn—they have no one to speak for them" (Marcus and Churchville 1985). The focus on morality—rather than religion—emphasizes that the fetus is a human being, regardless of personal belief;

> we in the Pro-Life movement (what a glorious affirmation!) are not 'demanding to make abortion a crime.' To the victimized child in the womb, abortion is already the foulest of crimes. What we are striving to do is secure for the unborn the same legal protection and guarantee of civil rights as are enjoyed by their fellow human beings (Lynch 1984).

Defining the pro-life argument as a moral statement creates a discourse that is quite vague in nature, but at the same time able to broaden the base of support for the pro-life movement.

The tendency to limit the use of religious references when justifying the pro-life approach, however, is less evident in the pro-life websites. Out of 109 organizations that use fetus-centered arguments, 52 (48 %) include some type of religious argument as a justification for this approach. Out of the 52 websites, only 11 (21 %) are organizations with a direct link to church bodies, such as Priests for Life or Lutherans for Life.[5] Similar to the discourse that appears in newspapers, the religious arguments used by both religious and nonreligious organizations often frame the pro-life position as a moral decision. However, the websites often emphasize the religious basis of this approach, arguing that this position is rooted in the Bible and is thus unchangeable. The Bible,

---

[4] The emphasis on universal—rather than religious—arguments for the sanctity of life continues even today. Between 1995 and 2015, the argument that the fetus is a human being appeared 253 times, while in only 64 cases it appeared together with some religious reference.

[5] Out of the 152 websites surveyed, 19 websites had such religious affiliation. Of the 19 websites, 8 focused either on women—mainly support centers for women who have had an abortion—or on men, who lost their child as a result of abortion.

according to these websites, establishes that human life is sacred; "So God created man in his own image, in the image of God he created him; male and female he created them" (Focus on the Family 2015).[6] Since human life starts from the moment of conception and ends with natural death, "abortion is the act of killing a human person and it is always wrong without exceptions" (Stand True 2015).[7] This human being is not only in the image of God; "God Himself was born as a child. The greatness of a person does not depend on size, for the new-born King is very small. Let us pray for an end to prejudice against the tiny babies threatened by abortion" (Priests for Life 2015). While we need to see Christ in the face of all human beings, this is especially important when regarding those who are not seen by society as humans, or as fully humans; "Seeing Christ in the faces of others as they stand smiling before us is easy, but we need to see him, as Mother Teresa did, as an Untouchable covered in filth and flies and in a handful of undifferentiated human cells" (Maier 2005).

Out of the 109 websites that include fetus-centered arguments, 57 (52 %) do not use religious references in their discussion of the sanctity of the life of the fetus, and 30 (28 %) present neither religious nor scientific arguments as the justification for this claim. The nonscientific and nonreligious discourse includes the same general language as appears in the newspapers in these cases. For example, the mission of National Right to Life is to "protect and defend the most fundamental right of humankind, the right to life of every innocent human being from the beginning of life to natural death." As part of their "Sanctity of Human Life Guide," Focus on the Family states:

> We believe that human life is of inestimable worth and significance in all its dimensions, including the preborn, the aged, the widowed, the mentally and physically challenged, the unattractive and every other condition in which humanness is expressed from the single-cell stage to natural death. In short, human life is sacred and respect for human life should be at the center of all we do (Rosati 2015).

[6] All quotes used in this section reflect arguments and statements that are often used by pro-life websites, thus highlighting common trends and tendencies rather than unique or extreme cases.

[7] The organization Survivors of the Abortion Holocaust, for example, also makes a very similar argument, using almost exactly the same language.

The fact that the fetus is a human being means, "abortion is meant to cause death. Every single time an abortion is performed, the goal is to kill a human being. Sometimes it kills a baby and a woman. Sometimes a baby escapes the procedure but is murdered for being a survivor" (Concerned Women for America 2015). In addition, Life Dynamics defines this debate as circular—"If it is not a baby, you are not pregnant"—while Abolish Human Abortion adds that it is illogical; "If the fetus were merely a collection of isolated cells, each cell undergoing its own developmental process, if left alone wouldn't each cell develop into its own separate fetus?"

Thus, while the frequency of the use of religious references differs between the sources, including newspapers and websites, in both, the argument regarding the sanctity of life plays a part in the pro-life discourse. The moral argument, with its central role in this discourse, remains underdeveloped in most of the arguments to eliminate access to abortion. Additionally, the claim that the fetus is a human being is justified by use of scientific arguments and evidence. This justification, which appears in both the newspapers and websites, is often used together with the religious argument, to provide a comprehensive argument for the need to protect the life of the fetus.

The Scientific Argument for the Fetus as a Human Being

From its inception, the pro-life movement has been using science to argue that the fetus is a human being. In this case, science is used in two different—and sometimes opposing—ways. First, science is used to argue that there is a clear answer to the question of when life begins, which is from the moment of conception. When society realizes this answer, pro-life activists believe, it will change public opinion on abortion. Furthermore, it will lead to the repeal of *Roe*, since the decision to legalize abortions was influenced by the absence of a clear answer regarding when life begins. Second, the constant development in scientific knowledge, pro-life activists argue, clarifies that science is unable to introduce a fixed and unchanging timeline of viability or definition of when life begins. Therefore, scientific developments that allow premature babies to survive outside the womb, allows for conception to serve as the moment when life begins. While both of these claims introduce a different understanding of science, one as immutable and fixed, the other emphasizes constant change, these arguments nevertheless conclude with the same assumption that life begins at the moment of conception.

The first argument is that the scientific community has always considered the fetus to be a human being. Eugene Diamond, the President of the American Association of Pro-Life Pediatricians, argued that researchers and scientists agree that the answer to the question of when life begins is conception. The current debates over the issue are a new development, influenced by social and political interests and not by scientific data; "Prior to 1973 (when Roe v. Wade became law), embryology and obstetrics textbooks stated unequivocally: 'Life begins with the fertilization of the ovum by the spermatozoa.' Furthermore, the "life" in question was obviously viewed as uniquely and indisputably human: The zygote thus formed represents the beginning of life for a new unique individual" (1992). Different doctors and researchers, Diamond stated, agreed with this statement. As a proof, he quoted professionals who said "by all of the criteria of modern molecular biology, life is present from the moment of conception"; "It is scientifically correct to say that an individual human life begins at conception.... Our laws, one function of which is to help preserve the lives of our people, should be based on accurate scientific data"; and, "this straightforward biological fact (the beginning of life is conception) should not be distorted to serve sociological, political, or economic goals" (Diamond 1992). Jerry Falwell makes a similar argument in his book *Listen, America!*, arguing that the people in the scientific community agree

> that an 'individual organism (the zygote) cannot be a part of the mother... it has entirely different set of chromosomes...it has a separate and unique life.'...the moment of birth is not a moment of magic when a potential being is transformed into an actual being. The unborn child is merely moving from a required aquatic environment to a required gaseous environment so that it can develop into its next stage of life (1981: 168).

The use of scientific knowledge arguing that the fetus is a human being appeared early in the pro-life discourse. One of the ways in which the scientific argument was utilized was through fetal imagery, showing that the fetus is a baby, helping people to identify its humanness (Crenshaw 1995; Petchesky 1987). Schaeffer and Koop were among the first to employ the use of fetal imagery in an antiabortion campaign, a strategy that was later embraced and expanded by John Willke in his best-selling *Handbook on Abortion* (1979). In the 1980s, the use of this imagery became common and widespread among the pro-life movement. According to the pro-life movement, the benefit of these technological developments is that they allow the public to see what was always known in the scientific community: that despite being in the womb, the fetus is already a baby. According to this approach, the technological developments allow us to acknowledge the real nature of the fetus. Thus, while there is no change in the scientific knowledge, or in the fact that the fetus is a human being, the ability of the public to access this knowledge and information does change.[8]

The second way in which science was used to argue that the fetus should be treated as a human being is by focusing on scientific and medical developments that have changed the moment of viability. These developments prove that our current knowledge should not be used to determine when life begins; since the advancement of science changes the definition of viability, it is thus clear that we should not use the current definition of viability—or this concept altogether—as a way to determine when life begins. As Schaeffer and Koop argued, "it is impossible for anyone to say when a developing fetus becomes viable, that is, has the ability to exist on its own. Smaller and smaller premature infants are being saved every year!" (1979: 37). The issue of fetal viability, and how it changes following medical and technological developments, is addressed also in newspapers. For example, according to John Willke, while in 1989 the survival rate of babies born in week 23 was only around 10 %, "he had seen newspaper accounts of babies born at 20 weeks of pregnancy and survived…'There have been no survivors that anyone knows of below 20 weeks,' he added, 'but it could be that next week we'll save an 18- or 19-weeker'" (Kolta 1989). According to this statement, although 24 weeks might be the point of viability today, current and future technological developments might change it. Scientific developments thus make evident the inability to establish viability through scientific tools, and further prove that life starts at conception.

Despite being part of the argument regarding the sanctity of life, the scientific argument was never very common in the pro-life discourse,

---

[8]The assumption that fetal imagery is one way in which the public can recognize the humanity of the fetus also stands at the center of some legislation, mainly laws that require mandatory ultrasound (The Guttmacher Institute 2015e). According to this belief, showing pregnant women this image essentially humanizes their fetus, deterring them from having an abortion. While there is significant controversy regarding the effect of this viewing on a woman's decision to abort, the most recent data available on the effect of ultrasound on rates of abortion seems to conclude that women who are interested in having an abortion are not influenced by these images (Gatter et al. 2014).

as it appears in newspaper items. Between the years 1973 and 1994, scientific arguments were mentioned 41 times, accounting for 16 % of all fetus-centered arguments. Until the early 1990s, these references were spread almost evenly, with one to three references every year starting in 1978. While in the early and mid-1990s the number of references increased to four to five per year, the late 1990s were again characterized by a decline in the number of references, which remain low until today; between 1995 and 2015 there are only 30 scientific references used as the basis for the argument that the fetus is a human being, which account for only 8 % of all fetus-centered arguments. Similar to the first argument regarding the sanctity of the life of the fetus, the scientific and medical references often do not include explicit calls for women not to abort their fetuses. Instead, the assumption is that proving the fetus is a human being is enough to promote antiabortion sentiments and policies among people who have some pro-choice tendencies or preferences. For example, a pro-life supporter writes that as every high school student knows, "the life of every organism, human or not, begins when the chromosomes of the sperm fuse with the chromosome of the ovum" (Walker 1981). The pro-life motivation of saving lives is thus based on the "clear, scientific evidence that each fertilized human ovum is an individual human person, and is therefore entitled to the same rights to life and liberty (including privacy) that other children and adults have" (Montanaro 1991). The conclusion of this scientific evidence and use of imagery is clear; "You see sonograms, you see five fingers. If it really is alive, and has a heartbeat, then why is it legal to kill? To me, it's hypocrisy" (Goodstein 1998).

The scientific-based discourse, however, is much more prevalent in the websites than in the newspapers. Out of 109 pro-life websites that use the fetus-centered claim, 39 (36 %) use scientific arguments to develop their claim that the fetus is a human being. Out of these 39, 12 (23 %) websites use this argument together with religious arguments regarding sanctity of life. These websites include current scientific information and citation, showing that life begins at conception. For example, on the website, Science for Unborn Human Life (2015), it is stated that "as noted in Williams Obstetrics (20th edition, 1997: 151), 'The status of the unborn child has been elevated to that of a patient, who, in large measure, can be given the same meticulous care that obstetricians provide pregnant women.'"

One example of the common argument that the question of when life begins is not debated among the scientific community is evident in

National Right to Life's website; "The question of when life begins is not an issue of theology or philosophy; it can easily be answered by elementary biology. For more than 100 years, medical science has known conclusively that every individual's life begins at the moment of fertilization" (National Right to Life 2015b). The answer to the question of when life begins is thus unchanging, and is affected neither by new data nor by technology. A similar argument is made by the Charlotte Lozier Institute, a research and education institute that aims to "promote deeper public understanding of the value of human life, motherhood, and fatherhood, and to identify policies and practices that will protect life and serve both women's health and family well-being." The humanity of the fetus, they argue, is clear and has never been questioned:

> the scientific basis for distinguishing one cell type from another rests on two criteria: differences in what something is made of (its molecular composition) and differences in how the cell behaves. These two criteria are universally agreed upon and employed throughout the scientific enterprise. They are not 'religious' beliefs or matters of personal opinion. They are objective, verifiable scientific criteria that determine precisely when a new cell type is formed (Charlotte Lozier Institute 2015b).

The use of fetal imagery is common within the pro-life movement. The website of the organization National Right to Life, for example, includes a section titled "Baby Rose photo album," which contains photos of Rose from a 6-week-old fetus through her birth and until her second birthday. The photos are accompanied by titles such as "Tiny, cute, and so perfectly formed!" and "Guess what? My brain waves can now be detected. I am going to be a smart girl!" (National Right to Life 2015a). The ultrasound images are thus used to create a photo album that starts within the womb, while the birth is described as an event that takes place after 9 months of life. According to this account, published on the website Abortion Facts (2015), "personhood is properly defined by membership in the human species, not by stage of development within that species. A living being's designation to a species is determined not by the stage of development but by the sum total of its biological characteristics." The use of scientific facts regarding fetal development, together with ultrasound and other fetal images that have become available through technological developments, promotes the claim that the physical attributes, behaviors, and capabilities are already developed within fetuses.

One topic with an increasing presence in pro-life websites is the issue of fetal pain, which is used to emphasize the humanity of the fetus.[9] Out of the 109 websites that address fetus-centered concerns, at least 16 (15 %) websites include a detailed explanation of the scientific evidence regarding fetal pain; most maintain that the fetus can feel pain at 20 weeks and, thus, abortion after that time is torture. In the attempt to frame this discussion as scientific, most of the websites use scientific information and testimony of researchers and medical professionals. For example, the website for Minnesota Citizens Concerned for Life, quotes Dr. Paul Ranalli, saying that "at 20 weeks, the fetal brain has the full complement of brain cells present in adulthood, ready and waiting to receive pain signals from the body, and their electrical activity can be recorded by standard electroencephalography (EEG)." The Charlotte Lozier Institute website also uses research to argue for early fetal responses to painful stimuli; "The earliest reactions to painful stimuli motor reflexes can be detected at 7.5 weeks of gestation [5.5 weeks post-fertilization]" (Charlotte Lozier Institute 2015a). According to the 2004 testimony of Dr. Kanwaljeet "Sunny" Anand before Congress, fetuses experience more intense pain than adults, since "mechanisms that inhibit or moderate the experience of pain do not begin to develop until 32–34 weeks post-fertilization. Any pain the unborn child experiences before these pain inhibitors are in place is likely more intense than the pain an older infant or adult experiences when subjected to similar types of injury" (Charlotte Lozier Institute 2015a). As in the case of other scientific arguments, the statements regarding fetal pain appear with no explicit call for women to avoid abortion. Instead, this conclusion is assumed to be obvious, in light of this scientific evidence that proved the humanness of the fetus.

The last issue addressed by pro-life websites regarding technological and medical developments is the increasing ability of medical professionals to detect fetal abnormalities. This ability, pro-life activists argue, often results in abortion, thus requiring the pro-life movement to address this issue directly.[10] As a response to this trend, some pro-life organizations that oppose abortion even in the case of a birth of a dead baby emphasize

[9] The issue of fetal pain is mentioned in some newspaper pieces in the early 1980s, such as in the case of articles in *The Washington Post* from 1982 to 1984, in which pro-life activists mention the pain that the fetus feels. However, statements from the 1980s regarding fetal pain are rare, and often without mentioning scientific research on the topic. The focus on fetal pain is more clearly evident in legislation, as will be discussed later in this chapter. While antiabortion restrictions based on fetal pain have become common in the last few years (Robertson 2013), the first bill addressing this issue appeared in 1983 (H.R. 203).

[10] While this information is difficult to verify, pro-life organizations, such as LifeNews, claim that 9 out of 10 fetuses diagnosed with Down syndrome are aborted (2013b).

the important role of perinatal hospice and care. Out of 109 websites that focus on the fetus, 11 (10 %) organizations focus on perinatal care for parents who decide to carry the pregnancy to term if their fetus suffers from fetal abnormalities that will most likely lead to a stillbirth or death shortly after the birth. In contrast to organizations that target parents whose children will most likely die at a young age, the focus on perinatal care primarily takes place when the fetus is within the womb. It is argued that this service provides women the gift of time with their baby, even if their life is limited to before birth. The idea of embracing life, regardless of its nature or length, is reflected in the website Perinatal Hospice: A Gift of Time (2015);

> if you are here because of a prenatal diagnosis that indicates your baby likely will die before or after birth, we are so sorry. Perhaps you are considering continuing your pregnancy and embracing whatever time you may be able to have with your baby, even if that time is only before birth, while your baby is cradled safely inside of you.

Abortion, according to this approach, is never an acceptable solution, not even if the child is going to die a few hours after birth, or be born dead. Continuing the pregnancy is

> a parenting decision that honors the baby as well as the parents. It allows you to parent your baby as long as possible and to protect your child for as long as he or she is able to live. Ultimately, it allows you to give your baby—and yourself—the full measure of your baby's life and the gift of a peaceful, natural goodbye. Continuing the pregnancy is not about passively waiting for death. It is about actively embracing the brief, shining moment of this little life (Perinatal Hospice).

The argument that the fetus is a human being, even during pregnancy, leads to the conclusion that abortion is never justified;

> Just because the baby is likely to die through a natural delivery, that does not justify an intentional killing. For example, if a rescuer is venturing into a burning vehicle to try to save its injured occupants, and is only able to save one of the two occupants, is it justifiable for him to then take out his gun and shoot the occupant he was unable to save? Of course not! Intentionally killing those you were not able to save is never justified in healthcare. We have the technology and expertise to provide quality healthcare to a pregnant woman without intentionally killing her unborn baby, regardless of the severity of her disease (Association of Pro-life Physicians 2015).

Abortion as Genocide or the Holocaust

The third type of argument that constitutes the fetus-centered discourse is the claim that abortion is an act of genocide, similar to the Holocaust. This comparison emphasizes that abortion is not only murder, but it is actually a systematically immoral act, a social phenomenon that signifies the lack of morality and values in society today. This comparison also highlights the severity of the act, and the lack of moral disagreement regarding the nature of abortion. While today this discourse often emphasizes race—arguing that abortion policies are meant to disproportionately affect African Americans and are thus used as a form of genocide—earlier references to these arguments focus less on race and more on the systematic and immoral nature of abortion.

The link between abortion and the Holocaust appears already in Schaeffer and Koop's book, which starts with a reference to Yad Vashem, Israel's official memorial to the victims of the Holocaust. This reference is used to remind us of the unlimited capacities of human evil. Abortion, they argue, allows human beings to decide who should live and who should die, just like Nazism and slavery. This comparison has since then become an integral part of the pro-life discourse surrounding abortion. Ron Paul, for example, warned in 1981 that in the case of abortion,

> the State protects the 'right' of some people to kill others, just as the courts protected the 'property rights' of slave masters in their slaves.... Unlike Nazi Germany, which forcibly sent millions to the gas chambers (as well as forcing abortion and sterilization upon many more), the new regime has enlisted the assistance of millions of people to act as its agents in carrying out a program of mass murder (Meagher 2008: 169).

The idea that individuals are allowed to kill a human being reminds us "an earlier time in our nation's history, a time of marked embarrassment to all American people, when individuals were permitted to determine for themselves whether those with black skin were human begins to be respected as such, or property to be used according to one's will" (Bachiochi 2004: 27). Nellie Gray, an organizer of the March For Life, also used a similar discourse when she warns that legislators who vote for abortion "will be held accountable, just as the Nuremberg trials found individuals personally responsible for crimes committed against humanity" (Isaacson 1981: 27). Abortion is thus a moral wrong, which although not yet recognized, should be universally accepted as such in the future.

The analysis of the newspaper items reveals that the references to the Holocaust or genocide appeared as early as the mid-1970s. Between 1973 and 1994, the comparison of abortion and genocide or the Holocaust, or references that create such a link, appeared 36 times, which accounts for 14 % of all fetus-centered claims. For example, the keynote address in the National Right to Life convention in 1979, given by William C. Brennan, was entitled "Medical Holocaust." The lecture

> compared abortions in America in the 1970s to the extermination of Jews by Nazi Germany in the 1940's. 'American doctors have, since the Supreme Court Decision in 1973, destroyed over six million unborn human beings'... Licensed physicians, he said, are 'the executioners,' the bureaucrats who provide support services are the 'medical mercenaries,' and the Upjohn Company, which manufactures medicines and devices used for abortions, is the I.G. Farben, a reference to the German Company that made chemicals used in mass executions (Herbers 1979).

The comparison between abortion and the Holocaust, pro-life activists argue, clarifies that abortion is even a bigger problem than the Holocaust; "It is high time that someone remind these pro-abortionists that there is a holocaust going on that dwarfs even the horrible Jewish one, taking 50 million lives every year, worldwide" (Cooper 1995).

The argument regarding the immorality of abortion is made also by linking abortion to slavery, thus emphasizing the immoral nature of the ruling as well as the practice. For example, in 1980, Carolyn Gerster, president of the National Right to Life Committee, stated, "In 1857, the supreme court voted seven to two in the Dred Scott decision that a slave in not a person.... And just as that mistake had to be corrected by the 13th and 14th amendments to the constitution, the mistake of 1973 will have to be corrected by the Human Life Amendment" ("Right to Life Committee Plan Drives" 1980). In this case, the reference to slavery is used to argue that despite current social assumptions, in the future we will recognize the moral wrong of abortion. Thus, while morality is fixed, it sometimes takes time for society to recognize it. In other cases, however, pro-life activists use the comparison between abortion and slavery to explicitly highlight the racial aspect of the practice, arguing that abortion influences African American communities more significantly than white communities. This discourse, while rare, appears in newspaper items with pro-life-discourse; between 1973 and 1994, the link between abortion and race was mentioned only eight times (3 % of the fetus-centered references), less than the 28 references (10 %) to genocide or the Holocaust. This tendency did not change much in later years; between 1995 and 2015, the pro-life discourse found in newspapers included references to genocide or the Holocaust in 8 % of the fetus-centered arguments, and slavery in 5 % of the cases. As in a letter to the editor from 1994, the references to slavery often emphasize the higher rates of abortion among blacks to argue for the need to remind "black abortion clinic staff that abolitionists, black and white, did not fight and die so that future generations of black women could achieve equal access to the abortion clinic" ("Pro-Life Preacher" 1994). As such, these references, while small in numbers, link abortion to the mission to change demographics in a systematic and horrific matter (Mason 1999).

The analysis of websites reveals different tendencies in the comparison between abortion and race, though the comparison of abortion and genocide or the Holocaust remains at a similar level; out of 109 websites that use the fetus-centered discourse, 14 (13 %) include some reference to genocide or the Holocaust. The link between abortion and race, however, appears in 29 (19 %) of the 152 websites surveyed. Out of these 29 websites, 21 are fetus centered, while the other 8 websites focus mainly on the influence of abortion on the parents, including the fathers. The analysis of the websites thus shows an increase in the use of the argument that abortion is a racist practice. While some websites still emphasize the link between abortion and genocide or the Holocaust, the majority of the websites use these references to highlight issues of race; 9 of the 14 websites that include references to genocide or the Holocaust include also references to race or slavery.

When introducing the link between abortion and race, numerous organizations argue that "abortion, by the numbers, is a racist institution… abortion kills minority children at more than three times the rate of non-Hispanic, white children" (Abort 73 2015). The racist aspect of abortion is proven through the comparison of the percentage of blacks and minority in the population against their percentage among women obtaining abortion. For example, a quote used by dozens of pro-life websites, as well as numerous news websites and activists, argues that

> according to 2010 census data, African–Americans make up 12.6 percent of the U.S. population but the Centers for Disease Control (CDC) reports that black women accounted for 35.4 percent of all abortions in 2009. The Guttmacher Institute puts the percentage of black abortions at 30 percent

of the U.S. total. Their most recent numbers are from 2008. Similarly, the Guttmacher Institute reports that Hispanic women accounted for 25 percent of all U.S. abortions in 2008, although Hispanics make up just 16.3 percent of the U.S. population. The CDC lists the percentage of Hispanic abortions at 20.6 percent. Comparing those numbers to non-Hispanic whites, who make up 63.7 percent of America's population, but account for only 36 percent of all U.S. abortions (or 37.7 according to the CDC) (Abort 73 2015).

The higher percentages of black and minority women who obtain abortions, these websites argue, indicate that abortion is an action that not only affects the fetus and their family. Rather, abortion holds significant implications for the social structure and lives of minorities; "Abortion's negative impact has significantly contributed to African–Americans being the only minority in America whose population is in decline. Hispanics are now the largest minority group in the country. If the current trend continues, the black community may cease to make a significant positive contribution in society" (Protecting Black Lives 2015). Therefore, as the organization, *Too Many Aborted* argued, abortion is the biggest civil rights struggle of our day.

How can we rise if our future is flushed down the drain? And we mean, literally, flushed down the drain. Over 1000 times a day, the body parts of black babies are torn from their mother's womb, ground in garbage disposals and washed away like sewage. This is the reality of 'choice' that often scares women away from any other option that doesn't end in death. Despite the reality that more black babies are aborted than born alive in NYC (although all abortions are a tragedy), the nation's largest black 'civil rights' groups have done nothing to address this epidemic (Bomberger 2013).

As part of their strategy, the organization's billboards include statements such as "Black children are an endangered species" and "Gone: 15 Million and Counting." The phenomenon of billboards emphasizing the racial aspect of abortion was also used in 2011, when 200 billboards sponsored by the group Life Always appeared throughout the U.S., mainly in cities and neighborhoods with a predominately African American population (Fried 2013). The billboards included a picture of a young, African American girl, stating, "The most dangerous place for an African–American is in the womb." This systematic targeting of minorities is intentional; "As Supreme Court Justice Ruth Bader Ginsburg said in 2009, *Roe v. Wade* enabled them to address 'the population we don't want too many of.' The numbers do not lie" (Life Restoration Project). Therefore, African Americans need to realize that the fight against abortion is the civil-right struggle of the day.

In the attempt to highlight the link between abortion and race, a few organizations focus on Planned Parenthood, a nonprofit that provides reproductive health services including abortion. Two of the websites surveyed—Klan Parenthood and Stop Planned Parenthood (STOPP)—are organizations that focus their struggle against abortion primarily on eliminating Planned Parenthood. In addition, 30 other organizations (20 %) mention Planned Parenthood in their websites, often referring to it as an "abortion company" or an "abortion mill." While in most cases Planned Parenthood is mentioned in relation to issues of race or genocide, other references address the issue of funding for abortions, and the risk that the organization introduces to women's health and safety.

The racial references made in this discourse often establish a link between Planned Parenthood and Margaret Sanger, a birth control activist from the early twentieth century, emphasizing her ties to the science of eugenics. For example, the website Too Many Aborted mentions Margaret Sanger and her project from 1939 to get rid of the "poor, black, and undesirable."[11] Her connection to Planned Parenthood explains why "today, the same mouthpieces for Planned Parenthood are claiming 'lack of access' while black women visit abortion clinics at five times the rate of white women. This is by design. Abortion kills more black lives (363,705) than *all other causes* of death **combined** (285,522)" (Too Many Aborted 2015). The organization Black Genocide also argues that there is a link between Planned Parenthood and racism;

> We are the only minority in America that is on the decline in population. If the current trend continues, by 2038 the black vote will be insignificant. Did you know that the founder of Planned Parenthood, Margaret Sanger, was a devout racist who created the Negro Project designed to sterilize unknowingly black women and others she deemed as undesirables of society? The founder of Planned Parenthood said, 'Colored people are like human weeds and are to be exterminated.' Is her vision being fulfilled today? (Black Genocide 2015)

[11] The accusations against Sanger have been used often by pro-life activists, as well as by politicians such as Herman Cain in his campaign for presidency (Kessler 2011). The reality is much more complex; Sanger believed in family planning, not based on class or race, and believed in the right of women to express their sexuality while also choosing not to give birth. She was associated at one point with the Eugenics Movement, but before the Holocaust.

Also, these organizations often emphasize the geographical location of Planned Parenthood clinics, arguing that the locations are part of their racist strategy. For example, the organization High School Students for Life includes a statement that even today, "the abortion industry continues to target and disproportionately affect the black population. Seventy nine percent of Planned Parenthood abortion clinics are located in minority communities. Black women are 3× more likely to get an abortion than a white woman. About 1000 black children are aborted every day" (2015) The organization Population Research Institute claims "four out of five Planned Parenthood clinics are located in minority neighborhoods, with blacks as the primary target. About one-third of all abortions are performed on blacks, even though they make up only 13 percent of the population (Population Research Institute 2015)."

The organizations and discourse focusing on Planned Parenthood are often the more extreme within the pro-life movement. For example, one of the slogans of the website Klan Parenthood is "Because lynching is for amateurs." They develop this argument on their homepage explaining "The Ku Klux Klan lynching of blacks can't hold a candle to Planned Parenthood when it comes to killing black children. Lynching by the Klu Klux Klan isn't as efficient at killing Blacks as Planned Parenthood abortions. Thanks to them, in America today, almost as many black babies are killed by abortion as are born (Klan Parenthood 2015)." Mark Crutcher from Life Dynamics provides an additional example in his response to tweets by Planned Parenthood after the Ferguson grand jury decided not to indict Police Officer Darren Wilson in the shooting death of Michael Brown. In his response he states, "This is an absolute and utter disgrace what these people are saying, because the fact is that in the history of the United States the Klu Klux Klan has done far less damage to the African–American community than Planned Parenthood has done to them and continues to do to them every day—and we've proven this" (Butts 2014).

One of only a few websites that uses the terms "Holocaust" and "genocide" without reference to the racial aspect of abortion is Survivors of the Abortion Holocaust. This organization argues that everyone who was born after 1973 is a survivor of the abortion Holocaust. Its activities focus on reaching out to those in schools and colleges, emphasizing their role of survivors—the two-thirds of this generation that were not killed in the abortion Holocaust—in changing the future of abortion in the USA;

Compelled by the Gospel of our Lord Jesus Christ and our respect for life, the Survivors of the Abortion Holocaust speak out on behalf of over 56,000,000 children lost to abortion in America since 1973. Dedicated to defending the right to life of future generations, **we are engaged in a battle to end America's genocide.** We recognize the urgency of this war, as over 3500 children die each day in the United States because of abortion…It happened to us—we are its target (Survivors of the Abortion Holocaust 2015).

Fetal Rights Versus Women's Rights

The last type of justification that makes up the fetus-centered discourse is the argument that the fetus' right to life stands in opposition to women's right to choose. Since there is a clear tension between the interests of the preborn and pregnant women, society, pro-life activists argue, needs to protect the fetus rather than the mother. Placing fetal rights in direct conflict with women's rights led the pro-life movement to largely ignore the issues facing women during the first few decades after *Roe*. This is evident in the analysis of newspaper items; while the fetus-centered discourse was mentioned 287 times between the years 1973 and 1994, women-centered concerns or arguments were mentioned only 69 times, reflecting 21 % of all pro-life arguments made during these years. Most of the references that addressed issues concerning women—61 %—start appearing in the late 1980s, with only 12 instances before 1989.

While most organizations rejected or avoided women-centered arguments until the mid-1990s, one exception is the organization Feminists for Life (FFL). The organization, founded in 1973, argued early on that the danger in abortion is that it allows men to exploit women, while at the same time freeing the state from the need to make sure that women can balance caretaking with their career. Patricia Goltz, one of the founders of the organization, called abortion "an insidious form of enslavement to the Playboy's 'right to fuck' [that] has no place in the women's movement" (Ziegler 2013: 238). As part of their concern over women's exploitation, the organization was also one of the first to address issues of informed consent for abortion. The organization's unique approach led them to support other initiatives that were mostly rejected by the pro-life movement, including the ERA, and actions by the state to address the reasons that led pregnant women to choose abortion, mainly social and economic concerns. For example, they demanded the removal of any mention of illegitimacy from birth certificates in the case of unwed mothers, arguing that reducing the stigma is one way to reduce abortion rates within this population. The influence of FFL within the pro-life movement declined in the late 1970s and early 1980s, when the alliance between the pro-life movement and the Christian Right shifted the movement's agenda, which now emphasized conservative family values and opposition to the ERA.[12]

One of the most common approaches that framed fetal rights in opposition to women's rights was developed partly as a response against the feminist movement, which was seen as supporting women's rights and rejecting family and religious values. Falwell, for example, identifies this conflict when he argued,

> the second weapon against the family is the feminist revolution. This is the counterreaction to the cult of the playboy. Many women are saying, 'Why should I be taken advantage of by chauvinists? I will get out and do my own thing. I will stand up for my rights. I will have my own dirty magazines.' Feminists are saying that self-satisfaction is more important than the family. Most of the women who are leaders in the feminist movement promote an immoral lifestyle (1981: 124).

The feminist movement, according to this account, is threatening not only pro-life assumptions about the sanctity of life but also traditional family values and gender norms. Therefore, there is a need to clarify that the decision over abortion cannot be based on the feminist concept of women's choice. The Family Manifesto of Moral Majority, for example, argued, "we proclaim that parental responsibility for reproductive decisions is joint. Hence we deny that reproduction is solely a 'woman's choice'" defining the issue as beyond just a women's concern (Dowland 2009: 616).

Despite the centrality of the fetus-centered argument, the pro-life discourse in the 1980s nevertheless includes some references to women and the impact of abortion on their lives. This discourse often emphasizes the natural role of women as mothers, and the threat that the feminist move-

---

[12] The uniqueness of FFL among the pro-life movement is evident even today. For example, they argue, "Abortion is a reflection that we have not met the needs of women. Abortion masks the unmet needs of women in the workplace, schools, home, and society. In society—the poor, the working poor, women in difficult and often abusive relationships, and students and women in the workplace whose basic needs are ignored: (FFL 2015)." This claim that abortion is a sign that society failed to meet the needs of women is as exceptional today within the pro-life discourse as their arguments were in the 1970s. More on the organization and its role in the development of the women-centered strategy is presented in Chap. 3.

ment poses—to society, but particularly to women—when they oppose family and traditional values. Thus, abortion hurts women because it acts against "a woman's call to be a wife and mother, which is the highest calling in the world" (Falwell 1981: 124). The shift to feminist values is danger-ous, argued in a letter to the editor, published in '*The Washington Post*' in 1988, since "in women's efforts to be made 'equal,' they have lost complete respect for the role we play, which God has given us and which no man can ever hope to equal—the role of mother! Heaven help us all ("The Abortion Debate Rages" 1988).." These types of arguments, with their concern for the fetus, and also for women, seem to also fit the women-centered strategy, which became prominent in the mid-1990s. However, while this later strat-egy is based almost entirely on scientific language and medical arguments, the discourse of the 1980s that addresses women's concerns, besides being limited and rare, is characterized by a more traditional version of women's natural roles and tendencies, with limited discussion of women's needs. As evident from Falwell's statement from 1986, what women need is help sav-ing their babies, not necessarily themselves; "millions of babies were being killed, and I would go on fighting to save their lives, but what about the other victims of abortion, the mothers of those babies who desperately need help to save their babies?" (Harding 2001: 187).

In light of all of this, women need to be protected from the feminist movement by a strong pro-life movement;

> the no. 1 goal of the women's liberationists is, in the words of Bella S. Abzug, 'to enforce the constitutional right of females to terminate preg-nancies that they do not wish to continue.'…I like being a woman—pro-life, pro-church, pro-children, and all that stands for being a woman…I was asked if I could live in a feminist world. The answer to that question is no. I'm terribly afraid of the feminist. If they want to be identified as men, more power to them. But leave the rest of us alone. Don't let them take away the right to be a woman (Lengers 1978).

This point also appears in Schaeffer and Koop's book, which rarely dis-cusses the needs of mothers, or the effect that abortion might have;

> 'why didn't anyone tell me?' is a fair question from girl suffering the after-effects of a recommended abortion. 'Why didn't anyone tell me I would feel like a mother with empty arms?' 'Why didn't anyone tell me I risked spoiling the possibility of having a normal pregnancy, because of the damage that might be done to my body by the abortion?'…we need to think about

the aborted human beings who have been deprived of a chance to live, but we also need to consider with sympathy and compassion the women being turned into 'aborted mothers'—bereft mothers—bitter in some cases, hard in some cases, exceedingly sorrowful in other cases (1979: 52).

Since, as will be discussed in Chap. 3, the women-centered approach changed significantly in the 1990s, it is not surprising that an examination of the organizations' websites—reflecting the nature of the discourse in 2015—reveals a different approach toward women's concern as compared to newspaper items and discourse from earlier decades. Out of 152 websites surveyed, 103 (68 %) include discourse that addresses the risk and harm of abortion for women. Seventy-one (69 %) of these websites, however, include both fetus-centered and women-centered discourses, while 32 (31 %) focus primarily or exclusively on mothers and fathers, mostly through emphasis on centers and programs dealing with the trauma of abortion. Thus, these organizations often argue against the need to side with either the mother or the fetus, instead claiming that the pro-life movement protects both. This argument is based also on refuting the claim that abortion is sometimes performed to save the mother's life; "Fact #8: Less than 1 % of all abortions are performed to save the life of the mother" (Abortion Facts 2015). In this context, only a small number of organizations today—around 4 % of websites surveyed—position women's rights in opposition to fetal rights. What all these organizations have in common is that they do not focus only on abortion. Instead, they all also fight to preserve family and religious values, opposing issues such as gay marriage and the elimination of school prayer. For example, the website Pro-Life—Ancient Order of Hibernians states "*Roe v. Wade* made the fetus out to be a predator, a threat to family happiness, another potential mouth to feed who might hamper the health and well-being of other family members already there. There would simply not be enough food and clothing and square footage of housing space to accommodate one more human being. The infant in the womb, the stranger in our midst, must go (Wallace 2015)."

In conclusion, the four different types of arguments that compose the fetus-centered strategy differ in nature and frequency; the arguments emphasizing the sanctity of the life of the fetus—based on religious, universal, or scientific claims—appear most often, although primarily without any justification beyond the claim itself. The argument that compares abortion to genocide, the Holocaust, or slavery is used to highlight the immoral nature of the practice, as well as the difficulty in relying on current social norms as the compass of morality. The claim that the rights of the fetus stand in opposition to the rights of women, an argument which later almost entirely disappears from the pro-life discourse, situates the right to life against the right to choose, arguing for the prioritization of the previous over the misguided and self-centered feminist argument. Despite this variation, the account presented here highlights the centrality of the fetus-centered discourse between 1973 and 1994. The centrality of this strategy is evident also in public policy during this period. The next section examines the legislative attempts made from 1973 to 1994, analyzing proposed and enacted bills at the federal and state levels.

4 ABORTION AND PUBLIC POLICY: 1973–1994

The ruling in *Roe v. Wade* invalidated an 1854 Texas statute that criminalized abortion in all cases except the life of the mother. In its ruling, the court recognized the right to privacy between a woman and her physician to decide if abortion is the best form of medical treatment, citing previous rulings that established this right to privacy. Following the court's ruling, almost all state laws concerning abortion were invalidated, particularly those that did not include exceptions for the health and safety of the mother (O'Connor 1996).

In light of this ruling, there were only limited avenues available for legislative intervention in women's decision to procure an abortion during the first trimester. However, the ruling concludes that states have interest in protecting the potential life during the second and third trimesters. Thus, states may establish some restrictions on access to abortion during these trimesters (410 U.S. 113, 1973). Immediately after the ruling was announced, it was unclear how the state and federal courts would respond to legislative attempts to regulate this practice. For policymakers at the federal and state levels, this uncertainty meant that they had to navigate an uncertain legal environment as pro-life supporters lobbied officials to limit access to abortion. Furthermore, given the highly controversial nature of the procedure and the great structural and institutional differences between Congress and state legislatures, the policy responses to this issue varied significantly between these two levels of government.

The factors that led to the adoption of abortion laws have been studied extensively, particularly at the level of the state, although numerous studies also examine abortion law at the federal level (Adams 1997;

Ainsworth and Hall 2011; Brady and Schwartz 1995; Tatalovich and Schier 1993). Previous studies of abortion-related policy development at the level of the state have focused on constituent preferences or public opinion (Arceneaux 2002; Camobreco and Barnello 2008; Cook et al. 1992; Norrander and Wilcox 1999), while conversely other studies focus on elite preferences or those in public office to explain the development of abortion policy (Berkman and O'Connor 1993; Halva-Neubauer 1990; Medoff et al. 2011) or some combination of these forces (Kreitzer 2015; Strickland and Whicker 1992).[13]

The current project, while investigating the development of abortion-related public policy, examines the entire range of policies from 1973 to the present in the aggregate as a means to understand the impact of the pro-life movement on public policy. This analysis of public policy is designed to uncover the impact of the pro-life rhetoric on the type of pro-life policies that emanated from the federal and state legislatures. If the pro-life movement is effective in its attempts to affect attitudes toward the practice of abortion, and in turn public policy, proposed and enacted legislation at both levels of government should reflect policies designed to protect the rights of the fetus. Policies designed to protect various rights of the fetus would illustrate the effect of this discourse, while a more stark example of this impact of this discourse would be policies designed to ban the procedure altogether.

Between the years 1973 and 1994, hundreds of abortion-related bills and resolutions were introduced at the federal level, the majority of which were designed to limit or restrict access to the procedure. Specifically, 794 bills, amendments, and resolutions were introduced at the federal level during this 21-year time period, with 709 (89 %) of these measures being pro-life in nature. The first section of this analysis examines policy development in the first four sessions of Congress immediately after the court's ruling (the 93–96 sessions, from 1973 to 1980) followed by an analysis of the 97–103 sessions, from 1981 to 1994. Although we argue that the shift in discourse occurs in the mid-1990s, thus serving as the demarcation of a significant transformation within the pro-life movement, 1980 is also a turning point given the political changes occurring within the Republican Party at this time. With Reagan's election, and his highly visible pro-life stance, the growing pro-life movement became increasingly mainstream

---

[13] This is in no way serves as an exhaustive list of studies on abortion-related policy development.

and entrenched within the Republican Party, which began its growth in political power during this time period as well.

1973–1980: From 1973 to 1980, 355 bills, amendments, and resolutions were introduced; 342 (96 %) of these measures were pro-life in nature and 278 (78 %) were intended to protect fetal rights. This was attempted primarily through the human life amendment, as well as some proposed bans on fetal research. The remaining 22 % of legislation addressed issues associated with third-party actors such as taxpayers or health professionals (18 %) and women (4 %). Despite the magnitude of legislation introduced during these years, particularly in the years immediately following the ruling, little was enacted into law and the vast majority of these successful legislation efforts addressed issues indirectly associated with the procedure. Proportionally, a similar phenomenon occurred at the state level, with a relatively small number of enacted abortion restrictions in place by the mid-1970s.

From 1973 to 1980, the most frequently proposed measure was the human life amendment, introduced through 266 independent proposals, representing 75 % of all abortion-related proposals introduced during this 8-year period. Despite some variations in the wording of these proposals, the primary purpose was clear: to amend the US Constitution to overturn the decision in *Roe v. Wade*. This amendment—if successful—would give legal status or "personhood" to a fetus from the moment of conception. Further, the amendment would restrict the jurisdiction of the Supreme Court on the issue of abortion, returning this authority to the states. Many of these measures propose to afford due process and equality protections to all persons "irrespective of age, health, function or condition of dependency, including the unborn" (H.J. Res 464, 1977). Others declare that the protections afforded "persons" under the 5th and 14th Amendments extends to all human beings, "including unborn offspring at every stage of biological development" (S.J. Res 10, 1975).

A smaller proportion of human life amendments focused on limiting the jurisdiction of the Supreme Court on the issue of abortion, returning the authority to regulate back to the states. For example, H.J. Res 527 would amend the US Constitution to "grant the States power to regulate or forbid the voluntary termination of human pregnancy" (1975). This attempt by members of Congress to overturn the ruling in *Roe* through an amendment to the constitution—in this instance by removing jurisdiction from the Supreme Court over abortion—related case law—is not unique to this particular instance. Initiatives to limit the jurisdiction of the court has occurred a number of times in the past, particularly after rulings on controversial issues such as school prayer and busing, and will no doubt continue in the future (Kay 1981). Despite the intense drive toward enacting this constitutional amendment, to date any such proposal has died in committee.

As a constitutional amendment establishing personhood and limiting the court's jurisdiction over abortion remained out of reach, members of Congress achieved abortion restrictions through other means. Despite this focus on fetal rights in the vast majority of proposed measures, the legislative successes at the federal level were achieved mainly in two other areas: refusal clauses and funding restrictions, both of which focus on the rights of third-party actors. Following the decision in *Roe*, Congress quickly passed the Church Amendment during the 93rd session (1973), which was added to the Health Programs Extension Act, prohibiting public officials from requiring individuals or facilities to provide abortion services if they receive public funds (42 U.S.C. § 300a–7(b)). This conscience clause continues to be in effect today, although the number and breadth of conscience clauses enacted at the federal level have increased overtime. Beside the Church Amendment, there was very little success in enacting abortion restrictions at the federal level during this time period, particularly with those measures most commonly proposed.

Restrictions on payment or funding for abortions—both therapeutic and elective—were included in numerous spending bills, beginning with the Foreign Assistance Act of 1973 (22 U.S.C. 2151a). Between 1973 and 1980, 11 appropriations bills included restrictions on funding for abortion. These acts range from the Social Security Act, Department of Defense spending bills, Department of Health, Labor, Education, and Welfare appropriations, to the District of Columbia appropriations act. As part of numerous riders that fund or prohibit funding for various projects and procedures, these bills included restrictions on funding for abortion. In practice, in the intermediate aftermath of the *Roe* ruling, and despite the intense controversy surrounding the ruling and the procedure more generally, the primary legislative success to limit abortion was achieved through funding restrictions on annual appropriations for a range of departments and services.[14] Thus, despite the attention given to fetal rights or establishing personhood for the fetus, the only legislative success pro-life officials found included funding

---

[14] Both refusal clauses and funding restrictions will be examined in greater detail in Chap. 4.

restrictions (11), refusal or conscience clauses (3), and an amendment to the Legal Services Act.[15] Congressional reaction to the *Roe* ruling, while swift and intense, was largely unsuccessful in achieving an overturning of the precedent or establishing significant restrictions access to the procedure in general.

At the state level, the court's ruling in *Roe* overturned virtually all state laws, including outright bans on the procedure as well as bans that were too vague in nature. As a result, from 1973 to 1980, 37 states and the District of Columbia enacted 104 abortion-related laws. During this time period, Illinois and Massachusetts produced the greatest amount of legislation (seven and five bills, respectively), with little variation among the states as a whole. Out of the 104 laws, only one pro-choice law passed at the state level, in Washington, DC. This law established a minor's right to consent to receive medical treatment for pregnancy or its lawful termination (D.C. Mun. Regs. Subt. 22-B, § 600). As expected, the legislation emanating from the states varies in nature from that which emerged in Congress during this time period. While at the federal level, all personhood or fetal rights proposals either died in committee or failed to pass, at the state level, there was some success with regard to fetal rights policies. At the state level, 32 % of the laws passed during this time period included some protection of fetal rights; 22 of these fetal rights measures (67 %) are restrictions on abortions after viability.

In *Roe*, the court established that a woman's right to an abortion, without significant burdens imposed by the state, extends until viability. Viability, defined by the ruling, is the potential ability of the fetus to live outside the womb, usually placed at 27 or 28 weeks (410 U.S. 113, 1973). The laws that restrict post-viable abortions at the state level vary in their definition of the point of viability. For example, Idaho's ban declares that no abortion may be performed after viability, construed as when a fetus is "potentially able to live outside the mother's womb, albeit with artificial aid" (Idaho Code § 18-604, 1973). Similarly, Nebraska's ban states, "no abortion shall be performed after the time at which, in the sound medical judgment of the attending physician, the unborn child clearly appears to have reached viability, except when necessary to preserve the life or health

---

[15] The Legal Services Act of 1974, attached to the Economic Opportunity Act of 1964, provides pro bono legal services for the indigent. The Act prohibits the provision of legal services for use in litigation associated with attempts to procure a nontherapeutic abortion or to compel an individual or institution to perform an abortion (42 U.S.C. 2996 et seq.)

of the mother" (Neb. Rev. Stat. §§ 28-325, 1977). Thirteen other states ban abortions after viability, without a clear definition of the term or reference to the mutability of viability. Four states offer greater clarity with regard to the point at which abortions may not occur; three states banned abortions after 24 weeks (Massachusetts, Nevada, and Oklahoma), with Iowa prohibiting this practice after the second trimester and Florida during the third trimester (Iowa Code Ann § 707.7, (1)–(2), 1976; Fla. Stat. Ann. § 390.0111, 1979). The other fetal rights measures passed at this time include statements regarding the importance and respect necessary for personhood (9), post-abortion fetal disposal requirements (7), and bans on fetal research (5).

In addition to the laws focusing on fetal rights, states were also successful in passing pro-life laws protecting third-party interests. Twenty-two state laws put restrictions on state funding of abortion, through either limitations on the use of Medicaid funds for the procedure (18) or restrictions on the use of state funds to refer, provide, or counsel for abortions (8). Further, while at the federal level there were just a handful of conscience clauses imposed, at the state level 37 clauses passed into law. Out of the 37, 32 refusal laws prohibited public officials from requiring individual health professionals or facilities to perform abortions. This prohibition is similar to the Church Amendment, which passed in Congress in 1973. Similar protections were extended to insurance companies or health maintenance organizations (HMOs) in five states.

Finally, at the federal level no laws pertaining to women's rights or women's health and abortion passed between these years. In addition, very few laws addressing these issues were proposed in Congress. At the state level, however, laws addressing women's health or women's rights were the most common type of abortion-related legislation during this 8-year period, representing 54 % of all legislation. Only one policy—the District of Columbia's parental notification—was pro-choice, thus all other state laws enacted during this time period were pro-life in nature. The most common issue addressed concerns the physicians that provide abortions and the facilities in which they occur. These laws include licensing requirements for physicians (32), regulating the type of healthcare professional that can provide abortions. Laws addressing clinic regulations (6) were meant to ensure these facilities are adequately designed and equipped to protect women's health and safety while undergoing the abortion procedure. While there is some variation in the content and scope of these laws, in general they establish basic standards and requirements that are also found in other areas of medicine.

In sum, the laws passed at the state level are distinct from those passed by Congress during this period, with the clearest divergence in the policy concerning women's health and safety. Not only were women's health- or rights-related laws unsuccessful at the federal level during this time period, only 4 % of all proposals brought before Congress addressed these issues. In the years immediately following the decision in *Roe v. Wade*, federal legislators are clearly focused on pursuing fetal rights policies, with virtually no attempts to address women's issues as it pertains to abortion. The focus of Congress (albeit with some measures dealing with third-party issues, some of which were successful) clearly reflects the rhetoric and mission of the pro-life movement at this time, demonstrating the impact of this movement on policymakers. Although the pro-life movement was not yet clearly aligned with the Republican Party during these early years following *Roe*, legislators pursuing abortion-related policy at the federal level have adopted the movement's rhetoric and overarching mission. The greater variability found in public policy at the state level reflects the impact of state political culture, ideology, partisanship, and structural differences found among the states. However, there is a strong focus on fetal rights legislation, with a substantial number of measures being passed at the state level. It is clear that there is greater acceptance of fetal rights claims and policy at the federal and state level in the years immediately following *Roe* that is very similar in nature to the strategy and rhetoric of the pro-life movement.

1981–1994: During these years, some changes begin to emerge at both the federal and state levels, although the basic trends persist. Of the 439 proposals introduced at the Congressional level from 1981 to 1994, 166–38 %—were focused on fetal rights. There was an increase in proposals that address the rights of third party actors (197, or 45 %), as well as that concerning women (76, or 17 %). Three hundred and sixty seven measures—84 %—are pro-life in nature, and while still a substantial proportion of the legislation from this time period, this number represents a decline in pro-life policies overall.

Fetal rights proposals, still the majority of measures introduced in Congress during this time period, primarily consisted of reintroductions of the human life amendment or similar measures that would establish personhood for the fetus (129). There were 95 proposals introduced that would amend the Constitution to protect the right to life of the unborn;

additionally, there were 34 bills introduced that would establish person-hood for the fetus without amending the US Constitution. Of the remaining fetal rights proposals, nine would prohibit the use of fetal tissue in research; one measure was introduced that was intended to study the relationship between abortion and child pornography, unemployment, non-payment of child support, and child abuse (H. Amend. 583, 1984). The other fetal rights laws include measures that would prohibit sex-selective abortion (5), and ensure the federal government will prohibit the states from enacting restrictions on late-term abortions (10). The fetal rights legislation introduced at this time is similar in nature to that enacted in the years immediately following the decision in *Roe*, although the amount of enacted legislation is in slight decline. As found in the years from 1973 to 1980, there were no fetal rights bills passed into law from 1981 to 1994.

At the state level, changes in the type of legislation begin to emerge in the years 1981–1994. Fetal rights laws become the most infrequent type of abortion-related measures passed during this time, representing 17 % of all state-level legislation. Bans on abortion procedures after viability were the most common bills passed during this time period (15), followed by personhood bills (10), and laws prescribing the requirements for fetal disposal following an abortion (8). Fetal rights laws, slowly on the decline at the level of the state, represent the only fetal rights laws that were successfully enacted in this first era following passage of *Roe v. Wade*.

From 1981 to 1994, laws concerning women's health and safety and third-party actors became increasingly prominent, particularly in the late 1980s and early 1990s. The Supreme Court rulings in *Webster* (1989) and *Casey* (1992) opened the door for some restrictions on access to abortion; while these rulings did not produce the flood of legislation expected by some (Devins 2009), there was an increase in efforts to restrict access to abortion, more so than in the first decade following the ruling in *Roe*. While the legislation that was passed was primarily related to women's health and wellness, and third-party interests, there remains an effort to initiate legislation to protect fetal rights.

5   ANALYSIS

The analysis of the impact of the pro-life discourse on public policy between 1973 and 1994 reveals the centrality of the fetus-centered strategy, as well as the variation within it; while the discourse focuses mainly on normative arguments, often with implicit links to religion, the widespread legislative efforts represent the attempt to limit abortion by any means possible. In addition to the influence of the fetus-centered approach on public policy, it also carries broader social and political implications. Specifically, we are interested in the implications of the fetus-centered strategy for our understanding of human rights, reproductive rights, and right-wing politics. These three areas are strongly influenced by the abortion debate, thus this analysis explores the implications of the pro-life strategy on social and political issues.

Human Rights: The Fetus' Right to Life

Until the 1990s, the pro-life movement did not explicitly use the human rights discourse. Instead, as evident from the analysis of the newspaper items, the arguments regarding the sanctity of life were introduced without addressing or developing the justification for the claim; between 1973 and 1994, 43 % of all pro-life arguments included some reference to this concept, without including references to religious or scientific justifications as the basis of their claim. In addition, the references to the sanctity of life also did not utilize the concept of human rights. The result is a statement that lacks any justification for the claim, as in the case of a pro-life demonstration in 1989, in which Governor Martinez of Florida shouted to the crowd "I stand with you because you are the voice of the unheard, those who have rights but no one has listened to. We're talking about an unborn baby who's seeking life…it's a heartbeat, a heartbeat that must be heard and seen" (Schmalz 1989).

The absence of any human rights' claims or discourse also characterizes the pro-life legislative efforts during this period. Despite hundreds of proposals for a human life amendment in Congress, the most commonly used language invokes themes from American law and legal principles rather than that of the human rights discourse. The rights intended to be granted to the fetus are predicated upon the protections established in the US Constitution, specifically the 14th Amendment, which prohibits the deprivation of "life, liberty, and property" to all persons without due process of law. For the pro-life movement, and in particular, for the authors of the human life amendments, the fetus' right to life is clearly established in these constitutional protections afforded all citizens. Other human life amendments are not as specific in their references to the essential protections afforded to unborn children. In these cases they either simply affirm that the U.S. Constitution does not establish the right to abortion, or aim to overturn the precedent in *Roe* by returning legislative authority over this issue to the states. Thus, despite the sanctity of life being seen as a paramount or natural right granted to all persons, including unborn children, the attempts to codify this protection do not use the terminology of human rights.

The limited references—in both discourse and legislation—to human rights concepts during these decades are not surprising. First, during the 1970s and 1980s, the human rights discourse has not yet been commonly used and widely legitimated (Beitz 2011). Thus, defining a certain act as a human rights violation did not yet become one of the most effective and acceptable ways to argue for the immorality of an action (Haule 2006). Second, during the 1980s, the human rights discourse was still often understood as conflicting with religious beliefs, as is in the case of Schaeffer and Koop's book (1979), which situates humanism in opposition to religion. Third, the conceptualization of the fetus-centered strategy as protecting the rights of the fetus against the rights claims of women also limited the use of the human rights discourse. While the human rights discourse respects a wide array of rights, the focus of the pro-life movement was solely on the right to life, arguing that other rights are secondary or marginal in comparison to the fetus' right to life. As such, the human rights discourse was less effective and relevant to the pro-life movement, since it undermines the ability to argue merely for one right.

In the last few decades, however, there has been an increase in the use of the human rights discourse by the pro-life movement. This shift has been influenced not only by the growing acceptance of human rights claims but also by the existing alliance between moral arguments and human rights claim; in this "age of human rights," human rights claims are seen as equivalent to moral arguments. It is within this context that the pro-life movement began using the human rights discourse. This shift, Peter Toon (1998: 33) argues, is not easy; while the legitimacy and frequency of the human rights discourse has changed,

> from a traditional Christian viewpoint it would appear that talk of 'rights-bearing subjects' only truly makes sense within the context of political and social ethical discourse in which a human being is considered as truly possessing dignity in his individuality and personhood. As such, he or she is considered an independent and autonomous person whose relation to others is contractual and self-determined and whose perceived relation to any 'God' is also self-determined.

While the use of the language of rights is crucial for participation in the political and social spheres today, "to be heard in the modern world, he may have to use 'rights talk' in a limited and wise way to argue for what is good for man in God's world and is achievable by political action" (Toon 1998: 34). This type of discourse is based on a universalist conceptualization of human rights, arguing that all human beings (which, pro-lifers argue, include fetuses) have the right to be born, regardless of the context in which they were conceived or the opinion of pregnant women.

The introduction of women-centered concerns into the pro-life strategy in the 1990s facilitated the adoption of the human rights discourse. The use of both strategies—the fetus centered and the women centered—allowed the pro-life movement to argue that it does not define women's rights as secondary to those of the fetus but, rather, aims to promote everyone's rights. In practice, however, the human rights discourse appears almost exclusively with regard to the fetus. The concern for women, while receiving significant attention in discourse and policy, nevertheless does not translate into the adoption of a human rights discourse.[16]

One prominent example regarding the use of the human rights discourse, as part of the fetus-centered strategy, is the 2015 March for Life, which was covered in the pro-life media as "the biggest human rights rally in the world."[17] In an interview with Catholic News Service, Micaiah Bilger, education director of the Pennsylvania Pro-Life Federation, said, "It's important for us to stand up in our nation's capital and say, 'Abortion is a human rights injustice and we want to see all life protected'" (Catholic News Service 2015). In his speech during the rally, March for Life Chairman Patrick Kelly said, "history is on our side, because history is always on the side of those who fight for human dignity and human life" (Andersen 2015). Jeanne Monhan, President of March for Life Education and Defense Fund, said, "Today, the March for Life has grown to become the largest human rights demonstration in the world. We will continue to March until the human rights abuse of abortion is brought to an end"

[16] One of the reasons why the women-centered strategy is not used together with the human rights discourse is that this strategy is characterized by identifying the subject as lacking autonomy and independence. As a result of these traits, the discourse of this strategy focuses on protecting women rather than recognizing their agency. This approach, which will be discussed at the end of Chap. 3, introduces some challenges to the human rights discourse.

[17] This language appeared in multiple pro-life websites, including catholicnews.com, catholiccitizens.org, ncronline.com, and thebostonpilot.com.

(Lopez 2015). The analysis of pro-life websites also highlights the increase in the use of human rights discourse; out of 152 websites surveyed, 33 (22 %) argue that the fight against abortion is a human right issue. Fifty-four percent of these websites include both fetus-centered and women-centered arguments, while the rest are almost equally divided between websites that focus only on fetus-centered arguments or women-centered claims. Furthermore, some of the websites focus exclusively on defining the abortion debate as a human rights issue; the organization Human Rights For All Ages, for example, uses the UDHR as a background to its website, in the attempt to clarify that pro-life organizations are inherently classified as human rights organizations.

Despite the attempts of some in the movement to define the pro-life struggle as a human rights issue, this link has not been accepted by human rights organizations, especially at the international level. The question of who is the bearer of human rights has always been debated and challenged throughout history, such as in the case of women and slaves, or more recently criminals, terrorists, and migrants. In the current human rights discourse the question whether the right to life, which is the most basic human right, is—or should be—extended to fetuses has been generally answered with a firm no. The UDHR, human rights organizations emphasize, starts with the statement that "all human beings are born free and equal in dignity and rights." Other human rights declaration—such as the European Convention of Human Rights, the International Covenant on Civil and Political Rights, the Convention on the Rights of the Child, and regional human rights declarations—also do not recognize the rights of the fetus. In addition, there is a widespread agreement among most human rights scholars that human rights conventions and international law focus solely on born individuals (Cook and Dickens 2003; Copelon et al. 2005; Penovic 2011).

The proposition that the fetus does not possess human rights and should not be protected by human rights treaties is also influenced by the approach taken by pro-life organizations, which is understood as prioritizing the rights of the fetus over that of the mother, even in those instances in which the life of the mother is at risk. In opposition to the pro-life discourse, the human rights discourse on women's reproductive rights emphasizes the need to prevent maternal mortality that is associated with illegal abortions, in order to secure the health of mothers (Yamin and Maine 1999). The issue of women's health and reproductive rights—as well as their right to have control over these decisions—is recognized under the

UDHR, as well as other treaties such as the International Convention on Economic, Social, and Cultural Rights (ICESCR) and the Convention of the Elimination of all forms of Discrimination Against Women (CEDAW). The emphasis within the human rights discourse on maternal health also sets the groundwork for a future in which the right to abortion is explicitly stated and accepted by human right organizations and institutions as a human right; some organizations, such as Human Rights Watch, already recognize access to safe and legal abortion as a human right. Within this context, the pro-life mission of defining the right to life of the fetus is understood as a threat to women's health and, at times, women's right to life. Thus, proposals to add protections for human beings from the moment of conception have been systematically rejected; for example, the International Conference on Population and Development (ICPD) in 1994 agreed to attach human rights to birth, a proposal that was approved almost unanimously. This decision was particularly meaningful, since it attached their goals on population and development to women's control over their reproductive choices (Copelon et al. 2005).[18]

In sum, despite the challenges—mainly by activists and leaders of human rights organizations and institutions—in the last few decades the pro-life movement has been increasingly relying on the human rights discourse as part of their fetus-centered strategy. Additionally, there has been a movement to establish a link between pro-life arguments and the human rights discourse and institutions, including attempts to promote the conceptualization of abortion as a human rights violation. While these attempts have failed at the international level—the current trend in the UN is to push toward greater protection of women's reproductive rights—nevertheless the use of the human rights discourse has been expanding beyond pro-life activists; Speaker of the House John Boehner stated, "abortion is a defining human-rights issue of our time" (Ricker 2013). While the pro-life movement has not provided justifications or explanations for this link, the lack of theoretical rationale is not unique to the pro-life movement. Rather, it is a common trait of the human rights discourse, in which the

---

[18] Despite this relative agreement within the human rights discourse, some researchers argue for the inclusion of the fetus under human right declarations and treaties. Flood (2006) and Joseph (2009), for example, argue that the life of unborn individuals is already protected under these conventions and laws, even if this responsibility is not explicitly stated in these documents. The applicability of these rights to unborn individuals, they argue, is either assumed—thus not requiring explicit references to the preborn—or excluded from the documents because of pressure from some countries.

debate over the origin and basis for human rights is often either a point of contention or assumed. Within this context, the lack of foundational arguments for the claim that the fetus is entitled to human rights does not in itself exclude the pro-life movement from employing the human rights discourse. Thus, the claim that the fetus is a human being already grants the fetus all human rights, with no need to justify this claim.

Reproductive Rights

The decision in *Roe* established two circumstances in which the interest of the state to regulate abortion may supersede women's right to abortion: the protection of women's health and safety and the protection of the potentiality of human life, with appropriate exceptions in place (410 U.S. 113, 1973). In the early years following the ruling, the fledgling pro-life movement very purposively focused on the rights of the fetus in its attempt to articulate to the general public and policymakers the imperative of overturning this ruling. With the focus of the pro-life movement primarily fixated on the fetus-centered strategy, at least until the mid-1990s, the advocacy of women's rights and interests came almost solely from the pro-choice movement.

By focusing on the fetus' right to life, the pro-life movement avoided any engagement with some of the most central public health issues that pushed many toward support for liberalizing abortion laws in the 1960s. The stories of women who traveled across the country or even abroad to locations such as Great Britain that had already legalized the procedure as well as the injuries and mortality rates associated with illegal abortion were still at the forefront at the public's understanding of this issue (Benson Gold 2003). These concerns were at the center of the public discussion before *Roe*, and were the primary reasons the majority of Americans were supportive of some access to abortion in the 1960s and 1970s (Petrocik 1987). Within this context, the fetus-centered strategy represented an attempt to shift the debate from women's health and reproductive rights to a discussion of the beginnings of life. The debate over the reproductive health and life of the mother was transformed into a moral debate concerning the sanctity of life and immorality of women who obtain abortions.

The fetus-centered strategy of the pro-life movement thus had two effects on reproductive rights. Regarding the discourse, the abortion debate became less about women, and more about the right to life, and who has the right to enjoy it. In the short term, this strategy resulted in few gains for the pro-life movement, at least with respect to their broader goals of banning the procedure or severely restricting access. While the restrictions imposed limited access for some women, abortion nevertheless remained accessible for most during this time period. In Congress, members failed to enact any fetal rights laws, despite the overwhelming proportion of proposals introduced. At the state level, while some fetal rights laws were introduced, the majority of enacted legislation concerns other parties such as women, taxpayers, and health professionals. The reported abortion rate grew steadily during the 1970s, peaking in the 1980s and remaining fairly steady through the early 1990s. Further, the number of abortion providers in the USA also grew during the 1970s, peaking in the mid- to late 1980s, indicating the greater availability of health professionals who provide this service in the years immediately following *Roe* (Henshaw and Kost 2008). Immediately following the decision in *Roe* the abortion rate increased dramatically, indicating that women were able to access abortion or turned to legal avenues for this procedure rather than relying on illegal or self-induced abortions. Thus, while making the abortion debate less about women's rights and health, the pro-life movement nevertheless failed limiting access to or frequency of abortion. The main achievement of this approach was in solidifying the support of the most ardent pro-life supporters.

In the long term, the intensity of some in the pro-life movement led to increasingly dramatic—and at times violent—efforts to restrict access to abortion. Protests outside of abortion clinics became increasingly common, creating a hostile environment for women and medical professionals as well as other patients entering or leaving the medical facility. Further, by the mid-1990s, an increase in the acts of violence perpetrated by pro-life extremists, which targeted abortion providers, clinics, and at times, the women attempting to procure an abortion, led many to associate pro-life movement with violence and murder (Rose 2007). The rise in violence from within the pro-life movement contributed to the highly contentious nature of abortion and reproductive rights, more generally.

One of the most distinct and defining features of reproductive rights during this time period concerns what is not addressed or included within the pro-life discourse and public policy outcomes. Reproductive rights encapsulate more than just abortion; access to birth control—which established the basis for the right to access abortion—remains a key issue under the umbrella of reproductive rights. Among pro-choice advocates, birth control, and in general, reproductive health are as critical to their understanding of reproductive rights as is abortion. However, during the first few decades following the decision in *Roe*, the discussion surrounding reproductive rights—among the general public, pro-life movement, and political leaders—focused squarely on the issue of abortion. While pro-choice advocates viewed access to abortion as essential for women's autonomy and equality (Carabillo et al. 1993; Ginsberg 1985; Siegel 2010), the public and political debate over reproductive rights in the years following *Roe* remain centered on the issue of abortion rather than a broader debate over women's equality and reproductive health.

Right-Wing Politics

In the 1970s, the Republican Party—and conservatives, more generally—were going through a transformation, in terms of both ideology and structure. As political leaders and intellectuals innovated to expand the party base, the coalitions that made up both parties also began to shift. Partisan change began to occur more significantly in the 1970s and 1980s as race and social welfare issues began to take prominence in the political sphere, in effect dividing the coalitions that had made up the Democratic Party since the 1930s (Abramowitz and Saunders 1998; Adams 1997; Petrocik 1987). Specifically, the adoption of the 1964 Civil Rights Act and the 1965 Voting Rights Act drove many conservative Democrats—particularly white, Southern Democrats—to the Republican Party. As this evolution began to occur, Republican leaders also began to incorporate social issues into their national platform, leading the party further to the right. The adoption of an antiabortion stance within the party platform in the 1980s further solidified the conservative shift of the Republican Party, eventually allowing for the alignment of the party's social conservatives with the pro-life movement. While the full expression of this secular realignment did not become apparent until the Reagan and post-Reagan years, the beginnings of this change was clearly established in the 1960s, preceding in many ways the growth and evolution of the pro-life movement (Green et al. 2004; Petrocik 1987).

Prior to this evolution, however, social issues such as abortion were not partisan in nature. In the 1960s and early 1970s, for example, Republicans in the electorate supported access to abortion at a slightly higher rate than Democrats, as the evolution of abortion into a highly partisan issue did not fully occur until the late 1980s (Adams 1997). It is within this environment, in which the public and party leaders are generally in support of some access to abortion and the issue itself is not yet highly partisan or salient, that the pro-life movement attempted to establish itself (Petrocik 1987). As the realignment of both parties occurred, the pro-life movement began its own period of evolution and growth. The ruling in *Roe*, and the backlash to the ruling, served as a perfect catalyst to stimulate the growth of this movement; the increased public attention to the issue of abortion not only created the ideal environment for the movement to grow, but it also structured the type of opposition that emerged.

The ruling in *Roe*, and thus the foundation from which the movement began to transform, established abortion as a private, personal matter, emphasizing a woman's right to privacy and freedom from unnecessary state intrusion. The libertarian nature of the ruling—specifically, the prohibition on excessive government intervention in this decision—in turn led to a political backlash that was also largely libertarian in nature. The policies that were successful, particularly at the federal level, concerned restrictions on government funding for abortion or abortion-related services, or more generally, policies that prevent the state from aiding or assisting in the process. As such, this legislation protects the interests of taxpayers and other third-party actors from the actions of the state. Even the final goal of the pro-life movement—to establish personhood for the fetus—fits a libertarian approach to legislating restrictions on abortion; after recognizing the fetus' right to life, there is no need for further legislation or intervention by the state, since this definition is enough to require all existing laws and protections to be granted to preborn individuals. Thus, the focus of the pro-life movement on personhood, if successful, will signify the end of the state intervention in this matter. The libertarian nature of the legislation is also evident in the numerous conscious clauses, which regardless of focusing on religious freedom emphasizes individual rights and freedom from government intervention.

The libertarian nature of the fetus-centered strategy during the first few decades after *Roe* aligned with the GOP and conservatives' vision of what government should be and how it should operate. In order to support the pro-life mission, Republicans are not required to strongly oppose abortion. Instead, it is enough for them to support limited government intervention and limitations on public funding in order for them to support pro-life legislation. Thus, the pro-life movement was able to appeal to conservatives and the Republican Party in an age when social issues were not yet commonly accepted as partisan issues that divide the two parties. This strategy of the pro-life movement, and particularly the legislative successes regarding third-party actors, is thus able to create an ideological alignment between the pro-life movement and the Republican Party, particularly with respect to beliefs about regulation and government intervention, and later also with regard to social norms regarding abortion.

6   CONCLUSION

Regardless of the relative consistency between discourse and legislative attempts regarding the fetus-centered strategy, and the alignment of the GOP with the pro-life movement, the movement failed to restrict access to abortion at the state and federal levels. In addition to the failure in reversing *Roe*, public support for abortion also did not significantly change; while in the mid- to late 1970s around 20–22 % of those surveyed said they support abortion under any circumstances and in the mid-1990s the percentage of people who supported this approach was in the low to mid-30s (Gallup). Furthermore, during the 1990s (Newport et al. 1999) there was a sharp rise in the amount of violence associated with the pro-life movement; "Between 1991 and 1998, there were 23 murders or attempted murders of physicians who perform abortions or staff members at clinics that provide abortion services. At the same time, the incidence of bombings, vandalism, death threats, acid attacks, and other forms of violence increased dramatically. For example, in the 13-year period between 1977 and 1989, there were 70 reported death threats against abortion providers; in the following 6 years, 1990–1995, there were 196" (Munson 2009: 88). The surge in violence, and public discussion of this violence, also influenced what pro-life activists were asked about in the news, or the type of arguments and justification they focused on in their statements; of the 66 times between 1973 and 2015 that the pro-life discourse in *The New York Times* and *The Washington Post* included some references to pro-life violence, 43 items (65 %) appeared between 1992 and 1998.

The increase of violence was also accompanied by public concerns regarding the racist and anti-Semitic sentiments of the extremist parts of the movement, as well as by supposedly mainstream politicians like Pat Buchanan (Schneider 1990). These extremists "complained about 'Jewish abortionists' making a profit off of the deaths of the unborn" leading to concern and disgust among many in the general public (Meagher 2008: 176–177). Some of this concern focused on the links between some pro-life groups and national militia movements. A report of *Planned Parenthood*, for example, stated,

> Joe Holland, the national director of the North America Free Militia, told a reporter, 'I have been referred to by some in the press as a "tax protestor." I cannot support the United States government until such time as it stops carrying out abortions in its murder clinics and stops supporting the national advancement of homosexuals'…Holland threatened a Montana judge with a letter asserting that law enforcement officers will be killed and 'sent home in body bags' if they challenge the militia (DuBowski 1996).

Although these acts were supported by only a few pro-life activists and abhorred by most, they nevertheless became associated with the pro-life movement and its strategy. As a result, while the violence and other extremist acts reflect small factions within the pro-life movement, the pro-life movement found itself defending its actions and activists, in a climate that undermined public support for the pro-life movement (Rose 2007).

In addition to the impact of violence and extremists on the public support of the pro-life approach, the pro-life movement also started doubting the decision to focus almost solely on the fetus-centered strategy. This approach, it was concluded, was successful in clarifying that the fetus is a human being, but not necessarily in changing public perception regarding abortion. Pro-life leaders argued that, "almost no one now speaks of the unborn as 'tissue,' a 'blob,' or an internal organ of the mother" (Bradley 2014) and that, "nearly 80 percent of the public will now admit that abortion involves the destruction of a human life, even though many in this group still believe abortion should be legal. In fact, studies show that at least 70 percent of aborting women believe what they are doing is morally wrong or at least deviant behavior" (Reardon 1996:ix). However, at the same time pro-life activists recognized that this approach had not successfully increased pro-life support among the public. As Bradley states, "we established that the unborn are persons, but somewhere along the way, our fellow Americans revised their view about what counts as *justified* killing" (2014). The problem, Beckwith (2004) argues, is that many Americans treat abortion as a question of personal preference;

> A recent study found that over two-thirds of those surveyed 'say that, regardless of their own feelings on the subject, the highly personal decision to obtain an abortion should be left to a woman and her doctor. Even more striking, while 57 percent of respondents say they consider abortion to be murder, more than half of that group agree that a woman should have the right to choose an abortion' (56–57).

Thus, while pro-life activists found the fetus-centered argument convincing, they "were increasingly encountering people capable of dismissing it. Perhaps all the people susceptible to it had already been reached and converted. For the remainder, whom we termed 'the mushy middle,' it was falling on deaf ears. We didn't know why" (Mathewes-Green 2004). The reason the argument fell on deaf ears, Willke (2001) argues, was that it "did not address the new argument of women's rights. This had to be answered, but we did not know what the effective answer [was]." The pro-life movement had to change strategy. After some research, the pro-life movement "found out that the answer to their 'choice' argument was a relatively simple straightforward one. We had to convince the public that we were compassionate to women. Accordingly, we test marketed variations of this theme. Thus was born the slogan 'Love them Both'" (Willke 2001).

The combination of the legislative failure, the inability to expand the base of support, and the negative image of the movement as violent extremists led to the development of a new strategy, which focused on the same subject as the pro-choice movement—women. However, the new focus did not lead the pro-life movement to abandon the fetus-centered strategy. Instead, the movement diversified,

> each person and group trying out strategies as they occurred to them. Some, of course, would continue to present the 'It's a baby and it deserves protection' message. This is the backbone of the pro-life movement and our final motivation, and we aren't about to abandon it. But others looked at subsets of the pro-choice population and began crafting ways to reach them. We didn't all set out in the same direction. The pro-life movement is diverse, and it's a good thing, because our target audiences are too (Mathewes-Green 2004).

This new women-centered strategy, which started in the mid-1990s, complementing the fetus-centered strategy, is the focus of Chap. 3.

REFERENCES

Abort 73. Abortion and race. http://www.abort73.com/abortion/abortion_and_race/. Accessed 24 Feb 2015.

Abramowitz A, Saunders K. Ideological realignment in the U.S. electorate. J Polit. 1998;60(3):634–52.

Adams G. Abortion: evidence of an issue evolution. Am J Polit Sci. 1997;41(3):718–37.

Ahern PV. The wrong label for the abortion issue. The New York Times. 1982 Mar 1.

Ainsworth S, Hall T. Abortion politics in congress: strategic incrementalism. New York: Cambridge University Press; 2011.

Andersen K. 'The largest human rights March in the world:' hundreds of thousands join in D.C. Catholic Citizens. 2015 Jan 23.

Arceneaux K. Direct democracy and the link between public opinion and state abortion policy. State Polit Policy Q. 2002;2(4):372–87.

Association of Pro-Life Physicians. Are there rare cases when an abortion is justified? http://prolifephysicians.org/app/?p=59. Accessed 24 Feb 2015.

Bachiochi E. Coming of age in a culture of choice. In: Bachiochi E, editor. The cost of choice: women evaluate the impact of abortion. San Francisco: Encounter Books; 2004. p. 22–32.

Berkman M, O'Connor RE. Do women legislators matter? Female legislators and state abortion policy. Am Polit Q. 1993;21(1):102–24.

Beckwith FJ. Choice words: a critique of the new pro-life rhetoric. Touchstone. 2004.

Beitz CR. The idea of human rights. Oxford: Oxford University Press; 2011.

Bennetts L. Thousands March in capital, seeking abortion ban. New York Times. 1980 Jan 23.

Benson Gold R. Lessons from before Roe: will past be prologue? Guttmacher Rep Public Policy. 2003;6(1).

Black Genocide. Planned parenthood. http://www.blackgenocide.org/planned.html. Accessed 12 Feb 2015.

Bomberger R. Civil rights gone wrong. http://www.toomanyaborted.com/civil-rights-gone-wrong/. Accessed 5 March 2015.

Brady D, Schwartz E. Ideology and interests in congressional voting: the politics of abortion in the U.S. Senate. Public Choice. 1995;84(1–2):25–48.

Bradley GV. The pro-life movement, forty-one years after roe. public discourse, The Whitherspoon Institute. 2014. http://www.thepublicdiscourse.com/2014/01/11929/. Accessed 12 Feb 2015.

Butts C. Pro-abortion tweets piggyback on ferguson tragedy. Onenewsnow. 2014 Apr 26. http://www.onenewsnow.com/pro-life/2014/11/26/pro-abortion-tweets-piggyback-on-ferguson-tragedy. Accessed 30 July 2015.

Camobreco J, Barnello M. Democratic responsiveness and policy shock: the case of state abortion policy. State Polit Policy Q. 2008;8(1):48–65.

Carabillo T, Meuli J, Csida JB. Feminist chronicles, 1953–1993. Women's Graphics. 1993.

Catholic News Service. March for life set for washington return. Catholic Herald. 2015 Jan 21.

Charlotte Lozier Institute. Science supports pain-capability of unborn by 20 weeks. https://www.lozierinstitute.org/science-supports-pain-capability-of-unborn-by-20-weeks/. Accessed 19 Feb 2015a.

Charlotte Lozier Institute. A scientific view of when life begins. https://www.lozier-institute.org/a-scientific-view-of-when-life-begins/. Accessed 19 Feb 2015b.

Concerned Women for America. When is it ok to kill a baby? http://www.cwfa.org/. Accessed 14 Jan 2015.

Cook EA, Jelen T, Wilcox C. Between two absolutes: public opinion and the politics of abortion. Boulder: Westview Press; 1992.

Cook RJ, Dickens BM Human rights dynamics of abortion law reform. Hum Right Q. 2003;25(1):1–59.

Cooper M. Debate on role played by anti-abortion talk. The New York Times. 1995 Jan 15.

Copelon R, Zampas C, Brusie E, Devore J. Human rights begin at birth: international law and the claim of fetal rights. Reprod Health Matters. 2005;13(26):120–9.

Crenshaw C. The 'Protection' of 'Woman': a history of legal attitudes toward women's workplace freedom. Q J Speech. 1995;81(1):63–82.

Devins N. How planned Parenthood v. Casey (pretty much) settled the abortion wars. Yale Law J. 2009;118(7):1318–54.

DeWitt K. Rights plan foes celebrate its difficulties with a gala. The New York Times. 1979 Mar 23.

Diamond EF. Word wars: games people play about the beginning of life. Focus on the Family Physician (November–December 1992):1–5.

Dowland S. 'Family values' and the formation of a christian right agenda. Church Hist. 2009;78(3):606–31.

DuBowski S. Storming wombs and waco: how the anti-abortion and militia movement converge. Front Lines Res. 1996;2(2):1–10.

Falwell J. Listen America! New York: Bantam Books; 1981.

Feminists for Life. Question abortion. http://www.feministsforlife.org/question-abortion/. Accessed 12 Mar 2015.

Flood PJ Does international law protect the unborn child? Life Learn. 2006;XVI.

Focus on the Family. Be a voice 2015. http://www.focusonthefamily.com/social-issues/promos/advocacy/be-a-voice. Accessed 19 Feb 2015.

Fox-Genovese E. Wrong turn: how the campaign to liberate women has betrayed the culture of life. Life Learn. 2002;XII:11–22.

Freeman J. Feminism vs. family values: women at the 1992 democratic and republican conventions. Polit Sci Polit. 1993;26(1):21–8.

Fried MG. Reproductive rights activism in the post-roe era. Am J Public Health. 2013;103(1):10–4.

Gatter M, Kimport K, Foster DG, Weitz TA, Upadhyay UD. Relationship between ultrasound viewing and proceeding to abortion. Obstet Gynecol. 2014;123(1):81–7.

Ginsberg RB. Some thoughts on autonomy and equality in relation to *Roe v. Wade*. North Carolina Law Rev. 1985;63(2):375–86.

Goodstein L. Rockers lead new wave of anti-abortion fight. The New York Times. 1998 Jan 21.

Green DP, Palmquist B, Schickler E. Partisan hearts and minds: political parties and the social identities of voters. New Haven: Yale University Press; 2004.

Greenhouse L, Siegel R. Before (and after) *Roe v. Wade*: new questions about backlash. Yale Law J. 2011;120:2028–87.

Halva-Neubauer G. Abortion policy in the post-*webster* age. Publius. 1990;20:27–44.

Harding S. The book of Jerry Falwell: fundamentalist language and politics. Princeton: Princeton University Press; 2001.

Haule RR. Some reflections on the foundation of human rights: are human rights an alternative to moral values? Max Planck UNYB. 2006;10(1):367–95.

Hyer M. Catholic bishops warn against dissent on abortion. The Washington Post. 1985 Oct 3.

Henshaw S, Kost K. Trends in the characteristics of women obtaining abortions, 1974 to 2004. New York: Guttmacher Institute; 2008.

Herbers J. Convention speech stirs foes of abortion. The New York Times. 1979 June 24.

High School Students for Life. February event-in-a-box: planned parenthood & genocide. http://highschool.studentsforlife.org/feb-eib/. Accessed 24 Feb 2015.

Isaacson W. The battle over abortion. Time. 1981 April 6.

Joseph R. Human rights and the unborn child. Netherlands: Brill; 2009.

Kay KR. Limiting federal court jurisdiction: the unforeseen impact on courts and congress. Judicature. 1981;65:185–9.

Kessler G. Herman cain's rewriting of birth-control history. The Washington Post. 2011 Nov 1.

Kihass P. 10,000 antiabortionists attend a protest rally. The New York Times. 1976 July 12.

Klan Parenthood. Homepage. http://www.klannedparenthood.com/. Accessed 22 Mar 2015

Klatch R. Women of the new right. Philadelphia: Temple University Press; 1987.

Klemesurd J. Are mormons against feminism? Not exactly. The New York Times. 1978 May 5.

Klusendrof S. The vanishing pro-life apologist: putting the "life" back into the abortion debate. CRJ. 1999;22(1).

Kolta G. Survival of the fetus: a barrier is reached. The New York Times. 1989 Apr 18.

Koop CE, Schaeffer FA. Whatever happened to the human race? Westchester: Crossway; 1979.

Kreitzer RJ. Politics and morality in state abortion policy. SPPQ. 2015;15(1):41–66.

Lengers A. Do women's liberationists play a destructive role? New York Times. 1978 Feb 12.

Life News. Selfish convenience: why people abort children with Down's Syndrome. https://www.lifesitenews.com/opinion/selfish-convenience-why-people-abort-children-with-down-syndrome. Accessed 13 Oct 2013b.

Lopez KJ. Every life is a gift. National Review Online. 2015 Jan 21. http://www. nationalreview.com/corner/396853/every-life-gift-kathryn-jean-lopez. Accessed 30 July 2015.

Luker K. Abortion & the politics of motherhood. Berkeley: University of California Press; 1985.

Lynch M. Abortion's distinction among immoral acts. The New York Times. 1984 Sept 22.

Maier CT. Killing for kindness. Touchstone. 2005;18(8).

Mason C. Fetal subjects, feminist positions. In: Morgan LM, Michaels MW, editors. Minority unborn. Philadelphia: University of Pennsylvania Press; 1999.

Marcus R, Churchville V. Antiabortion March nears; protesters arrive by the busload. The Washington Post. 1985 Jan 20.

Mathewes-Green F. Doing everything we can: a response to Francis J. Beckwith. Touchstone. 2004.

McBride DE. Abortion in the United States: a reference handbook. Santa Barbara: ABC-CLIO; 2008.

McDonagh E. The case of the missing frame: abortion as self-defense. Hist Methods. 2007;40(4):187–91.

Meagher Jr RJ. Discourse, framing, and the conservative coalition. Ph.D. Dissertation, The City University of New York, 2008.

Medoff M, Dennis C, Stephens K. The impact of party control on the diffusion of parental involvement laws in the U.S. states. SPPQ. 2011;11(3):325–47.

Montanaro AJ. The abortion pill: a new battleground. The Washington Post. 1991 May 26.

Munson ZW. The making of pro-life activists: how social movement mobilization works. Chicago: University of Chicago Press; 2009.

National Right to Life. Baby rose. http://www.nrlc.org/abortion/babyrose/. Accessed 19 Jan 2015a.

National Right to Life. When does life begin? http://www.nrlc.org/abortion/ wdlb/. Accessed 19 Jan 2015b.

Newport F, Moore D, Saad L. Long-term Gallup poll trends: A portrait of American public opinion through the century. 20 Dec 1999. http://www.gal- lup.com/poll/3400/longterm-gallup-poll-trends-portrait-american-public- opinion.aspx.

Norrander B, Wilcox C. Public opinion and policymaking in the states: the case of post-Roe abortion policy. Policy Stud J. 1999;27(4):707–22.

O'Connor K. No neutral ground: abortion politics in an age of absolutes. Boulder: Westview Press; 1996.

Penovic T. Human rights and the unborn child (review). Hum Right Q. 2011;33(1):229–43.

Perinatal Hospice. http://www.perinatalhospice.org/. Accessed 19 Feb. 2015.

Petchesky R. Fetal images: the power of visual culture in the politics of reproduc- tion. Fem Stud. 1987;13(2):263–92.

Petrocik J. Realignment: new party coalitions and the nationalization of the south. J Polit. 1987;49(2):347–75.

Population Research Institute. Stopping genocide: planned parenthood targeting of alaska natives. http://pop.org/content/stopping-genocide-1247. Accessed 24 Feb 2015.

Priests for Life. Pro-life meditations on the mysteries of the Holy Rosary. http://www.priestsforlife.org/index.aspx. Accessed 15 Jan 2015.

Pro-life preacher denies charge of anti-semitism. The New York Times. 1994 Nov 13.

Protecting Black Lives. Facts about abortion. http://www.protectingblacklife.org/facts-about-abortion/. Accessed 25 February 2015.

Reardon DC. Making abortion rare: a healing strategy for a divided nation. Springfield: Acorn Books; 1996.

Ricker W. Abortion is a human rights issue. Life Site. 1 Mar 2013.

Right to life committee plans drive for anti-abortion amendment. The New York Times. 1980 Jun 30.

Robertson J. Fetal pain laws: scientific and constitutional controversy. Bill of Health: Petrie-Flow Center. 2013 Jun 26.

Rosati KM. Genocide and sanctity of human life. Sanctity of Human Life Guide: Focus on the Family. 2014: 46–7.

Rose M. Safe, legal, and available? Abortion politics in the United States. Washington, DC: CQ Press; 2007.

Rosenthal A. Jane roe has a part in drama of high emotion. The New York Times. 9 April 1989.

Rubin ER. The abortion controversy: a documentary history. Westport: Greenwood Press; 1994.

Sanger C. Seeing and believing: mandatory ultrasound and the path to a protected choice. UCLA Law Rev. 2008;56:351–408.

Schneider SW. The anti-choice movement: bad news for Jews. Lilith: Independent, Jewish, and Frankly Feminist. 1990: 9–11.

Schmalz J. Lawmakers spurn curbs on abortion in florida session. The New York Times. 1989 Oct 11.

Science for Unborn Human Life. What has science shown us? http://www.sfuhl.org/g_what_has_science_shown.htm. Accessed 19 Feb 2015.

Siegel R. Abortion and the 'Woman Question': Forty years of debate. Ind Law J. 2014;89:1365–80.

Siegel R. Dignity and sexuality: claims on dignity in transnational debates over abortion and same-sex marriage. Int J Const Law. 2012;10:335–79.

Siegel R. Roe's roots: the women's rights claims that engendered Roe. B U Law Rev. 2010;90:1875–907.

Siegel R. The new politics of abortion: an equality analysis of woman-protective abortion restrictions. U Ill Law Rev, Baum Lecture. 2007:991–1054.

Siegel R, Blustain S. Mommy dearest?: woman-protective antiabortion argument. Am Prospect. 2006 Oct;22–26.

Siegel R. Dignity and the politics of protection: abortion restrictions under Casey/
Carhart. Yale Law J. 2008a;117:1694–800.

Stand True. Mission statement. http://www.standtrue.com/mission-statement/.
Accessed 22 Feb 2015.

Strickland RA, Whicker ML. Political and socioeconomic indicators of state restric-
tiveness of toward abortion. Policy Stud J. 1992;20(4):598–617.

Survivors of the Abortion Holocaust. Who are the survivors? http://www.survi-
vors.la/who-are-the-survivors/. Accessed 21 Mar 2015.

Suter S. The 'repugnance' lens of Gonzales v Carhart and other theories of reproductive rights: evaluating advanced reproductive technologies. Geo Wash Law
Rev. 2008;76(6):1514–98.

Tatalovich R, Schier D. The persistence of ideological cleavage in voting on abortion legislation in the house of representatives, 1973–1988. Am Polit Res.
1993;21(1):125–39.

The abortion debate rages. The Washington Post. 17 April 1988.

The Guttmacher Institute. Requirements for Ultrasound. *State Policies in Brief.*
August 1, 2015e.

Too Many Aborted. Number one killer. http://www.toomanyaborted.com/
numberonekiller/. Accessed 20 Jan 2015

Toon P. Christianity and subjective human rights. Touchstone. 1998;11:31–5.

Walker P. A view of abortion, with something to offend everybody. The New York
Times. 1981 Jun 8.

Wallace EJ. Pro-Life. http://www.aoh.com/pro-life/. Accessed 8 July 2015.

White M, Falwell J. If I should die before I wake. Nashville: Thomas Nelson;
1986.

Williams DK. God's own party: the making of the christian right. New York:
Oxford University Press; 2012.

Willke, JC. Handbook on abortion. Right to Life League. 1979.

Willke JC. Life issues institute is celebrating ten years with a new home. Life Issues
Connector. 2001 Feb. http://lifeissuesorg/connector/01feb.html. Accessed
20 May 2015.

Yamin AE, Maine DP. Maternal mortality as a human rights issue: measuring compliance with international treaty obligations. Hum Right Q. 1999;21(3):563–607.

Ziebart E. Diverse crowd marches to the drumbeat of 'life'; from grandmothers to
schoolchildren, protesters denounce abortion, pray for amendment. The
Washington Post. 1985 Jan 23.

Ziegler M. Women's rights on the right: the history and stakes of modern pro-life
feminism. Berkley J Gender Law Justice. 2013;28:232–68.

CHAPTER 3

Love Them Both: Pro-life Is Pro-women

1 INTRODUCTION

The mid-1990s were met with a sense of failure by the pro-life movement. Despite the significant growth in the organization and activism, not much has changed regarding public support of abortion. The limited changes that did occur reflect mainly the decline in the support of pro-life arguments in the mid-1990s; according to a Gallup poll, while in the mid- to late 1970s, around 19 % of Americans believed that abortion should be illegal in all circumstances, in the mid-1990s the number declined to approximately 13 %. The main increase during these years was in the number of people who believed that abortion should be legal under any circumstances (Adams 1997; Newport et al. 1999). The lack of significant changes in the public's attitudes toward abortion has been especially surprising in light of changes toward other social issues such as gay marriage (Leonhardt and Parlapiano 2015).

The attempt to repeal *Roe* in its entirety or limit access to abortion through legislative intervention was also largely unsuccessful; at the federal level, the pro-life legislative successes were limited mainly to restrictions on federal funding, including appropriations for the Department of Defense, the Peace Corp, and foreign assistance for public spending on abortion. Conscience clauses, which passed at the federal as well as the state level, prevent government intervention in providers' decision to participate or not participate in abortion. However, they do little to restrict access and

© The Editor(s) (if applicable) and The Author(s) 2016
A. Von Hagel, D. Mansbach, *Reproductive Rights in the Age of Human Rights*, DOI 10.1057/978-1-137-53952-6_3

the availability of this service, as desired by the pro-life movement. The relative failure of the pro-life movement—manifested in both insufficient legislative success and lack of change in public support of abortion—was driven by the focus of the movement on the fetus-centered strategy. David C. Reardon, for example, the director of the Elliot Institute that will play a central role in transforming the pro-life strategy, states, "for pro-abortionists, this women versus 'fetus' strategy has been highly successful. By framing the debate in this way, they are attempting to push pro-life candidates into a box labeled 'Uncompassionate Anti-Woman Ideologues'" (Reardon 1994).

In addition to the perceived failure of the fetus-centered strategy, market research conducted by the National Right to Life Committee (NRLC) found that a discourse centered on women's rights would be more effective, particularly among people who do not have a clear position on the issue of reproductive rights. These findings contributed to the shift of the pro-life movement to a strategy that includes concerns for the protection of women's rights and health. This women-centered approach—also called the New Rhetorical Strategy (NRS) (Reardon 2002)—is based on the assumption that abortion is detrimental to women's health, and is contributing to women's exploitation by coercing women to have an abortion against their will and own interests. In order to protect women, supporters of the women-centered strategy argue, there is a need to limit or restrict abortion. This new strategy aims to challenge the perception of the movement as intolerant, hostile, and potentially violent, instead promoting the same sense of compassion and caring for women as for the fetus (Rose 2007; Shields 2009; Willke and Willke 1997). While different activists and organizations disagree whether the fetus-centered and women-centered strategies may be promoted simultaneously (Beckwith 2001), in general, the new strategy has been used together with the fetus-centered strategy, focusing now on two subjects who need protection: the fetus as well as the mother.

This chapter analyzes the development and use of the women-centered strategy by the pro-life movement starting in the mid-1990s. This analysis reveals how this new strategy transforms both the pro-life discourse and policy. The women-centered discourse is often scientific in nature, framing the arguments as facts based on research, highlighting the danger of abortion to women. The legislative attempts that follow from this discourse focus less on overturning *Roe*, as the fetus-centered strategy aims to do.

Instead, the women-centered strategy primarily focuses on restricting or limiting access to abortion. The women-centered discourse and legislation defines women as a vulnerable subject in the abortion debate, rather than an enemy. As a result of the focus on women, the pro-life movement no longer debates with the pro-choice movement who is the subject whose rights need to be protected, thus modifying the relation between the two movements. At the same time, however, the women-centered strategy of the pro-life movement introduces a different image of women than the pro-choice movement had, one that is easily coerced and misguided, and thus whose rights need to be protected by state and federal regulations.

The first section examines the development of the pro-life strategy, and its relationship to pro-choice and feminist arguments in the abortion debate. This account traces the change in the approach of the pro-life movement from a conservative pro-family focus to a movement that aims to protect both pro-family and pro-women values. The second section introduces the evolution of the women-centered strategy, mainly between 1995 and 2014, based on analyses of the discourse and legislative attempts of that period. This section analyzes the different justifications that are used by pro-life activists to highlight the danger of abortion, focusing mainly on informed consent and the emotional and health risks of this practice. The third section of this chapter examines the way in which this strategy has been influencing the development of human rights, reproductive rights, and right-wing politics. This analysis shows that while being very conservative and interventionist in nature, the women-centered strategy has been effective in expanding the pro-life discourse, while also promoting incrementalist—and effective—pro-life legislation.

2   THE DEVELOPMENT OF PRO-LIFE WOMEN-CENTERED STRATEGY[1]

The introduction and development of the women-centered strategy have been influenced by the growing public support of women's rights during the decades since *Roe*. This strategy aims to address the claim made by pro-choice activists that only they support women, while pro-lifers are concerned only about the fetus. The pro-choice link between the right to

---

[1] The term "women-centered" is commonly used to refer to this discourse (Bachiochi 2004; Cannold 2002). Other terms include "women-protective claims" (Siegel 2008a, 2012; Ziegler 2013).

have an abortion and women's rights is relatively new. It was not part of the justification in the legalization of abortion in *Roe*, and was not common before the 1970s, since at that time abortion was seen as harmful to women, both physically and mentally. During the 1960s and 1970s, the criminalization of abortion started to be understood as a tool of an oppressive system, which controls women's bodies and limits their ability for autonomous decision making, in general, and of control over their reproductive decisions, in particular (Rose 2011; Schreiber 2002, 2012; Siegel 2012).

The rise of the women-centered strategy among pro-life supporters in the mid- and late 1990s took place after more than a decade of focusing mainly on fetal-centered arguments, which emphasized religious and pro-family messages. Before the mid-1990s, only a few pro-life movements incorporated pro-women-centered arguments. The most famous and vocal one was Feminists for Life (FFL), which was founded in 1973 by Pat Goltz and Cathy Callaghan, who left the National Organization for Women (NOW) out of dissatisfaction with its position on abortion. In the early 1970s, FFL played a significant role in the NRLC, which was the largest pro-life organization. Their influence, for example, helped them add to the NRLC's pre-*Roe* position the statement that the organization is "in favor of a legal system that protects the life of the unborn child, while recognizing the dignity of the child's mother, the rights of its father, and the responsibility of society to provide support and assistance to both the mother and child" (Ziegler 2013: 239). In the attempt to challenge the link created in the 1960s and 1970s between abortion and women's rights, FFL activists argued that in the past, women's movements have always opposed abortion, understanding that practice not as women's rights but, rather, as "women's wrong" (Derr 1995: 133). According to this account, the opposition of early feminists to abortion was not only influenced by the health risks associated with the practice at that time. Instead, they opposed any attempt to define groups of human beings as nonhuman, including fetuses. It is thus their sensitivity to oppression, and the way in which society treats marginalized groups, that led to strong pro-life positions among feminists.

The use of the women-centered strategy within the pro-life movement, however, declined in the late 1970s and remained insignificant until the mid-1990s. This decline is related to the rise in the late 1970s of the religious right within the pro-life movement, a connection that brought financial as well as public support to the pro-life movement; while in 1978,

NRLC was $25,000 in debt, the Moral Majority was raising $1 million a week in mail contributions (Ziegler 2013). The leadership role taken by the Catholic Church in the pro-life movement led to the shift to a frame of traditional Christian morality (Rose 2011; Ziegler 2013). Although FFL continued to be active, their focus and activism did not reflect the pro-life approach during these years, and the movement had very little influence and virtually no presence in Washington (Reynolds 1989). Instead, during the late 1970s and throughout the mid-1990s, the women's organization that played a central role in the pro-life movement was Concerned Women for America (CWA), which included conservative figures like Phyllis Schlafly and Beverly LaHaye. CWA was explicit in its opposition to feminism, stating that it presented an alternative to these evil ideas (Schreiber 2012). Like Schlafly, CWA combined arguments against abortion with antifeminist arguments, situating pro-family claims in opposition to feminist ones. Together with a new emphasis on social issues, the focus on the family became part of the Republican Party's platform, which in 1980 stated, 'We will work for the appointment of judges at all levels of the judiciary who respect traditional family values and the sanctity of innocent human life.' The platform plank associated and equated pro-life and pro-family causes—and was repeated verbatim for years thereafter" (Siegel 2012: 1374). While in the mid-1980s, some leaders of the pro-life movement urged president Ronald Reagan's Surgeon General, C. Everett Koop, to follow the model of the antismoking campaign and to publicly state that abortion poses a risk to women, this argument did not become central in the pro-life discourse until a decade later (Siegel 2007).

The rise of the pro-life women-centered strategy in the 1990s was shaped by different factors, among them significant court rulings, and strategic decisions on the part of the movement (Greenhouse 2008). Between the late 1980s and mid-1990s, a number of Supreme Court rulings validated restrictions on access to abortion, although the basic framework of *Roe* was preserved. Cases in which the court accepted limited restrictions on abortion included *Webster v. Reproductive Health Services* (1989) and *Planned Parenthood v. Casey* (1992). In *Webster*, the court upheld Missouri's ban on the use of public facilities or state funds for abortion. Additionally, the court found the state's provisions requiring counseling prior to an abortion, as well as restrictions on abortion after viability, to be legally permissible under *Roe*. This ruling opened the door for greater restrictions on abortion, as the court approved a requirement for viability testing in the second trimester as well as prohibited abortion after viability. Given the nature of the ruling—and the court's apparent increasing acceptance of restrictions on abortion—it was expected that this ruling would produce a groundswell of legislative activity among the states (Devins 2009).

In *Casey* (1992), the court, while upholding the framework established in *Roe*, accepted an expansion of state regulation of the procedure itself. Providing greater deference to the states to regulate this practice, the court accepted all but one requirement established by the state of Pennsylvania, including informed consent, 24-h waiting period, and parental notification requirements for minors. The opinion established the "undue burden test," allowing for restrictions on abortion prior to fetal viability to "accommodate the state's interest in potential life" (505 U.S. 833, at 838). This ruling—in addition to *Webster*—indicated that the courts were willing to accept greater restrictions on access to this procedure. As these rulings opened the door to increased regulation by the states, legislators responded with increased efforts to limit access to abortion premised on women's health and safety.

In addition, the development of the women-centered approach was also a strategic decision, partly in response to what the pro-life movement recognized as a failure to expand its base of support. This failure was attributed not only to the negative image of the movement as violent and extremist but also to the limitations of the fetus-centered strategy. The premise of the fetus-centered strategy—that realizing that the fetus is a human being will lead people to oppose abortion—proved to be wrong; research conducted by pro-life organizations revealed that, "while three-fourths or more of the people in the USA now admitted this was a child who was killed, two-thirds of the same people felt that it was all right to give the woman the right to kill" (Willke 2001). The failure of the fetus-centered strategy, pro-life activists argue, has been influenced by the focus of the movement on moral arguments, and the assumption that others think within the same moral framework; "Our message is not being well-received by this audience because we have made the error of assuming that women, especially those facing the trauma of an unplanned pregnancy, will respond to principles we see as self-evident within our own moral framework, and we have presented our arguments accordingly" (Swope 1998).

At the same time, the failure of the fetus-centered strategy was further made evident by the success of the pro-choice movement over the abortion debate. At the federal level, the 1992 Congressional election cycle—often referred to as the Year of the Women—brought in the highest proportion of female members of Congress to date. In the Senate, the number of female Senators increased from three—Barbara Mikulski (D) of Maryland and Nancy Kassebaum (R) of Kansas, with Diane Feinstein (D) of California entering the Senate by special election in 1992—to seven, including Kay Bailey Hutchison from Texas, elected in a special election in 1993. In the House of Representatives, the number of female representatives increased from 28 to 46. Many of these new elected legislators—all of the Democratic females and several of the female Republicans—were supportive of reproductive rights, advocating for increased access to contraceptives and abortion (Delli Carpini and Fuchs 1993; Tumulty 2012).

The introduction of many new female Democrats and supporters of reproductive rights in Congress corresponds with a rise in pro-choice abortion-related proposals in the mid-1990s. Between 1995 and 2014, there were 217 women-centered policies introduced in Congress; 118 of them were pro-choice in nature. The majority (75) of these measures focused on the lifting of funding restrictions on abortion. Sixty of these measures attempted to repeal the domestic funding restrictions for abortion or abortion-related services imposed in the annual appropriations budgets for the Department of Defense, Medicaid, federal family planning programs, federal healthcare insurance plans, and for escort services for women in prison. The other 15 measures focus on annual appropriations for foreign assistance, which restrict funds from going to nongovernmental organizations (NGOs) that provide abortion or any abortion-related services, even if these services are funded through segregated accounts containing non-US funds. For example, the House and Senate introduced the Global Democracy Promotion Act, which would allow NGOs to be eligible for foreign aid for reproductive health services as long as the organization was operating within the bounds of their own nation's law (H.R. 2738, 2013). Despite being introduced repeatedly over this time period, the bill never made it out of committee to the floor for a vote.

The other proposals offered by pro-choice legislators include acts that reassert women's right to abortion (8), ensuring women receive accurate and nonfraudulent information about reproductive services (16), and measures protecting clinic access or condemning clinic violence (6). The latter measures were a response to the escalation of violence directed toward abortion doctors and abortion clinics that had begun in the 1980s and early 1990s. The murder and attempted murder of numerous health professionals, use of arson, assault, and battery, and death threats culminated in the early 1990s, producing substantial reaction on the part of legislators as well as some within the pro-life movement who were quick to condemn such actions (Rose 2007). In the 102nd session of Congress (1992–1993), the Freedom of Access to Clinic Entrances Act was passed into law, prohibiting the use of physical force or threats to prevent access to a reproductive health center, committing violence against an employee or patient at a reproductive health center, or intentional damage or destruction of such a facility (18 U.S.C. § 248, 1994). Following the passage of this federal law, and a number of similar laws at the state level (17, including Washington, D.C.) violence against abortion clinics and abortion providers did decline, although threats of violence and other forms of clinic obstruction continued.

The legislative focus on women's rights was accompanied by a relatively united pro-choice movement, which was able to shift the debate from concerns regarding the fetus to women's issues; the pro-choice movement, pro-life activists protested, "changed the question. No longer was our nation arguing about killing babies. The focus, through their efforts, had shifted off the humanity of the unborn child to one of women's rights. They developed the effective phrase of 'Who Decides?'" (Willke 2001). In light of this change, the focus of the pro-life movement on the fetus was understood by some as ignoring women by defining women's interests as in conflict with those of their fetuses (Crenshaw 1995). Pro-choice organizations such as NARAL and NOW criticized the growing connection between the pro-life movement and the New Right, accusing their opponents as excluding women and their concerns from their organizations.

This critique was shared by some within the pro-life movement, who raised both moral and practical arguments against the exclusive use of the fetus-centered strategy:

> We have steadily criticized our 'fellow' pro-lifers who seem to care more about in utero life than life that passed through the birth canal; but we also believe that these types of pro-lifers are on the decline. Pro-lifers, after all, make no profit from their stand. Unlike abortionists and playboys (who are among the most liberal contributors to abortion rights organizations), they are not fighting to protect an economic investment or individual rights (Derr 1995: 148).

Other pro-life activists discussed their

frustration with the fetal rights focus of the pro-life movement, stating: 'I used to wonder if I was the only one who realized people just weren't persuaded by the pictures of tiny feet. I would think, you know, sure, it persuaded you, and that's why you're standing in front of Planned Parenthood every week, but it's not working for all the girls that are walking right past you and that's the point that some of us are missing. We need to speak to them, not all the other people standing on the corner with us' (Trumpy 2014: 171).

While this critique was prominent mainly among the activists of FFL, in the mid-1990s even CWA began to argue that the pro-life movement should focus not only on helping the fetus but also on protecting women and their health (Ziegler 2013). As a result of this pressure and critique, the pro-life movement started using both the fetal-centered and the women-centered strategies, in the hope of making "their position more attractive to potential adherents that were not swayed by or interested in the original framing" (Trumpy 2014: 177). In the attempt to answer also the "choice" argument, pro-life activists started addressing the issue of women's rights, in general, and the concern for the emotional and health effects of abortion on women, in particular. This argument, according to John Willke, was "a relatively simple straightforward one. We had to convince the public that we were compassionate to women. Accordingly, we test marketed variations of this theme. Thus was born the slogan 'Love Them Both'" (2001). The "Love Them Both" approach was meant to appeal to the more moderate audience, which resents the approach that blames women for abortion, but is nevertheless open to a movement that aims to "help a woman to reevaluate what she perceives as the three 'evils' before her" (Swope 1998). This new strategy "will result not only in making abortion rare, but in making American culture more pro-life" (Beckwith 2001: 119).

David C. Reardon was a central figure in the development of the women-centered discourse. His books *Aborted Women, Silent No More* (1987), and *Making Abortion Rare* (1996) established the concept of "pro-life, pro-women." In his writing, Reardon recognizes the need to expand the base of support to include more parties, so that we can convincingly show that it is we who are defending the authentic rights of both women and children. In short, we must insist that the proper frame for the abortion issue is not women's rights versus the unborn's rights, but rather women's and children's rights versus the schemes of exploiters and the profits of the abortion industry" (Reardon 1994).

By highlighting their concern for women, the pro-life movement will be able to appeal to "the middle majority (who are uncomfortable with abortion, but sympathetic to women in crisis)," (Reardon 1994), who do not necessarily share the religious and moral beliefs with the Christian right. This approach requires to "always remember that the two chief concerns of the middle majority are: (1) the desire not to interfere with the autonomy of women; and (2) the desire not to condemn those women who have already had abortions...Specifically, we must recognize that the middle majority will only open their hearts to concern for the unborn *after* the concerns of women have been addressed" (Reardon 1996: 25). In order to do so, pro-life activists must highlight their compassion to women, which "must be voiced both first and last in all our arguments, and in a manner which shows that our concern for women is a primary and integral part of our opposition to abortion" (Reardon 1996: 26).

Today, many pro-life organizations incorporate the women-centered discourse and strategy, including the Elliot Institute, Women Affirming Life, Operation Outcry, and the Silent No More Awareness Campaign (Siegel 2012; Trumpy 2014). The women-centered discourse is not used in isolation. Instead, the pro-life movement has conceptualized it as a "mutual benefits" argument, emphasizing the "aligned interests rather than competing rights, insisting that both women seeking abortions and people opposed to abortion are better off if the law restricts or prohibits abortion" (Friedman 2013: 52). This discourse moves away from the discussion on the legal rights of women, instead recognizing that the decision to have an abortion—and the effect this decision has on the woman—is complex (Rose 2011). This political strategy became central not only among pro-life organizations but also in politics. In 2012, for example, the Republican Platform incorporated this statement: "We, however, affirm the dignity of women by protecting the sanctity of human life. Numerous studies have shown that abortion endangers the health and well-being of women, and we stand firmly against it" (Friedman 2013: 52–53).

The use of the women-centered strategy is evident also in legislation and judicial proceedings. One example of the use of this strategy in legislation is the 2006 Women's Health and Human Life Protection Act in South Dakota (Friedman 2013; Hill 2008; Ivey 2008; Manian 2009; Rose 2011; Shields 2012; Siegel 2008a, 2012; Smith 2008; Suk 2010). The South Dakota Act, which was drafted with the help of Reardon and his research newsletters, was passed by the state legislature in 2006 and repealed in a voter referendum later that year. The Act significantly restricted access to abortion, almost to the point of prohibiting the practice altogether. This bill was a product of the 2005 report from the South Dakota Task Force to Study Abortion, which was prepared by state legislators, justifying the prohibition of abortion in order to protect women's rights.

The report, which includes testimonies and written statements from a range of medical professionals, mental healthcare professionals, and pregnancy help center counselors, argued that the process of obtaining informed consent is inadequate for ensuring the protection of women's interests. Specifically, the Task Force concluded that the failure to provide the "objective, scientific fact" that abortion causes the killing of a "whole separate unique living human being" means that women are not able to give their informed consent, and doctors are unable—professionally and morally—to secure this consent (South Dakota Task Force Report 2005, 5, 9–10). An additional concern identified by the Task Force is the health risks associated with abortion. Testimony and written reports submitted to the Task Force cite post-traumatic stress disorder (PTSD), depression, and suicidal ideation as potential psychological disorders resulting from an abortion, together with an increased risk of breast cancer, Post-abortion syndrome (PAS), or death. While the majority of the medical community does not recognize a relationship between these psychological and medical conditions and abortion, the report maintains that restrictions on abortion will protect women from these and other related conditions.

The Task Force identified women's exploitation in abortion as another justification for the need to restrict this procedure. It presented testimony from women who have gone through this procedure and concluded that the vast majority felt coerced to have an abortion, either by the unborn child's father, their own doctor, or by the society. In making the decision to abort, a woman is asked to perform a task beyond her capability, namely the killing of her unborn child. Thus, the restrictions on abortion not only protect women's individual rights, but protect her "very nature as a mother" and her relationship with the child (2005, 56). Therefore, in order to protect women, who in actuality do not want to abort their fetus, from the coercive influences that render their decision involuntary, there is a need to restrict abortion.

The arguments raised in the Task Force report for limiting access to abortion reflect the main justifications used in the women-centered strategy: the argument regarding the lack of a meaningful process of informed consent, which results in women who are coerced into consenting to abortion without knowing and understanding the implications of their act, as well as the interrelated arguments that abortion causes health and emotional risks to women. The next section analyzes these three arguments, as they appear in pro-life discourse and legislation, revealing that in the case of the women-centered strategy, the discourse and legislative efforts are more closely linked.

3   ABORTION HURTS WOMEN: THE WOMEN-CENTERED DISCOURSE AND POLICY

This section analyzes both the discourse and public policy as it appears in the women-centered strategy, focusing on the period between mid-1990s until 2014. The analysis of the discourse is based on several sources. Data was obtained mainly from 1235 articles published in *The New York Times* between the years 1995 and 2015,[2] which included references to "abortion" and "pro-life." The analysis focuses especially on the 124 pieces (10 %) that include pro-life discourse, namely, the quotes, slogans, or statements made by pro-life activists and supporters. Out of the 1447 pieces published in *The Washington Post* between these years, 339 (23 %) include pro-life discourse.[3] Within these 463 discourse pieces, there were 478 pro-life arguments made. Three hundred and twenty-six (68 %) of these justifications were classified as emphasizing fetus-centered justifications—focusing on arguments regarding the need to prevent abortion for the sake of the life of the fetus—while the other 152 pieces (32 %) were classified as women-centered concerns. In comparison, before 1995— during the period characterized by the fetus-centered strategy—women-centered justifications appeared only 69 times, which amounts to 21 % of

[2] The data from both newspapers includes publications until May 31, 2015.

[3] While this project does not address the differences between the newspapers, the higher percentage of *The Washington Post* articles that include discourse can be explained by the tendency of this newspaper to have longer and more in-depth pieces on this topic.

the references. In addition, in both newspapers, in almost all subcategories—for example, the argument that abortion causes psychological harm, health risk, and regret—the number of times that the women-centered justification was mentioned increased after the mid-1990s.[4]

In addition, the analysis of the women-centered discourse also includes data from the 152 websites of pro-life organizations surveyed. Out of these websites, 103 (68 %) include women-centered justifications, either exclusively (32) or together with fetus-centered arguments (71). Furthermore, in the attempt to trace the change in strategy, this section also uses central primary sources written during these years by prominent pro-life leaders, among them Bachiochi (2004), Beckwith (2004), Derr (1995), Fox-Genovese (2002), Reardon (1994, 1996), Swope (1998), and Willke (2001).

The analysis of public policy focuses on federal legislation (proposed and enacted), as well as state legislation (enacted), between 1995 and 2014. During this time period, 524 abortion-related bills, amendments, and resolutions were introduced at the federal level. The vast majority (77 %) were pro-life in nature, a slight decline from the previous era in which 89 % of all measures introduced at the federal level reflected a pro-life agenda. The legislative focus during these years is characterized by a decline in legislation regarding fetal rights, and increased attention to women's health and safety, both before and during the abortion procedure. Forty-one percent of all abortion-related bills, amendments, and resolutions involved women-centered proposals, with 26 % pertaining to fetal rights. The remaining 33 % of federal policies introduced during this period centered on the rights of third-party actors such as health professionals and taxpayers. These ratios represent a change from the previous era; between 1973 and 1994, only 90 proposals (11 %) addressed women and women's issues. The most significant decline is found among proposals addressing fetal rights, which consisted of 56 % of all measures proposed between 1973 and 1994.

The women-centered strategy that focuses on the need to protect women from abortion is based on three main justifications that appear both in the pro-life discourse and in public policy. The first is the need for a more meaningful process of informed consent. According to the pro-life

---

[4] One exception is the number of times in which the argument that abortion causes health risk was mentioned in *The New York Times*, four times between 1973 and 1994, but only twice between 1995 and 2015. When combining the two newspapers together, however, all the women-centered subcategories show an increase in the later period.

movement, institutional and societal pressures push women—and even coerce them in some cases—to have an abortion. Within this context, women need to be protected against the misrepresentation of abortion, which is done mainly by doctors but also by partners and other individuals who have an interest in women having abortions. Therefore, the idea that abortion is a choice that women make by themselves and for themselves, pro-life activists argue, is misleading since "most women have abortion out of fear, not as a reasoned response to the crisis pregnancy: they fear that they cannot afford to care for the child, that they are too immature, that they will be ridiculed, that they will be abandoned by their family or by the baby's father" (Bachiochi 2004: 25). The answer to this pressure and fear is to target the problematic nature of the process of informed consent.

The inadequacy of informed consent, pro-life activists argue, is dangerous not only because of the coercion that women experience but also because of two other risks of abortion: the psychological harm and the health risks associated with the practice. Abortion, pro-life supporters argue, causes emotional harm, such as in the case of PAS. Even in cases that women—as well as men—do not experience such psychological harm, they nevertheless regret having an abortion, thus influencing their emotional state for the rest of their lives. In addition, the pro-life movement links abortion with health risks, such as breast cancer, and argues that in some extreme cases abortion—despite being presented by pro-choice supporters as safe—leads to the death of women. In contrast to the fetus-centered discourse, which often uses moral or religious arguments, this women-centered discourse relies more heavily on scientific language, emphasizing data and findings to support their claim regarding the harm of abortion. As such, the women-centered argument is often framed as a public health concern, and uses scientific language to appeal to a broader, and more secular, audience (Rose 2011; Siegel 2007, 2012).[5]

While some in the pro-life movement, mainly the FFL, had raised women-centered arguments in the 1970s, this current strategy does not closely resemble those arguments; FFL often claimed that existing social

[5] Since this chapter aims to analyze the arguments made by the pro-life movement, it includes very few references to the critique of this discourse by feminist thinkers, who often criticized the women-centered strategy as reinforcing traditional and stereotypical understanding of women and their role in society (Siegel 2008a; Manian 2009). In general, this chapter does not question the "true-nature," sincerity, or even medical accuracy of these arguments.

and economic conditions lead women to choose abortion. Thus, in the attempt to eliminate abortions, pro-lifers should also focus on changing the social and economic conditions that cause women to choose this option. The current women-centered strategy, however, does not promote such claims. Instead, it is based on more traditional views of women and motherhood, emphasizing the biological and natural connection between the mother and her child, and questioning their ability to make rational decisions regarding pregnancy and, mainly, stopping pregnancy (Siegel 2007). The transformation of the organization Susan B. Anthony's List (SBAL) represents this shift; while the organization was established by FFL's activists as a political action committee designed to help women opposed to abortion to secure elected office, by the late 1990s, SBAL became much more conservative, opposing many of the initiatives that were supported by FFL. By 2000, the pro-life feminism of the 1970s, which favored social welfare, funding for daycare, and contraception, had all but disappeared (Ziegler 2013).

Informed Consent

Much of the women-centered discourse of the pro-life movement focuses on the problematic nature of consent given by women in the process of seeking an abortion. The basic assumption is that "abortion kills a living human being and mutilates another. Surgery done on a healthy body is mutilation, and such surgery done without adequately informed consent is battery. Legalized abortion without even minimal informed consent is widespread, epidemic battering of women. Women deserve a straightforward acknowledgment by government of this fact" (MacNair 1995: 245). Therefore, it is wrong to assume that abortion is a result of an active and informed decision by women. Rather, "abortion takes away real, affirming choices and replaces them with women who have abortion because they feel they have no choice" (Keech 1995b: 241).

Strategically, the focus on informed consent is an effective way to broaden the support for the pro-life movement since everyone—including pro-choice activists—is interested in preventing coercion in the process of abortion. Defining the pro-life mission as promoting a meaningful process of informed consent is thus seen by the movement as a way to unite people who often disagree about abortion; "Polls show that the vast majority of the public supports informed consent requirements. Most people understand that a woman's 'right to choose' means nothing without a corresponding 'right to know'" (Reardon 1994). Opposing the fight for informed consent, Rachel MacNair, president of FFL, claims, proves that the practice is coercive; "You can't be free choice and willing to fight against providing information on the procedure. If abortion practitioners are willing to fight against informed consent, then they are admitting that the procedure is not as safe as they claimed" ("Abortion Opponents Set Strategy" 1989). By focusing on informed consent, the pro-life movement frames the attempts to regulate or limit abortion as protecting the woman, who is the patient; like in the case of other medical procedure, "women have a right to full disclosure of the nature of the abortion procedure, the risks and potential complications, and alternative support services, as well as the father's responsibilities" (Foster 2004: 37). The issue of informed consent shifts the focus of the pro-life movement from religious and moral arguments to issues of oppression and coercion, thus helping the pro-life movement to broaden its base of support beyond the religious or conservative crowd, which already supports the movement.

The analysis of both newspaper sources reveals that the argument of informed consent is the single most common argument used within the women-centered discourse in the two periods. Between 1973 and 1994, while the women-centered arguments appeared in only 21 % of the pro-life discourse, in more than half of these cases the argument focused on the lack of informed consent. Between 1995 and 2015, informed consent remained the most commonly used argument within the women-centered discourse; of the 152 women-centered arguments that appeared in the newspapers, 63 (41 %) focused on informed consent. At the same time, however, the issue of informed consent is less central in the organizations' websites. Of 103 websites that include women-centered arguments as part of their pro-life approach, only nine websites address the issue of informed consent, most of them (7) while also mentioning some or all of the other women-centered justifications. This percentage is significantly small in comparison to the use of other women-centered justifications in the websites, as will be discussed later in this section.

The claim that abortion is done without meaningful informed consent is based on two different types of arguments. The first uses scientific language to argue that evidence shows the lack of a meaningful process for informed consent. A 2010 report of the Elliot Institute, which is widely quoted by pro-life websites and other publications, argues that abortion is forced on women;

Most abortions are unwanted are coerced and many are forced, sometimes violently. Escalating pressure to abort can come from employers, husbands, parents, doctors, partners, profit-driven abortion businesses, landlords, friends and family, or even trusted financial, personal, school or religious guides, gatekeepers or authorities. They may be negligent in telling young or vulnerable individuals or couples about available resources. They may misrepresent information or present false information as fact. They may threaten or blackmail" (2).

According to this report, abortion is a type of violence, similar to other forms of violence that are often experienced by pregnant women.[6] As part of the problem of coercion, pro-life activists argue that in the process of informed consent, women lack knowledge regarding the harm of abortion to their emotional stage and health; "women did not receive adequate counseling on abortion and that they were not told of the risk of sterilization, 'harm to their bodies' and post-abortion stress" ("Family is Aim of Clergy Group" 1988). In addition, pro-life supporters argue that women also lack knowledge regarding the effect of abortion on the fetus. The website of the organization Hope After Abortion states: "in every abortion a child dies—in an early stage of development before birth. The child's death is intended and carried out with the presumed consent of the mother (with or without the consent of the father) (Angelo 2011)." This discourse also focuses on fetal pain, an issue that will be introduced later, arguing that, "It would be my hope that a number of women, once informed of the pain in the womb that the child will experience, will hopefully just say 'I just don't want to do this'" (Toner 2004). In this case, the argument over informed consent is combined with fetus-centered arguments to emphasize that women who choose abortion do so because of their lack of understanding and access to real scientific data.

The second type of argument that proves the process of informed consent is insufficient is based on assumptions about the natural link between a mother and her child. The abortion process, according to this approach,

---

[6] The report includes dozens of references to other articles, as well as specific cases of violence against pregnant women. Out of the 30 sources that are cited for the statistics in the report, five sources are articles authored by Reardon himself, six are used in a way that may be interpreted as out of context, ten are nonscientific articles (newspaper reports or opinion pieces), and three are opinion polls. Six more sources prove that women who are pregnant have higher risk of experiencing violence—and even dying from it—than nonpregnant women.

"inherently lacks consent because a pregnant woman cannot make a truly informed decision to give up a relationship with a child until after the child is born" (Siegel 2012: 1010). Since the nature of motherhood prevents women from being able to get rid of their child, then it is clear that women who choose abortion are necessarily coerced, forced, or misled by others. Instead of discourse that emphasizes "choice," in this account "abortion becomes a product of pressure and coercion" (Suk 2010: 1248).

This approach to informed consent identifies the main individuals or groups that force women to have an abortion: their male partners and doctors. Male partners, pro-life activists argue, play a role in the decision of women to have an abortion; "in the July issue of Glamour magazine an article by Eric Goodman appeared entitled 'Men and Abortion.' It is an account of several men's experiences with their partners' abortion. The thread running throughout the article in nearly every instance was that the abortion was his idea—and the women agreed to follow his lead" (Keech 1995a: 238). As part of the campaign of the organization American Victims of Abortion, which is a project of the National Right to Life, Olivia Gans often talks about her own abortion; "she was 22 years old, eager to please her boyfriend and desperate to hide her pregnancy from her family when she decided to undergo the procedure, she says. 'I was being a good little girl,' said Ms. Gans…'I was going through with the abortion to solve everybody's else's problems'" (Toner 1989).

Some of the websites argue that women are coerced, but offer explanations that focus more on social structures as the source of coercion. For example, After Abortion (2015), a website that targets women who had an abortion and are suffering, states that women's suffering and feelings of regret is a result of the coercion that led her to choose to have an abortion; "You may have been denied the choice you wanted or the support you needed. Women's experiences vary widely. For some, it was a decision they made and later came to regret; for most, it involved some form of coercion. For still others, it was forced by those in positions of authority or power." These power differences mean that women are not to be blamed for having an abortion. As Hadley Arkes, a political science professor and pro-life activists argue;

> On the one hand there may be a young, unmarried woman, who finds herself pregnant, with the father of the child not standing with her. Abandoned by the man, and detached from her family, she may feel the burden of the crisis bearing on her alone, with the prospect of life-altering changes. On the other hand, there is the man trained in surgery, the professional who

knows exactly what he is doing—he knows that he is destroying a human life, either by poisoning a child or dismembering it. And in perfect coolness and detachment, and at a nice price, he makes the killing of the innocent his office-work ("Life After Roe" 2007).

Since "significant evidence led one sociologist to conclude that 'the attitude of the man is the most important variable in a woman's decision to have an abortion'" ("Life After Roe" 2007), women should not be blamed, or punished, for their actions. Instead of being the enemy, they are thus the victims, just like the fetus (Trumpy 2014).

In the attempt to prevent coercion, the website of Ramah International includes a legal warning:

> It is against the law for anyone to force you to have an abortion. Not even a husband or parent can require you to undergo an abortion against your will, even if you are a minor (under 18 years old). Pregnancy care centers exist to help you in any circumstance. They can help you discuss this choice with those closest to you that are influencing your decision. The law in many states also requires abortion providers to give you information on: (1) possible complications, (2) the development of the baby, and (3) organizations that provides alternatives to abortion (2015).

The issue of informed consent is addressed also in legislation, both at the federal and the state level. In theory, the two types of explanations of informed consent may lead to different types of legislation. On the one hand, the argument regarding women's lack of knowledge and information on the process promotes regulations that may improve the process of informed consent. On the other hand, the argument that women cannot consent to abortion because of their nature as mothers means that no regulation will make the process of informed consent more meaningful. In practice, however, the policy proposals follow mainly the first argument, focusing on ensuring that women are not coerced into obtaining an abortion, or that they do not do so without full information about the fetus and the health risks involved. The result of this type of legislation is that abortion is a unique medical procedure; the procedure is highly regulated. Many of the informed consent laws that have been imposed in the mid-1990s across the country, mandate doctors to include specific information, including statements that are not accepted by the mainstream medical community (Vandewalker 2012). Further, this analysis uncovers that many of these laws reflect the general sentiment that women are in need of additional protections to assist them in the decision-making process. For example, Pennsylvania's 1982 Abortion Control Act notes that the legislature has uncovered clear and compelling evidence that "many women now seek or are encouraged to undergo an abortion without full knowledge of the development of the unborn child or alternatives to abortion" (18 Pa.C.S.A. § 3202, 1982).

Some of the laws concerning informed consent appeared right after *Roe*. One focus of this legislation was spousal notification and consent. By the early 1990s, there were six states with spousal notification laws, which require pregnant women to notify their spouses prior to obtaining an abortion.[7] Spousal notification requirements were framed as a way to protect or ensure the father's rights in the abortion decision. Missouri's spousal notification law requires a pregnant woman's spouse to provide written consent to an abortion in the first trimester, unless the physician certifies it is necessary to preserve her life. This law is informed by the legislature's "perception of marriage as an institution," thus concluding that any major family decision is to be protected to ensure both are involved and come to a shared agreement. The law was overturned in 1976, with the court referencing the appellants' argument that this law grants the husband a unilateral veto over the decision, a power that, during the first trimester, is not held by the state or any other authority. Further, the law only requires this of married women, and thus imposes a different burden on women based upon marital status (428 U.S. 52, 1976).

The other spousal notification laws primarily deal with notification rather than consent, requiring women to notify their husbands prior to obtaining an abortion. Many of these laws have the stated intent to strengthen marriage and families through the inclusion of the father in this decision. For example, the Pennsylvania spousal notification requirement declared that the legislative intent was to "further the Commonwealth's interest in promoting the integrity of the marital relationship and to protect the spouse's interest in having children within marriage" (18 Pa.C.S.A. § 3209, 1989). This requirement existed only for married women; for single or unmarried women, the provisions requiring notification were waived.

In 1992, the Supreme Court ruling in *Casey* addressed the constitutionality of informed consent, including consulting requirements,

[7] Louisiana's spousal notification law requires minors who are married to obtain the consent of their spouse prior to obtaining an abortion; for minors who are single and pregnant, parental consent is required for an abortion (Louisiana Stat. Ann 40 § 1299.33, 1973). Additionally, two notification laws—Florida and Montana's—were ruled unconstitutional (Florida Stat. Ann. 390.001(4)(b), 1979; Montana Code Ann. § 50-20-107, 1974).

a waiting period, parental consent, and spousal notification. The court upheld some of the informed consent requirements in the Pennsylvania law, but ruled that the spousal notification provision for married women represented an infringement on women's right to obtain an abortion as established in *Roe*. The court maintained that this requirement created an undue burden for women, and could potentially exacerbate cases of spousal or child abuse (505 U.S. 833, 1992). At the same time, however, the court established the state's interest in protecting women's health and psychological well-being. Specifically, the ruling opinion declared that "in attempting to ensure that a woman apprehend the full consequences of her decision, the State furthers the legitimate purpose of reducing the risk that a woman may elect an abortion, only to discover later, with devastating psychological consequences, that her decision was not informed" (505 U.S. 833, at 882). Thus, the court reinforced the role of the states as a protector of women's health and well-being, validating the expansion of government authority and power in order to do so.

Despite the overturning of spousal notification laws in *Casey*, spousal notification bills have recently been introduced in a handful of states. Ohio state legislators introduced a "father's consent bill" in 2007 and 2008; this law would require women to present notarized consent from the father of the child prior to obtaining an abortion. Instances in which the father is unknown, a list of names regarding who could be the potential father must be submitted in order to determine paternity prior to proceeding with treatment (House Bill 252, 2009). A similar bill has been introduced in Missouri (House Bill 131, 2014), both of which would be unconstitutional if passed into law. While the lack of laws addressing spousal notification is influenced by the court's ruling as unconstitutional, they fit the women-centered approach; the decision of women to have an abortion is often influenced by their partner, who has his own interests in the matter.

Casey, while responsible for the elimination of spousal notification laws, also determined the other requirements constitutional. Thus, although the pro-life laws imposing requirements on women or abortion providers were introduced before the 1990s, since *Casey*, there has been an increase in the number of laws passed, as well as the scope and extent of the requirements included in these laws. Following the ruling, it is not surprising that the legislation after *Casey* focused on consulting requirements—including wait-time period and requirements to provide information and images about the development of the fetus and fetal pain—as well as the requirement for parental notification in the case of minors seeking abortions. These aspects were either approved in *Casey* as constitutional or not directly challenged. This legislation fits into the pro-life discourse over informed consent, since it is meant to address both the lack of knowledge of women regarding the effect and outcome of abortion, as well as their difficulty to make such a decision.

As of 2015, 35 states have some form of counseling requirement prior to obtaining an abortion. As part of the consultation, most laws necessitate the physician to describe to pregnant women the probable gestational age of the child, the risks of the procedure for women's health as well as alternatives to abortion, and the probable anatomical and physiological characteristics of the "unborn child" (Ky. Rev. Stat. Ann. § 311.725, 1998). In Kansas, the law also requires physicians to detail the options available to pregnant women, including the requirement of the father for child support and the prenatal resources provided by the state, as well as the following statement:

> Many public and private agencies exist to provide counseling and information on available services. You are strongly urged to seek their assistance to obtain guidance during your pregnancy. In addition, you are encouraged to seek information on abortion services, alternatives to abortion, including adoption, and resources available to postpartum mothers. The law requires that your physician or the physician's agent provide the enclosed information (Kan. Stat. Ann. § 65-6701, 1997).

In addition to the counseling requirements, 28 states require a specific wait time after women receive counseling before they are able to obtain the procedure itself. Of these 28 laws, 26 were passed after *Casey*. Under most laws, the wait times are 24 h, although two states (Alabama and Tennessee) have a 48-h mandatory wait time, and three (Missouri, South Dakota,[8] and Utah) impose a 72-h wait. In all three cases, the law of 72-h wait requirement passed in 2014 and replaced an earlier 24-h wait requirement. Thirteen states require the first visit to be in person, necessitating a second trip to undergo the actual procedure. These wait times are justified as increasing women's ability to decide whether or not to abort, without the pressures of family members or physicians.

At the federal level, attempts to ensure or protect the informed consent process in the decision to abort resulted in policy proposals to increase the funding for certain protective measures. After 1995, 21 proposals involved

---

[8] South Dakota's counseling law prohibits the inclusion of weekends and state holidays in the 72-h waiting period (South Dakota Codified Laws 34-23A-10.1).

ultrasounds prior to an abortion. Specifically, there were 14 proposals for the Department of Health and Human Services (HHS) to provide grants to community pregnancy centers for ultrasound equipment. These bills would require those receiving the grant to show the visual image of the fetus to the pregnant woman, give a full anatomical description, provide the approximate age of the fetus and information on alternatives to abortion, as well as state resources available to help women carry the fetus to term (H.R. 216, 2005). Seven of these proposals require providers to perform ultrasounds on women, as a necessary step before a woman can give informed consent for an abortion. Further, these 14 measures require all abortion providers to collect and report surveillance data, including information on the woman receiving an abortion, information about the fetus, and the type of procedure performed. One proposal requiring a wait time of 24 h was introduced in the 112th session of Congress; the bill died in committee and no other similar legislation has been introduced since (House Resolution 3802, 2012). Three informed consent measures were initiated as well, in the 109th and 110th sessions of Congress, none of which passed.

The attempt to teach women about the fetus and its development also shapes policy at the state level. As part of the process of informed consent, a majority of states (33) require women to receive information regarding the gestational development of the fetus as well as pictures or descriptions of the fetus at different stages of development. These requirements are often considered important so that women understand that the fetus is a "whole, separate, unique, living human being" (Mo. Rev. Stat. § 188.027(1)(2), 2011; S.D. Codified Laws § 34-23A-10.1(1)(b), 2011). The requirement to provide women actual pictures and descriptions is unique to abortion procedures; while informed consent is intended to provide information on the medical risks and benefits of the procedure, showing women images of the fetus is designed to influence their decision not based on the medical aspects of the procedure (Vandewalker 2012).

Similar to the imagery and ultrasound requirements, fetal pain laws, which have become increasingly common in the past 10–15 years, are also meant to provide women information and discourage them from having an abortion. The fetal pain requirements are based on studies, performed by medical doctors who are sympathetic to the pro-life movement, that document when the fetus is able to experience pain. This, they argue, happens at approximately 20 or 22 weeks.[9] At this stage, the

[9] While a fetus at 20 or 22 weeks may have developed the physiological capacity to experience pain, most scientists maintain that the development of neurological pathways that allow

fetus has sufficient physiological development of the spinal cord, nerve tracts, thalamus, and cortex that allow for the experience of pain. This scientific understanding of fetal pain has been used to limit abortion at 20 or 22 weeks, and the information regarding this issue is found in many informed consent requirements (The Guttmacher Institute 2015b; Vandewalker 2012).

Twelve states included in their informed consent requirements information on fetal pain, all between the years 2003 and 2013. For example, Indiana law requires that women be told that "objective, scientific information shows that the fetus can experience pain at or before 20 weeks of post-fertilization age" while South Dakota's fetal pain law does not specify any specific age at which the fetus may feel pain (Ind. Code § 16-34-2-1.1(a)(1)(G), 2011; S.D. Dep't of Health, 2012). In Texas, the counseling booklet given to women before an abortion declares that by the 12th week of gestation "the fibers that carry pain to the brain are developed; however it is unknown if the unborn child is able to experience sensations such as pain." Further, it is stated that at 20 weeks, "some experts have concluded that the unborn child is probably able to feel pain" (Texas Department of Health, 2003: 4–5). As in the case of the requirement for ultrasound or fetal imagery, these laws do not provide information on the medical risks and benefits of the procedure.

A different type of legislation concerning informed consent addresses the problem of decision-making process in the case of minors. Laws concerning parental notification requirements for minors are among the most prominent proposed and enacted laws, at both the federal and state levels. These measures, in general, establish and protect the role of parents to provide consent for a minor before obtaining an abortion. Since 1995, 42 parental notification bills were introduced in Congress, representing 41 % of all women-centered, pro-life proposals at the federal level. Almost all of these measures (33) would prohibit the transportation of a minor across state lines to obtain an abortion to circumvent a parental notification law in another state. For example, the Child Custody Protection Act—introduced 13 times during the 105th through 113th sessions of

for the conscious perception of pain does not occur until 28 weeks of gestation. The difficulty in making conclusive findings on the ability of the fetus to experience pain is compounded by the interpretation of "pain" or avoidance responses to a stimulus. The physiological markers used to measure pain remain that, only markers that we assume demonstrate an adverse reaction or pain response in the fetus as the subject cannot provide any description of their feelings (Lee et al. 2005).

Congress—prohibits transporting a minor over state lines for an abortion, which constitutes an abridgement of the rights of the parents in the state in which they reside (H.R. 1755, 2003). The remaining federal parental notification proposals are restrictions on the performance of abortion on minors by facilities or medical professionals that receive federal funding (1), the performance of abortion in Department of Defense facilities for minors who are dependents of a member of the Armed Forces (1), and the performance of abortion on a minor without parental consent (8).

The first round of state-level parental notification laws were passed shortly after the ruling in *Roe*; from 1973 to 1994, 23 states passed into law some form of parental notification or consent requirement. Of the 14 state laws that have been challenged in the courts, five were invalidated. All of the legal challenges to these parental notification laws concerned the absence of sufficient judicial bypass measures; for minors who became pregnant because of rape or incest, or are in situations of child abuse, judicial bypass measures are meant to protect access to abortion as well as protect the health and safety of these women. Of the five laws invalidated, all were later amended to include sufficient judicial bypass mechanisms. Of the 20 states that passed parental notification laws between 1995 and 2015, eight were challenged in the courts and the courts invalidated five. The judicial bypass measures during these years were also found lacking by the courts; three of which were amended by their respective state legislature. These laws vary somewhat, with some allowing grandparents or other family members to provide consent to the minor's abortion. Despite frequent challenges and changes to these new laws, only two states have had their parental notification law invalidated and have not, to date, drafted a new law.[10]

These policies range from the requirement of consent from one parent (18) or both parents (3) to requirements for parental notification and consent (5). In addition, other states require only notification, including 11 states that require notification of one parent and one state that requires notification of both. Many of these parental notification laws state that "immature minors often lack the ability to make fully informed choices that take into account both immediate and long-range consequences [of an abortion]," further declaring that "the capacity to become pregnant and the capacity for mature judgment concerning the wisdom of an

---

[10]Connecticut, Maine, and Washington, D.C. are the only locations in the USA that positively affirm a minor's right to obtain an abortion without parental notification.

abortion are not necessarily related" (Mont. Stat. § 50-20-202, 2013). According to this approach, the role of the state is not only to protect the woman from entering into this procedure without being fully informed; rather, the state also establishes protections for the family unit, ensuring the ability of parents to safeguard the physical and emotional health of their daughter. Thus, in 38 states, it is parents who are tasked with ensuring the decision to abort is fully informed, as their participation is required through their consent or notification of the procedure.

The focus on informed consent is the most common and effective argument within the women-centered strategy. It emphasizes physical and emotional risks that may be linked to abortion, and frames them as an issue that needs to be addressed through a better medical procedure and meaningful process of informed consent. In addition, however, the women-centered strategy also addresses these same issues—of mental and physical risks—separately from the issue of informed consent. These risks, pro-life activists argue, are the reason why abortion harms women, regardless of the process through which they consent to abortion.

The Emotional Toll of Abortion

The second argument at the center of the women-centered strategy is that women who have an abortion suffer from emotional toll and trauma. This argument is based on the idea that womanhood and motherhood are naturally connected. Since abortion is an act against this natural link, it causes long-lasting trauma to women (Trumpy 2014).[11] The court also recognizes the emotional effect of abortion, suggesting, in *Roe, Casey*, and *Carhart*, a willingness to restrict access to abortion in case it affects women's emotional state (Suk 2010). This argument contains two separate justifications. The first justification for the argument of trauma is that abortion is linked to a negative approach in society toward motherhood and care, thus undermining women's role in society and, as a result, also their own self-worth. The second justification focuses on PAS, which pro-life activists argue is caused when women are prevented from fulfilling their natural and social role of becoming mothers. Both these justifications are based on the assumption that abortion prevents women from ful-

---

[11] In the last few years, there has been a growing focus on the trauma experienced by men, mainly in cases that their partner made the decision without them or against their will. This discourse, however, is still marginal in comparison to the one that focuses on women.

filling their natural role. Thus, accordingly, it is not surprising that women who had an abortion experience it as traumatic, and as an emotionally damaging event for the rest of their lives.

This argument appears in the newspapers as well as in the organizations' websites. Between 1995 and 2015, the argument regarding emotional and physiological effects of abortion appears 33 times in the newspaper items, representing 22 % of all women-centered arguments. The claim that women regret having an abortion appears 20 times, a significant increase from the previous period, in which the topic was mentioned only once in 22 years. In addition, between 1995 and 2015, the argument that abortion is bad because of the natural link between womanhood and motherhood appeared in the newspapers 14 times, in comparison with twice in the earlier period. An analysis of the organizations websites, which trace the current use of such arguments, reveals a significant increase in the use of this discourse; of the 103 websites that include women-centered arguments, only 18 (17 %) do not include claims regarding these issues. Eighty-four websites (82 %) include the claim that abortion causes emotional trauma, and 29 websites (28 %) include statements or testimony of women regretting their abortion.[12] The natural link between women and motherhood appears in ten websites (7 % of all websites), arguing that since this act is unnatural to women, it causes them harm. This discourse often uses language that aims to show compassion for the difficult—even if wrong—decision that these women were forced to make. This type of discourse appears also in the 36 websites that target women who already had an abortion, emphasizing their trauma and need for healing, as well as the long-lasting effects of abortion.

As part of the women-centered discourse, the pro-life movement argues that one of the reasons why women choose abortion—against their natural tendencies and preferences—is the new ideas about women's role in society, and the growing emphasis of liberal concepts such as individualism and reason. As a result of these new ideas, practices that are important to women—such as compassion and care—are marginalized and undermined. Therefore, women, who want to be valued and respected, are pushed to adopt values and behaviors that are not necessarily natural to them. In the process of acting against their natural tendencies, some women "choose" abortion. However, this is not really a choice, due to the context in which this "choice" is made.

[12] Twenty-six websites include both arguments.

The argument about this natural link and the effect abortion has on women has been promoted in the 1970s by FFL. Daphne Clair de Jong, the founder of FFL in New Zealand, writes,

> the womb is not the be-all and end-all of women's existence. But it is the physical center of her sexual identity, which is an important aspect of her self-image and personality. To reject this function, or to regard it as a handi-cap, a danger or nuisance, is to reject a vital part of her own personhood. Every woman need not be a mother, but unless every women can identify with the potential motherhood of all women, no equality is possible (1995: 171–172).

As stated in the website Hope After Abortion, the trauma of abortion is related to the unnaturalness of the act;

> within a few days after conception, even before the tiny embryo has nested in her uterine wall, a hormone called 'early pregnancy factor' is found in her bloodstream, alerting the cells of her body to the pregnancy…She begins to think 'baby.'…But if she wants to have an abortion she must try to stop this process. She must deny the maternal feelings entering into her con-sciousness…If she has the abortion, the very cells of her body remember the pregnancy and know that the process of change that had been going on was stopped in an unnatural manner. Her body and her emotions tell her that she is a mother who has lost a child. And so it is not surprising that after the abortion, a pain begins to emerge from the depths of her heart. She has a loss to morn, but cannot allow herself to grieve (2015).

Motherhood, according to this approach, is central for the self-definition of women;

> A mother's benefits from her relationship with her child throughout her natural life are unique and irreplaceable. Often—and many would say normally—a mother's continuing relations with her child enhance her life and sense of self, bringing great joy and fulfillment, but even when chil-dren cause their mother pain, the mother continues to view her relations with them as integral to her sense of herself as a person—and as one of her greatest interests. It is inconsistent with the experiences of the vast majority of women to dismiss a woman's interest in her relations with her child as in any way peripheral to her sense of self (Fox-Genovese 2002: 7)

This natural connection, however, has been denied by the pro-choice movement, which had been able to convince "vast numbers of people, many of them decent people of good will, that women's prospects for happiness and self-realization depend upon unrestricted access to abortion" (Fox-Genovese 2004: 52). The legalization of abortion, according to this account, is one of the factors that hinders women's equality. Instead of recognizing the unique contribution of women to society, the pro-choice argument that abortion is a choice means that pregnancy, as well as raising children, is understood as a failure of women. Furthermore, since it was the mother's own choice to raise children, society assumes it is now her own responsibly to raise them, without the right to demand anything from the father. Thus, some pro-life supporters argue, the legalization and public legitimacy of abortion "has shifted primary (and often sole) responsibility for the bearing and rearing of children onto women's shoulders. Abortion has cheapened the moral fabric of American culture" (Comstock Cunningham 2004: 111).

According to this discourse, the natural link between womanhood and motherhood is not limited to the connection between women and their own children. Instead, women are naturally more caring than men. As Bachiochi states:

> I came to understand that the beauty of women lies in their desire to give of themselves for others, the less fortunate, the helpless, the weak. These were not attributes imposed upon women by men to keep us from achieving prestige in public offices and places of commerce. Rather, such feminine virtues have always, until quite recently, been understood as marks of true nobility in both women and men. For women, to consider these qualities of little worth in comparison with the competitive qualities hailed in the public sphere is to turn against both women themselves and those whom women have traditionally served (2004: 30–31).

Thus, the fight against abortion is not only a fight for an individual woman who is coerced into having an abortion but also a fight for feminine values, for a society where women can be true to themselves and still be respected. It is thus a fight against a way of life, against the attempt to replace values and concepts that women care about; "Abortion advocates propose a radical revision in what it means to be a woman – if not an abolition of the very substance and concept of woman" (Fox-Genovese 2004: 53). The fight against abortion is a fight to protect women, because "when those babies aren't born, that is a loss for their mothers" (Bazelon 2012). This sense of loss does not disappear; as stated in the website Abortion Recovery International, "Maybe it was 25 years ago. Maybe last year. Or last month. Or even yesterday! But you, or someone you know, may be struggling with one or more past abortions. Regrets of a past 'choice' are not just 'all in your head.' Abortion may have affected your life in ways you could have never expected" (2015).

The argument about the unnaturalness of abortion is expanded in some websites to include also men; 11 websites argue that men also experience trauma because of their partner's decision to have an abortion. In the case of men, it is often harder for them to recognize their experience of abortion as trauma; the website Life Institute states, "Many men acknowledge various problems in their life without connecting them to a previous abortion decision" (Mattes 2009). However, since men may have only limited power to influence the decision of their partner to have an abortion, some of them will experience strong feelings of loss and trauma. This point is made in the website Men and Abortion, where it is stated, "It may be especially hard on you if you wanted to have a baby with her or get married and she doesn't or is not ready. You may feel the loss more than she does" (2015).

The second argument used to prove that women who have an abortion experience an emotional and psychological trauma is the scientific-based discourse on PAS. PAS, according to pro-life accounts, occurs because of a few reasons. First, the trauma women experience after abortion is connected to the lack of meaningful process of informed consent, which was discussed earlier. This lack leads women to make wrong decisions, without a full understanding of the implications of their actions. Second, the trauma is an outcome also of the failure of these women to fulfill their natural role of becoming mothers. As Family Research Council's website states, "when certain practices violate human dignity and the intrinsic nature of womanhood and motherhood, they produce psychological problems based on the denial of the truth about the human person" (Siegel 2007: 1038). As such, in the women-centered discourse, PAS is presented as the outcome of a situation in which women are forced by society, as well as specific individuals, to act against their natural tendencies and instincts.

The idea that abortion is experienced by women as a trauma builds upon the feminist literature on the trauma of rape, which emphasized the link between acts done on the body and their emotional effect (Suk 2010). Such a link is evident in Derr's writing, where she states that the trauma of abortion is connected not only to the interference with the natural process of becoming a mother but also to the bodily trauma that is caused by abortion;

> Abortion cheats women of the intense pleasures natural to gestation, delivery and breastfeeding...the deepest part of the vagina, the part around the cervix, stores up the pain of rape, traumatic childbirth (often caused by undue medical interference in labor and delivery), and abortion. This pain must be released and resolved before a woman can attain the satisfaction she deserves (Derr 1995: 257).[13]

This language differs from the discourse on PAS that appears in the websites, which often uses scientific language and evidence-based arguments. Vincent Rue, the co-director of Institute for Pregnancy Loss, is one of the pro-life activists who developed and promoted the concept of PAS. He has played a central role in the development of pro-life legislation at the state level, mainly in Texas. In the case of PAS, the use of scientific language is also meant to create a link between this phenomenon and other cases of PTSD. One of the claims that appear in multiple websites, including, for example, Operation Rescue, is that "Post-Abortion Syndrome (PAS) is a type of Post-Traumatic Stress Disorder. It occurs when a woman is unable to work through her emotional responses due to the trauma of an abortion."[14]

The assumption that abortion causes emotional trauma appears also in federal legislation, which uses scientific data and language to argue for the need to conduct further research on the matter, or to develop programs that target the emotional effect of abortion. Between 1995 and 2014, there were seven proposals to fund research on post-abortion depression and psychosis as well as other problems that may result from an abortion,

---

[13] The question of whether this discourse is a reflection of conservative values or, rather, represents a feminist approach, is of course debated. On the one hand, feminist thinkers often reject the argument that certain biological attributes determine women's social roles, instead arguing that it is the social construction of gender that links women's ability to give birth with practices of care and concern. On the other hand, some pro-life activists argue that the pro-choice movement misunderstands feminism as promoting equality through sameness rather than difference. In addition, they argue, the feminist movement often ignores the complex relations between reproductive potential and patriarchy, as well as the fact that it is the patriarchy that defines physiology as a barrier to public achievement.

[14] Similar statements appear also on the websites for the organizations After Abortion, Christian Life Resources, Secular Pro-Life, among other similar organizations and groups.

including future infertility, cervical tearing, and death (Post-Abortion Services and Support Act, 2002). As part of the justification for the Post-Abortion Depression Research and Care Act, the law cites research arguing,

> The symptoms of post-abortion depression include bouts of crying, guilt, intense grief or sadness, emotional numbness, eating disorders, drug and alcohol abuse, suicidal urges, anxiety and panic attacks, anger or rage, sexual problems or promiscuity, lowered self-esteem, nightmares and sleep disturbance, flashbacks, and difficulty with relationships. Greater thought suppression is associated with experiencing more intrusive thoughts of the abortion. Both suppression and intrusive thoughts, in turn, are positively related to increases in psychological distress over time (H.R. 2805, Post-Abortion Depression Research and Care Act 2001).

The claim that some research findings document the emotional and psychological effects of abortion is used to justify the $3 million increase in the appropriations for the National Institute of Health (NIH). Further, the act notes many contributing factors to post-abortion depression and psychosis, including the lack of social support, the lack of understanding of this issue within the medical community and among the general public, and the social pressures to have an abortion. While all these factors have been uncovered in numerous research studies, the issue has not yet been investigated by the NIH. The remarks offered by the bill's sponsor, Joseph Pitt, as found in the Congressional Record, illustrate the presumption that this bill is designed solely to protect women's health and safety. He declares that much research has been conducted on the psychological consequences or effects of giving birth or of miscarriage, and yet the same is not true for post-abortion depression; he ends stating "why should women who choose to have an abortion be given any less care and concern than women who give birth or who miscarry" (Pitts 2001).

Eight proposals in Congress during this time period introduced increased funding for the different programs in the globalization (HHS) to address the social and emotional difficulties associated with pregnancy as an alternative to abortion. The legislative findings of the bill H.R. 7091, Care for Life Act, state that many women feel coerced (64 %) or do not want to be a single parent or report problems with the father of the child (50 %). Thus, these proposals are designed to ensure greater support services for pregnant women, assisting them in "overcoming the social and emotional difficulties" that may cause women to abort (Care for Life Act, 2008).

Health Concerns

In addition to addressing the emotional and psychological effects of abortion, the women-centered discourse also emphasizes the health risks associated with abortion, specifically the link between abortion and breast cancer, despite the rejection of this link by the mainstream medical community. In general, this discourse and legislation replace the moral or normative discussion, which characterizes the fetus-centered strategy but still appears in some of the women-centered strategy, with a discourse that is solely scientific in nature, using evidence-based argument regarding women's rights. This concern for women's health appears in the newspapers mainly in the 1990s; while between 1973 and 1994, the health risks associated with abortion were mentioned 16 times, and 22 times in the later period, two-thirds of all references were made in the 1990s. The argument that abortion causes health risks is widespread in the websites; it appears in 85 websites, which constitute 83 % of the websites that include women-centered arguments, thus making it the single most commonly used argument in the websites. The centrality of this discourse in the websites signifies the current trend of the pro-life discourse to use a more scientifically based argument, with 52 websites using scientific language as the basis for at least some of their arguments.

According to pro-life activists and research, one of the main health concerns associated with abortion is the higher risk that women have of suffering from breast cancer. This risk, according to pro-life publications, is a result of the fact that abortion prevents full-term pregnancy, which is associated with lower risk of breast cancer. This link—between giving birth and decreased risk of breast cancer—is relatively documented and accepted within the scientific community (Helewa et al. 2002). In addition, pro-life supporters argue, abortion independently increases the risk of breast cancer. Unlike the first claim, this is not supported by independent researchers outside of the pro-life movement; most research examining spontaneous as well as induced abortion found no increased risk of breast cancer, often raising political as well as methodological concerns about the research that identifies those links (Collaborative Group on Hormonal Factors in Breast Cancer 2004; Jasen 2005; NCI 2010).

Despite the rejection of this argument by most in the scientific community, the claim that abortion independently increases the risk of breast cancer is prominent within the pro-life discourse. In 2013, for example, four of the six annual newsletters of the Elliot Institute included pieces written by Dr. Joel Brind, a biology and endocrinology professor, all explaining why the existing data about the lack of connection between abortion and breast cancer is flawed. Brind's findings are used by many pro-life websites, including ProLife OBGYNS, Right to Life, American Right to Life, to argue for the established scientific link between abortion and breast cancer (Jasen 2005).

At the state level, numerous proposed and enacted laws invoke women's health and safety, as in the case of informed consent laws that include medical scripts that physicians are required to share with women prior to obtaining an abortion. Of the 35 informed consent laws described earlier, 27 include specific information the physician must provide to the patient; in five states (Alaska, Kansas, Mississippi, Oklahoma, and Texas), the medical scripts require physicians to assert that there is a link between abortion and breast cancer. The mandated medical scripts of 20 states includes a description of the potential implications of an abortion for one's future fertility. Finally, a description of the potential mental health effects of an abortion is mandated in 20 states, requiring statements on the psychological consequences of abortion; seven of the policies (in Kansas, Louisiana, Michigan, Nebraska, North Carolina, Texas, and Utah) provide a detailed account emphasizing all the possible negative emotional responses that may occur as a result of an abortion (The Guttmacher Institute 2015b).

Another type of public policies intended to address women's health in the abortion procedure includes clinic regulations and physician requirements. These policies, argued by many researchers and pro-choice organizations to represent unnecessary impediments to the procedure itself, are intended to protect women from the purported health risks associated with the procedure. While basic safety standards and regulations exist for all medical facilities, abortion is a unique procedure given the existence of dozens of additional state laws that go above and beyond previously established clinic regulations. Specifically, 24 states have laws such as these, addressing the location or facility in which this procedure can occur. These additional safety requirements apply to physicians' offices where abortions are provided (14) or any site that provides medication abortions as well as surgical abortions (17) (The Guttmacher Institute 2015b). For example, Kansas' law requires "separate locker rooms for patients and staff to store clothing and belongings, janitorial closets of 50 square feet per procedure room; and the maintenance of air temperature at between 70 and 75 degrees in patient recovery rooms, and between 68 and 73 degrees in procedure rooms," although this law has been temporarily enjoined by the courts (Kan. Admin. Regs. §§ 28-34-133 (3) (15), 2011). Even more specific requirements are present in Utah, which requires "specifications for the type of fabric used on window coverings, requisite ceiling heights for the boiler room, and a mandate that a provider have four parking spaces per procedure room" (Utah Admin. Code R432-600-29, R432-600-5(2), 2011).

Twenty-two states have licensing standards for clinics—or any location that provides any type of abortion—which is comparable to the standards for ambulatory surgical centers that also provide abortion. Eleven states specify the size the buildings' corridors must be and 11 states have certain requirements for the size of patient rooms. With regard to clinic regulations, 11 states have laws that require abortion clinics to be located within a certain distance from ambulatory surgical centers. These requirements maintain that hospitals must be within 15 min (Missouri and Utah) or 30 min (Michigan and Mississippi) from the abortion clinic, 15 miles (Illinois) or 30 miles (Arizona, Arkansas, North Dakota, and Ohio), or in the adjacent county (Indiana and Tennessee). Finally, clinician requirements are present in 13 states; these states require physicians that provide abortions must have admitting privileges at local hospitals (4) or admitting privileges or some type of alternative arrangement (9) (The Guttmacher Institute 2015b).

A final issue area in which the legislative concern for women's health has been manifested in legislation concerning FDA approval of RU-486 in 2000, which is used as an oral abortifacient taken in the first month of pregnancy. At the state level, there have been a number of laws enacted to prohibit or limit the use of telemedicine to provide access for medication abortion. Telemedicine is a growing phenomenon in the USA that allows physicians, therapists, or other health professionals to connect with patients via telecommunications and information technologies. Particularly for individuals in rural communities, telemedicine provides increased access to immediate and long-term care, while allowing for greater accommodation of both the providers and patients' schedules. In 2008, Planned Parenthood of Iowa began providing medication abortion—a combination of mifepristone and misoprostol—via telemedicine, a practice in which women who have undergone an ultrasound and have completed lab work, have a videoconference with a physician and the local clinician to determine what type of procedure is necessary. If medication abortion is the selected course of action, the woman is provided the first dose of medication at the local clinic, and the second dose is given to her to ingest at home the following day. The use of telemedicine for medication abortion can lead to a decline in later abortions as women take advantage of the access provided for early abortions (Semuels 2014).

Following the initiation of this service, the Board of Medicine of Iowa established a new policy requiring the physical presence of a physician at the time the abortion-inducing drug is provided. Further, a follow-up appointment at the same facility is required, within 12–18 days of the initial visit. One of the primary reasons for this policy was to protect patient health and safety. The opinion in the court ruling specifically emphasized this point, noting that the board did not pass the new rule in the interest of protecting fetal rights, rather it was to protect the health and interests of women (*Planned Parenthood of the Heartland v. Iowa Board of Medicine* 2015). In the case of Iowa, the court overturned this restriction established by the Board of Medicine, yet 18 states have since passed laws prohibiting the use of telemedicine for medicated abortion. These laws have all been enacted since 2011, with two states—Arkansas and Idaho—passing their restrictions in 2015.

During this time, a similar subset of laws emerged at the federal level. Twelve measures address the FDA approval of RU-486 or mifepristone in 2000, which remains controversial today. All 12 proposals advocate for some form of restriction on the distribution and use of the drug; six would establish restrictions on physicians who are able to prescribe the drug, including admitting privileges at a hospital an hour or less away, the requirement that the physician is licensed, is trained in surgical abortions, and has completed a program on the use of RU-486. The other measures addressing RU-486 proposed during this time period would require the suspension of FDA approval for the drug as well as a review of the approval process, performed by the Comptroller General. In the legislative findings section of the proposal, used to justify the legislation, it is stated that the use of mifepristone—in conjunction with off-label use of misoprostol[15]—

[15] The prescribed dosage of RU-486 was first investigated by the FDA in the 1990s, and approved in 2000. Since 2000, researchers have found that altering the dosage of the two drugs—mifepristone and misoprostol—is safer, more effective, and results in fewer side effects for most women. Off-label use of drugs such as this occurs quite frequently, and is accepted as long as there are medical studies demonstrating its effectiveness (FDA 2015; USA Today 2006).

has resulted in the death, near death, and "adverse reactions" (Senate Bill 511, RU-486 Suspension and Review Act, 2005). These laws—operating to restrict access to medicated abortion—were unsuccessful, dying in committee with no action taken.[16]

Recently, pro-life legislators have used the introduction of RU-486 as a way to address the problem of informed consent and regret after abortion. Medication abortion, they argue, allows for "abortion reversal," since it involves two separate drugs, taken at different points in time. George Delgado is one of the doctors who have championed the prospect of abortion reversals, encouraging women who have changed their minds after receiving the first dose of mifepristone, to receive an injection of progesterone to reverse its effects. While there is an extremely small amount of data to demonstrate that the mifepristone—the first dose administered in medication abortion—can be successfully reversed with no damage to the fetus,[17] Arizona now includes in their informed consent requirements a statement that medicated abortion can be reversed (Marcotte 2014). After the signing of Senate Bill 1318 in March 2015, the Center for Arizona Policy's President (a pro-life lobbying organization) declared "A woman who takes abortion pill has right to know her action may be reversible. Give women all the facts. Respect women. Yes on 1318" (Shumway 2015). The implementation of SB 1318 was put on hold as the law was challenged by three Arizona doctors and Arizona Planned Parenthood. The case is currently before a federal court, with hearings scheduled for October 2015. Nevertheless, soon after Arizona passed this law, Arkansas followed suit. In the wake of this growing attention to the prospect of legislating informed consent for "abortion reversals," Louisiana legislators have pledged to pursue this option as well.[18]

[16] In 2012, the Telemedicine Safety Act was introduced in Congress. The act would prohibit telemedicine abortions over state lines as well as restrict funds for facilities that provide telemedicine abortion (H.R. 5731, 2012).

[17] The American College of Gynecologists and Obstetricians (ACOG) maintain that taking the mifepristone alone, without also taking misoprostol, may cause a woman to not miscarry, regardless of whether an injection of progesterone is taken or not. They have challenged the assertions of Delgado, maintaining that there is no reliable data demonstrating that "abortion reversals" are effective, and may in fact be dangerous for women's health (Khazan 2015).

[18] Although Arizona and Arkansas are the only states that have created the legal requirement to include information on "abortion reversals," a number of crisis pregnancy centers around the country are offering this form of "treatment" (Kulze 2014).

The three arguments that build the women-centered strategy have been criticized by individuals and organizations that oppose the pro-life mission, as well as from within, by pro-life supporters. The critique from pro-life activists focuses mainly on the reliance of the women-centered strategy on medical and scientific evidence, rather than the moral argument that characterizes the fetus-centered strategy. Scientific data is always changing and can be—and often is—challenged by other researchers. Even pro-life supporters may challenge the scientific data that shows women are negatively affected by abortion (Beckwith 2004). For example, in the late 1980s, the pro-life Surgeon General Everett C. Koop criticized the use of the concept of informed consent to put limitations on abortion; in his statement in 1989 before the subcommittee on human resources and governmental relations of the house committee on government operations, Koop stated,

> review of published studies on the psychological sequelae of abortion by statisticians at NCHS and CDC indicated that the methodology in virtually all of those studies was seriously flawed. Our studies regarding the physiological outcomes of abortion could not be conclusive for several reasons: One, the lack of consensus regarding the symptoms, the severity, and duration of adverse mental reactions post-abortion; two, the lack of controls for psychological symptoms or disorders associated with life events experienced before or after the abortion; three, the methodological difficulties related to sampling to form an appropriate study group; four, finding a technique to surmount the fact that many as half the women who have had abortion are likely to deny it on a questionnaire; and finally, the paucity of long-term follow up on post-abortion women" (Rubin 1994: 277–278).

In light of the questionable scientific data, Koop urged the movement to avoid using "irrelevant and unproven claims about women" (Siegel 2007: 1016).

In addition, the move from fetus-centered arguments to arguments regarding the health and well-being of the woman puts too much emphasis on women as the ones who should make the decision. This opens the possibility for women to decide that despite the risks, they nevertheless are willing to have an abortion;

> although an appeal to self-interest may persuade some women not to have abortions, it is not clear how the choice not to abort under that pretense is equivalent to moral conversion and intellectual assent to the pro-life per-

spective. After all, if a nineteenth-century American slave owner chose to free his kidnapped Africans because he was persuaded to believe that it was not in his self-interest to continue owning them, such an act, although good insofar as sparing the slaves a tremendous indignity, would not be equivalent to the slave owner being converted to the belief that no person by nature is property and thus ought not to be owned by another (Beckwith 2001: 129).

Legislation that adds requirements to the process of informed consent also follows this line, emphasizing risks and adding limitations, but not completely blocking the possibility to have an abortion. Thus, convincing the American public that abortion is a serious moral wrong is the only way to stop abortions altogether, rather than merely reducing their number.

This tension—between the moral arguments of the fetus-centered strategy, which acts to overturn *Roe*, and the scientific approach of the women-centered strategy that in practice introduces limitations on access to abortion—explains the use of different discourses for different audiences. While it is clear that since the 1990s women-centered arguments have been shaping pro-life strategy in discourse and legislation, these arguments are not equally common within some pro-life supporters and organizations, mainly religious ones. This is also the case in the 184 issues of *Touchstone*, a Christian conservative journal, published between 1986 and 2015. An analysis of the 152 articles that address the topic of abortion reveals that most focus on fetus-centered arguments (126 times, or 82 %), while the minority of the articles includes references to women-centered arguments (27 times, or 18 %). In comparison to the newspapers and websites, the percentage of women-centered references is significantly lower in this journal, even after the mid-1990s; more than 50 % of the justifications focus on the argument that the fetus is a human being, with 45 (29 %) references to God or religion, and 42 (27 %) mentioning of general arguments regarding sanctity of life.[19]

In the few cases that they do appear, the women-centered references in *Touchstone* follow the same arguments introduced earlier, with an emphasis mainly on the emotional trauma and regret that follows abortion. For example, in a piece from 2001, Robert P. George, a jurisprudence professor and pro-life activist, recognizes some women-centered concerns

---

[19] The higher rate of religious references in *Touchstone*—29 % versus around 13 % in the newspaper items in both periods—is not surprising, given the religious nature of this publication.

when he argues that the legalization of abortion "has done immeasurable moral, psychological, and sometimes physical harm to women who are so very often, and in so many respects, truly abortion's 'secondary victims.'" While George includes a call for political and educational action, at the end of the day, it is God who will decide who will win and who will lose; "the victory is ultimately in his hands" (George 2001). Frederica Mathewes-Green, a FFL activist, also published in this journal, highlighting the problem in lack of emotional support after an abortion;

> Psychologists say the mechanism works like this: A woman has an abortion, but in her heart grieves for her baby, and unconsciously feels obligated to have another to 'make up for' the one that was lost. This is called an 'atonement baby.' But when she 'slips up' and becomes pregnant again, she finds she's still in the same bad situation. Circumstances are no more welcoming to a new life than they were before. She has a second abortion, and then has *two* atonement pregnancies to make up (Mathewes-Green 2001).

4   ANALYSIS

Evident from this account, the women-centered strategy has been influencing public discourse as well as policy concerning reproductive rights. In general, the use of both the fetal centered and women-centered strategy by the pro-life movement redefines the abortion debate; the debate is no longer over who is the subject in need of protection, the fetus or the mother. Instead, pro-life activists argue that their movement is now able to protect both subjects in need of protection. This is achieved by the use of both strategies simultaneously, which are seen as complementary rather than contradictory. In practice, however, while the fetus-centered and women-centered discourses can be used together to argue for the protection of the life of the fetus and the health and well-being of the mother, at the level of policy making, the relationship between these strategies is more complex. Specifically, each of these strategies leads to a different type of legislation; while the fetus-centered strategy calls for the criminalization of abortion and overturning *Roe* as the only way to stop the killing of unborn babies, the women-centered strategy, with its emphasis on lack of information and problematic decision-making processes, often leads to legislative proposals that add limitations and restrict access to abortion. At the same time, however, the women-centered strategy seems to be effective in limiting access to abortion; Mississippi's strict laws, for example, led to a reduction in abortions, and increase in women going out of state (Joyce and Kaestner 2001). Thus, in opposition to the attempt of the fetus-centered strategy to ban abortions, the incrementalist approach has resulted in much greater success, as "voters are not comfortable with abortion, but they aren't comfortable banning it" (Khazan 2014).

This focus on protection of women carries implications regarding the three topics that are at the center of this project: human rights, reproductive rights, and right-wing politics. In general, in comparison with the fetus-centered strategy, the women-centered discourse expands the rights that are included under the concept of human rights, while at the same time creating requirements and regulations that limit agency and autonomy. As a result, this strategy leads to an increase in state intervention in decision-making processes—mainly in the private sphere—as well as to a discourse that emphasizes protection of individuals rather than personal autonomy. As such, the women-centered strategy introduces a shift from the libertarian approach of the fetus-centered strategy to a strategy of increased intervention of the state in private matters, thus moving to a more conservative approach in legislation.

Human Rights

The concept of human rights introduced in the women-centered discourse is very different from the one used in the fetus-centered strategy. In the case of the fetus-centered approach, the human rights concepts and discourse were used to argue for the expansion of the subjects who should enjoy human rights, fetuses, in this case. This expansion of human rights claims to include the fetus has generally not been accepted by human rights organizations, which have been moving toward declaring the right to abortion as a human right (Zampas and Gher 2008). Nevertheless, this type of argument fits within the pro-life movement with its mix of conservative and libertarian arguments; this strategy calls to define the fetus as a human being, thus eligible for all human rights. However, the strategy focuses on the most basic right—the right to life—and understands human rights as negative; we have the responsibility to protect people from harm of others—such as in the case of abortion—but not to provide them conditions that will help them practice their rights. Thus, the fetus-centered argument uses human rights discourse but promotes policy of limited intervention of the state, especially in matters considered personal. Practically, the only requirement of the pro-life movement from the state and the human right regime is to define the fetus as a human being. This definition will naturally result in the criminalization of the act of abortion, since it will be understood as the killing of a human being.

The women-centered strategy, however, introduces a different approach to the issue of human rights, in general, and the right to health, in particular. First, the focus on women's health and well-being better fits the international human rights discourse, which aims to ensure women's control over their reproductive decisions, partly as a way to decrease cases of maternal mortality and deaths from illegal abortions. By emphasizing health concerns, the pro-life movement is able to provide an answer to the human rights regime, with its focus on women's reproductive rights; as in its response to the pro-choice movement within the USA, the women-centered strategy allows the pro-life movement to frame its position as protecting women, arguing that it promotes the human rights of all participating subjects.

Second, the women-centered strategy may be seen as introducing a positive concept of the right to health, thus shifting away from the more limited understanding of rights that characterizes the fetus-centered strategy. While the negative right to health is based on the idea of noninterference with medical treatment decisions, a positive concept of this right will require the government to play an active role in securing this right, including providing funding for securing this right (Hill 2008). According to the women-centered legislation and discourse, it is wrong to assume that the right to health is solely the responsibility of the woman. Instead, it is the role of the government to make sure that women become aware of the risks or implications of abortion on their health and well-being. This approach can be used to explain the women-centered discourse, which focuses on providing such information. The positive concept of the right to health also characterizes the pro-life legislation, which requires all parties involved in the processes—including physicians, abortion centers, and the state—to ensure women's emotional and physical safety.

While the women-centered approach expands the types of rights included within the human rights discourse, and the protections that need to be granted for securing these rights, this approach avoids using the human rights discourse. The lack of such a discourse does not surprise pro-choice activists, who question this women-centered approach, and specifically the idea that this approach is beneficial to women since it promotes the protection of women's health and well-being. The framing of the women-centered strategy as protecting women's rights is based on the assumption that abortion has a negative impact on women. This assumption, however, is not widely accepted by feminists and human rights activists, who instead argue that the pro-life legislation is meant to limit women's reproductive rights and choices, rather than to protect them. In addition, while the women-centered strategy seems to frame the right to health as a positive right—the legislation is defined as an attempt to make sure that women can exercise their right—in practice this approach is based on the assumption that women should have no autonomy over their reproductive choices (Smith 2008). Thus, the critics argue, the framing of the women-centered approach as protecting the rights of women is misleading, since it uses ideas and concepts of human rights but without adopting the basic assumptions regarding agency and autonomy of human beings (Siegel 2008b).

Reproductive Rights

The pro-life movement defines the women-centered strategy, with its emphasis on women's emotional and physical well-being, as pro-women; women need to be protected from making (wrong) reproductive decisions. First, women are easily coerced and they lack the resources or abilities to make independent decision. Second, as is evident in the discourse of emotional trauma and regret after abortion, pregnant women are especially vulnerable to coercion. In addition, social pressure also pushes women to question their maternal tendencies and natural link to their children. The result of these social and institutional pressures, which include liberal ideas and a powerful abortion industry, together with natural tendencies of women, especially in relation to their motherhood, is the need to protect women who are required to make life-and-death decisions. This understanding of women follows traditional views on gender and gendered power relations, defining women as a subject in need of protection; as stated in the website Abortion is the UnChoice, women are fragile and easily misled, just as in the case of the girl who "believed the guy in the letter jacket who said he loved her…and the guy in the white coat who said it's just a blob of tissue." Thus, women are vulnerable subjects, whose social and emotional weakness requires society to protect them, from other people but also from themselves. This vulnerability is further reinforced during pregnancy, a period that is known to be emotional as well as socially challenging. As a result of this characterization of women, the pro-life movement offers two different—and maybe even contradictory—types of legislation.

The first type of legislation is the one that frames the additional requirements for information and data—even if questionable by the scientific community—as an opportunity to allow women to make a meaningful choice. Among the requirements that fit this category are laws addressing counseling, ultrasound, and wait-time period, all defined by their supporters as ways to free women from social and institutional gendered relations, which undermine their ability for informed consent. In the attempt to help women make decisions that are right for them, the state not only requires physicians and clinics to provide information and chances to change their mind but also determines what is the information that women need to know and see in order to make this decision. Thus, these laws reinforce the role of the state as a protector of women from their own inadequate decision-making ability.

The argument that these measures are meant to empower women is criticized by feminist and pro-choice activists as further reinforcing oppression and marginalization; it denies women's agency and autonomy, replacing one form of coercion with another set of regulations meant to limit women's ability to make their own reproductive decisions (Manian 2009; Siegel 2008a). Nevertheless, and despite making the process of abortion more burdensome for women, so far these legislations did not lower the number of abortions. Instead, they cause delays, and in particular lower rate of first-trimester abortions (Henshaw et al. 2009; Bitler and Zavodny 2001). As such, in practice, this type of legislation corresponds with the pro-life discourse, emphasizing the need to require the informed consent process to address the risk of women being coerced by others, as well as the emotional and physical dangers of abortion, this without actually preventing women from having an abortion, if they so desired.

The second type of legislation, however, does not correspond with the discourse of informed consent. Instead, it emphasizes the dangers of abortion and the inability of women to make life–and-death decisions, thus calling for legislation that bans abortion, or at least certain types of abortions. The legislation that most closely reflects suspicion of women's ability for medical decision-making is spousal notification laws. While these laws were ruled unconstitutional in *Casey*, they nevertheless have been recently introduced in a handful of states. The assumption at the basis of these proposals is that reproductive decisions should be made within the family unit, and not by the pregnant woman. A similar approach is reflected in parental notification laws; these laws are predicated on the assumption, which is stated in the legislative findings of many state and federal parental notification laws, that minors are not able to fully comprehend the implications of this decision. In this particular case, the state has identified an outside party (the parents or legal guardians) to take part in the decision-making process. Parents are charged with determining what is best for their daughter with regard to her physical and emotional well-being. In granting parents this authority, essentially a veto power over the abortion decision, state legislatures promote their aim of preserving the family unit and "protecting minors from their own immaturity" (Alabama Code § 26-21-1, 1987).

In this type of legislation, the protection of women is achieved by taking away—or at least limiting—their ability to make their own reproductive decisions. The idea at the basis of this approach is that women are neither able to make such decisions—because of their maternal nature, among other reasons—nor should they make these decisions. This type of conceptualization of the "protection" of women—which protects them from their own inability to make decisions that promote their interests—has shaped many policies throughout history, including, for example, legislation regarding the protection of women in the workplace (Crenshaw 1995). One current practice that has been banned by states, and is no longer available for women to choose from, is partial-birth abortion, which became a prominent issue in the mid- to late 1990s. Partial-birth abortion laws, in general, prohibit a particular type of abortion procedure, intact dilation and extraction (D&X). This procedure is different from dilation and evacuation (D&E), a procedure also used in late-term abortions; while D&E entails the dismemberment of the fetus prior to extraction, thus preventing any damage to a woman's cervix, D&X, a procedure developed in the mid-1990s, allows for the extraction of the fetus intact, following the dilation of the cervix and puncturing of the fetus' skull (Rovner 2006).[20]

---

[20] Partial-birth abortion is not a medical term; rather, abortion opponents who characterize the procedure as infanticide, or the killing of a baby after its extraction from the womb developed it. The medical procedure, dilation and extraction, has been found to be the most effective and safe procedure for late-term abortion. This procedure is quite rare, and is used primarily in instances when women intended to keep the fetus but later found there are significant health risks for the fetus or mother if carried to term (Rovner 2006; Suter 2011). Although partial-birth abortion is not the medically correct terminology, and the phrase is ideological in nature, it is used here because it is the most common and prominently featured in the public discourse.

This type of procedure produced an intense degree of opposition and controversy, particularly as it was characterized as infanticide or the killing of a baby. Beginning in the mid- to late 1990s, state legislatures began to pass a flurry of legislation to prohibit the procedure. These measures, however, either have not been passed into law or have been overturned by the courts, with two cases reaching the Supreme Court. In 2000, the court overturned Nebraska's ban on partial-birth abortion, determining there were insufficient protections for women's health and that the law placed an undue burden on women's right to obtain an abortion. Further, given the vague definition of partial-birth abortion (which is not a medical term), the court determined this placed an undue burden on women's access to abortion (530 U.S. 914, 2000). In light of the court's ruling, states began to pass partial-birth abortion bans that clarify the procedure which is being banned, as well as—for the most part—including exceptions that are constitutionally required. To date, partial-birth abortion bans have been passed in 32 states, although 13 of these laws are not in effect or have been blocked by the courts. Of the 13 state laws that have been blocked or are not enforced, it is most often the vague definition of the procedure that is banned that prompts the court to block enforcement or overturn it in its entirety (Danne 2000). Despite the infrequent use of this particular procedure, partial-birth abortion bans have remained prominent among the general public and legislators.

At the federal level, members of Congress began introducing measures to ban partial-birth abortion in 1995. While this measure passed through both chambers of Congress in 1995 and again in 1997, President Clinton vetoed it. After introducing a ban on partial-birth abortion 22 times since 1995, the act was finally signed into law by President George W. Bush in 2003. In 2007, the federal partial-birth abortion ban came before the Supreme Court. In *Gonzales v. Carhart*, the court upheld this ban. The language of the bill specifically referenced intact dilation and extraction, thus rendering the federal law distinct from the Nebraska ban that was too vague and could be presumed to prohibit multiple procedures. The opinion, authored by Justice Kennedy, not only upheld the federal ban but did so through employing the pro-life, women-centered rhetoric used by the pro-life movement during this time period. Relying on affidavits and Amici Curiae brief from Operation Outcry (an organization that gathers testimony from women who had negative experiences following an abortion), the opinion cites the regret that some women encounter after going through an abortion as an important state interest. This regret can lead to "severe depression and loss of self-esteem," thus justifying state protection that takes, in this case, the form of prohibiting the use of intact D&E (550 U.S. 124, 2007). Justice Kennedy concluded women's profound regret, grief, and depression following this procedure is no surprise "when she learns, only after the event, what she once did not know: that she allowed a doctor to pierce the skull and vacuum the fast-developing brain of her unborn child, a child assuming the human form" (550 U.S. 124, 2007). Since "respect for human life finds an ultimate expression in the bond of love the mother has for her child" (Manian 2009: 255), the state has a legitimate role to protect women from future regret by limiting their access to the practice.

Justice Kennedy's emphasis of the negative implications of abortion, in general, and regret of women, in particular, framed the ban of partial-birth abortion as addressing concerns for women's health and well-being. These issues, however, were not included in the legislative findings within the law itself and did not serve as justification for the prohibition. Relying solely on the Amici Curiae briefs provided by antiabortion organizations, Kennedy accepted the women-centered, pro-life reasoning, justifying a ban on a particular type of abortion because of the professed need to protect women from the negative consequences of uninformed decision-making. Partial-birth bans are thus meant to shift the decision-making processes from the woman to the state, this in order to protect women from the negative impacts that the pro-life movement identifies with abortion. The use of women-centered arguments for banning certain types of abortion introduces a tension between the pro-life discourse and legislation; while the legislation supports certain bans—and might in the future call for banning abortion altogether because of the damage it does to women—the discourse focuses mainly in providing information and facts, as a way to deter women from choosing abortion.

The two types of legislation that follow from the women-centered strategy thus introduce significant implications to the issue of reproductive rights. The first type of legislation, which adds more and more requirements for women who are interested in having an abortion, makes the process long and difficult, but not necessarily impossible. At the same time, however, these requirements reinforce traditional ideas about women as emotional, impulsive, and in need of protection. This protection is provided either by the state or by the family unit, both assumed to be able to help women make a decision by freeing her from social pressures that are liberal in nature, as well as from men who will profit from her abortion. Women's reproductive choices, while they might still remain in the hands of women, are the responsibility of the state and family. As such, they need to be examined, discussed, and supervised by others besides the woman herself. The second type of legislation shifts the decision-making process away from the woman, thus making the process of reproductive rights the responsibility of the state, rather than the woman. Women, according to this account, have too many natural and social limitations and weaknesses—especially regarding motherhood and children—and are thus incapable of making their own reproductive decisions. At the end of the day, the women-centered strategy, with its focus on women's health and well-being, sees these goals as achieved when reproductive decisions are supervised and limited.

Right-Wing Politics

The success of this women-centered approach occurred as the movement and the GOP became firmly intertwined. As the pro-life movement began to become more politically powerful in the late 1970s and early 1980s, the adoption of a pro-life stance by members of the GOP brought greater numbers of Catholics to the Republican Party. Further, as the parties underwent a realignment, abortion served as one of the defining social issues in the culture war that has come to dominate the political sphere. Having established a very overt pro-life stance by the 1990s, the GOP solidified its connection with social conservatives, which will come to represent a significant part of the Republican Party base (Dowland 2009).

The presence and strength of social conservatives, including the pro-life movement, within the GOP establishment, come into conflict with the libertarian faction of the GOP. Unlike the fetus-centered strategy of the 1970s and 1980s, the women-centered approach has resulted in significant amount of laws and regulations over abortion, all calling for increased intervention of the state in personal matters and decision-making processes. The promotion of an interventionist strategy, particularly at the state level, has required increased government expenditures, including funding for crisis pregnancy centers, ultrasound equipment, and alternatives to abortion programs. In addition, this approach also resulted in greater government regulatory processes and oversight, as in the requirement for parental notification, admitting privileges, abortion provider requirements, and clinic regulations. This direction in policy making clearly establishes a prominent role for government to regulate, oversee, and participate in this medical treatment, to a much greater extent than has ever been established.

As such, this approach comes into conflict with the basic beliefs and values of libertarians, who aim to limit almost all forms of government oversight and intervention in economic or social life, in general, and private decisions, in particular. This tension is further developed by the adoption of a positive concept of the right to health; in addition to reflecting a clear expansion of the rights that need to be protected by the state, the adoption of a positive concept of right to health may be (mis)understood as translating into a support for some kind of mandated health insurance plan. The promotion—and success—of the interventionist policies by members of the GOP represents the current tension, as well as future potential conflict, within the GOP base. With regard to the issue of abortion, there are no loud voices within the GOP that call for a less interventionist approach but, instead an attempt to do what is possible to prevent and limit abortions. However, this type of debate—between an interventionist state that promotes conservative values and limited state that follows libertarian principles—does take place regarding other social issues such as gay marriage and the legalization of drugs (Leonhardt and Parlapiano 2015). As such, the tension within the GOP is about the more general question of the role and purpose of government.

The analysis of the women-centered approach revealed the significant shift in the pro-life movement's strategy from the fetus-centered approach. This change is not only at the level of discourse or specific legislation but it is mainly a shift to a conservative, interventionist approach, which aims to expand the dialogue and its legitimacy by addressing the American public, as well as pro-choice supporters and the human right regime. This shift, however, also has implications regarding right-wing politics, more generally; if this current regulatory approach toward abortion continues, it sets the stage for a substantial divide within the party base that may affect the trajectory of the party, and create tension in other similar, social wedge issues. The promotion of traditional sexual norms and gender roles by one segment of the Republican Party leaves the party at odds with changing attitudes toward marriage and family life. The way the GOP has been addressing—or solving—this tension, will be examined in the next two chapters, which trace the discourse and legislation of the pro-life movement regarding third-party actors, in general, and its strategy following the Hobby Lobby ruling, in particular.

REFERENCES

Abortion opponents set strategy for coming battle. The New York Times. 1989 July 5.

Abortion Recovery International. Abortion affecting you? http://www.abortion-recovery.org/afterabortion/abortionaffectingyou/tabid/218/Default.aspx. Accessed 8 July 2015.

Adams G. Abortion: evidence of an issue evolution. Am J Polit Sci. 1997;41(3): 718–37.

After Abortion. Help and healing. http://afterabortion.org/help-healing/ Accessed 4 Apr 2015.

Angelo EJ. Portraits of Grief in the Aftermath of Abortion. http://www.hopeafterabortion.com. 2011

Bachiochi E. Coming of age in a culture of choice. In: Bachiochi E, editor. The cost of choice: women evaluate the impact of abortion. San Francisco: Encounter Books; 2004. p. 22–32.

Bazelon E. Charmaine Yoest's cheerful war on abortion. The New York Times. 2012 Nov 2.

Beckwith FJ. Choice words: a critique of the new pro-life rhetoric. Touchstone. 2004.

Beckwith FJ. Taking abortion seriously: a philosophical critique of the new anti-abortion rhetorical shift. Ethics Med. 2001;17(3):155–66.

Bitler M, Zavodny M. The effect of abortion restrictions on the timing of abortions. J Health Econ. 2001;20:1011–32.

Cannold L. Understanding and responding to anti-choice women-centered strategies. Reprod Health Matters. 2002;10(19):171–9.

Collaborative Group on Hormonal Factors in Breast Cancer. Breast cancer and abortion: collaborative reanalysis of data from 53 epidemiological studies, including 83,000 women with breast cancer from 16 countries. Lancet. 2004;363(9414):1007–16.

Comstock Cunningham P. The Supreme Court and the creation of the two-dimensional woman. In: Bachiochi E, editor. The cost of choice: women evaluate the impact of abortion. San Francisco: Encounter Books; 2004. p. 103–21.

Crenshaw C. The 'Protection' of 'Woman': a history of legal attitudes toward women's workplace freedom. Q J Speech. 1995;81(1):63–82.

Danne WH. Validity, construction, and application of statutes requiring parental notification of or consent to minor's abortion. Am Law Rep. 2000;77(5).

de Jong DC. The feminist sell-out. In: Derr MK, MacNair R, Naranjo-Huebl L, editors. Pro-life feminism: yesterday and today. Woodmere: Sulzburger & Graham; 1995.

Delli Carpini M, Fuchs E. Year of the woman? Candidates, voters, and 1992 elections. Polit Sci Q. 1993;108(1):29–36.

Derr MK. Abortion and women's sexual liberation. In: Derr MK, MacNair R, Naranjo-Huebl L, editors. Pro-life feminism: yesterday and today. Woodmere: Sulzburger & Graham; 1995.

Devins N. How planned Parenthood v. Casey (pretty much) settled the abortion wars. Yale Law J. 2009;118(7):1318–54.

Dowland S. 'Family values' and the formation of a christian right agenda. Church Hist. 2009;78(3):606–31.

Elliot Institute. Forced abortion in America: a special report 2010. http://www. theunchoice.com/pdf/FactSheets/ForcedAbortions.pdf. Accessed 27 Apr 2015.

"Family is Aim of Clergy Group." The New York Times. 18 Sept 1988.

Foster SM. The feminist case against abortion. In: Bachiochi E, editor. The cost of choice: women evaluate the impact of abortion. San Francisco: Encounter Books; 2004. p. 33–8.

Fox-Genovese E. Wrong turn: how the campaign to liberate women has betrayed the culture of life. Life Learn. 2002;XII:11–22.

Fox-Genovese E. Abortion: a war on women. In: Bachiochi E, editor. The cost of choice: women evaluate the impact of abortion. San Francisco: Encounter Books; 2004. p. 50–60.

Friedman AD. Bad medicine: abortion and the battle over who speaks for women's health. William Mary Women L. 2013;20:45–72.

George RP. Our national sin. Touchstone. 2001.

Greenhouse L. How the Supreme court talks about abortion: the implications of a shifting discourse. Suffolk Univ Law Rev. 2008;42:41–59.

Helewa M, Levesque P, Provencher D, Lea RH, Rosolowich V, Shapiro HM. Breast cancer, pregnancy, and breastfeeding. J Obstet Gynecol Canada. 2002;24(2):164–80.

Henshaw SK, Dennis A, Finer LB, Blanchard K. The impact of state mandatory counseling and waiting period laws on abortion: A literature review. New York, NY: The Guttmacher Institute; 2009 Apr.

Hill JB. Reproductive rights as health care rights. Columbia J Gend Law. 2008;18(2):1–49.

Hope after abortion. After the abortion. http://hopeafterabortion.com/?p=109. Accessed 23 Mar 2015.

Ivey RE. Destabilizing discourses: blocking and exploiting a new discourse at work in Gonzales v. Carhart. Virginia Law Rev. 2008:1451–1508.

Jasen P. Breast cancer and the politics of abortion in the United State. Med Hist. 2005;49(4):423–44.

Joyce T, Kaestner R. The impact of mandatory waiting periods and parental consent laws on the timing of abortion and state of occurrence among adolescents in Mississippi and South Carolina. J Policy Anal Manage. 2001;20(2): 263–82.

Keech L. Better living (for men) through surgery (for women). In: Derr MK, MacNair R, Naranjo-Huebl L, editors. . Woodmere: Sulzburger & Graham; 1995a.

Keech L. The sensitive abortionists. In: Derr MK, MacNair R, Naranjo-Huebl L, editors. Pro-life feminism: yesterday and today. Woodmere: Sulzburger & Graham; 1995b.

Khazan O. Can an abortion be undone? The Atlantic. 2015 Mar 27.

Khazan O. Pro-lifers' existential crisis. The Atlantic. 2014 Nov 7.

Kulze E. An Iowa clinic is now providing 'abortion reversals.' Vocativ. 2014 Dec 5.

Lee SJ, Henry JPR, Eleanor AD, John CP, Mark AR. Fetal pain: a systematic multidisciplinary review of the evidence. JAMA. 2005;294(8):947–54.

Leonhardt D, Parlapiano A. Why gun control and abortion are different from gay marriage. The New York Times. 2015 Jun 30.

"Life After Roe." National Review Online. 2006 Apr 26.

MacNair R. Pro-life feminism: yesterday and today. In: Derr MK, MacNair R, Naranjo-Huebl L, editors. Would legalizing abortion set loose the Back-Alley Butchers? No-legalizing abortion did that. Woodmere: Sulzburger & Graham; 1995.

Manian M. The irrational woman: informed consent and abortion decision-making. Duke J Gender Law Policy. 2009;16:223–92.

Marcotte A. The newest crisis pregnancy center offer: 'abortion reversals.' Slate. 2014 Dec 8. http://www.slate.com/blogs/xx_factor/2014/12/08/_abortion_reversals_the_latest_anti_abortion_offer_from_crisis_pregnancy.html. Accessed 8 July 2015.

Mathewes-Green F. What women need. Touchstone. 2001.

Mattes B. The impact on men: Losing a child by abortion. Life Issues Institute. 2009 April 1. http://www.lifeissues.org/2009/04/impact-men-losing-child-abortion/. Accessed 5 July 2015.

Man and Abortion. Coping with a pregnancy decision. http://www.menandabortion.com/formen.html. Accessed 10 May 2015.

National Cancer Institute (NCI). Abortion, miscarriage, and breast cancer. National Institute of Health. 2010 Jan 12.

Newport F, Moore D, Saad L. Long-term Gallup poll trends: A portrait of American public opinion through the century. 20 Dec 1999. http://www.gallup.com/poll/3400/longterm-gallup-poll-trends-portrait-american-public-opinion.aspx.

Pitts J. Post-abortion depression and research act. Congressional Record—Extension of Remarks. 2001 Aug 3.

Ramah International. Abortion information. http://ramahinternational.org/abortion-information/. Accessed 24 Mar 2015.

Reardon DC. A defense of the neglected rhetorical strategy (NRS). Ethics Med. 2002;18(2):23–32.

Reardon DC. Making abortion rare: a healing strategy for a divided nation. Springfield: Acorn Books; 1996.

Reardon DC. Why politicians should be both pro-woman and pro-life. The Post Abortion Review, Fall 1994. http://afterabortion.org/1994/why-politicians-should-be-both-pro-woman-and-pro-life/. Accessed 25 Jan 2015.

Report of the South Dakota task force to study abortion. 2005 Dec.

Reynolds P. A different voice in the abortion debate 'I don't fit the mold at all.' The Boston Globe. 1989 Aug 11.

Rose M. Pro-life, pro-woman? Frame extension in the American antiabortion movement. J Women Polit Policy. 2011;32(1):1–27.

Rose M. Safe, legal, and available? Abortion politics in the United States. Washington, DC: CQ Press; 2007.

Rovner J. 'Partial-birth abortion:' separating fact from spin. NPR.org, 21 Feb 2006. http://www.npr.org/21 Feb 2006/02/21/5168163/partial-birth-abortion-separating-fact-from-spin.

Rubin ER. The abortion controversy: a documentary history. Westport: Greenwood Press; 1994.

Schreiber R. Righting feminism: conservative women and American politics, with a new epilogue. Oxford: Oxford University Press; 2012.

Schreiber R. Injecting a woman's voice: conservative women's organizations, gender consciousness, and the expression of women's policy preferences. Sex Roles. 2002;47(7–8):331–42.

Semuels A. The safer, more affordable abortion only available in two states. The Atlantic. 2014 Oct 10.

Shields JA. Review: the politics of motherhood revisited. ASA. 2012;41(1):43–8.

Shields JA. The democratic virtues of the christian right. Princeton: Princeton University Press; 2009.

Shumway J. Arizona senate committee approves abortion restrictions. AZ Central. 2015 Feb 11.

Siegel R. Dignity and sexuality: claims on dignity in transnational debates over abortion and same-sex marriage. Int J Const Law. 2012;10:335–79.

Siegel R. Dignity and the politics of protection: abortion restrictions under Casey/Carhart. Yale Law J. 2008a;117:1694–800.

Siegel R. The new politics of abortion: an equality analysis of woman-protective abortion restrictions. U Ill Law Rev, Baum Lecture. 2007:991–1054.

Siegel R. The right's reasons: constitutional conflict and the spread of women-protective antiabortion argument. Duke Law J. 2008b:1641-92.

Smith PJ. Responsibility for life: how abortion serves women's interests in motherhood. J Law Policy. 2008;17(97):97–160.

Suk J. The trajectory of trauma: bodies and minds of abortion discourse. C Law Rev. 2010;110(5):1193–252.

Suter S. Bad mothers or struggling mothers? Rutgers Law J. 2011;42:695–704.

Swope PF. Abortion: a failure to communicate. First Things. 1998 April.

The Guttmacher Institute. An overview of state abortion laws. State Policies in Brief. 2015b. Accessed 1 Aug 2015.

Toner R. Changing senate looks better to abortion foes. The New York Times. 2004 Dec 2.

Toner R. Personalities eclipse legalism in abortion debate. The New York Times. 1989 July 11.

Trumpy AJ. Woman vs. fetus: frame transformation and intramovement dynamics in the pro-life movement. Sociol Spectr. 2014;34(2):163–84.

Tumulty K. Twenty years on, 'year of the woman fades'. The Washington Post. 2012 Mar 24.

Vandewalker I. Abortion and informed consent: how biased counseling laws mandate violations of medical ethics. Mich J Gender Law. 2012;19:1–70.

Willke JC. Life issues institute is celebrating ten years with a new home. Life Issues Connector. 2001 Feb. http://lifeissuesorg/connector/01feb.html. Accessed 20 May 2015.

Willke J, Willke B. Why can't we love them both?: Questions and answers about abortion. Snowflake: Hayes; 1997.

Zampas C, Gher JM. Abortion as a human right: international and regional standards. Hum Right Law Rev. 2008;8(2):249–94.

Ziegler M. Women's rights on the right: the history and stakes of modern pro-life feminism. Berkley J Gender Law Justice. 2013;28:232–68.

CHAPTER 4

Defending the People: Third-Party Interests in the Debate over Reproductive Rights

1 Introduction

The debate over access to abortion and contraceptives has always included the question of the rights of third-party actors, who are considered by some to have interests in the debate over abortion. Generally, the discussion focused mainly on healthcare providers and taxpayers; the actions of these two groups—that either provide abortion services or pay for them through their taxes—have been understood by pro-life supporters as playing a role in the abortion process. Therefore, the pro-life movement argues, there is a need to protect third-party actors from participating in acts they do not support, or are merely not interested in paying for. While the exemptions for both abortion service providers and taxpayers have been introduced in the 1970s, the two types of exemptions are different in nature, and have been developed separately. In the attempt to protect taxpayer interests, the Hyde Amendment was introduced as one of the first funding restrictions imposed after the decision in *Roe v. Wade*. This amendment restricted Medicaid funding of all abortions except cases involving the life of the mother. The protection of the rights of healthcare providers who oppose abortion was achieved primarily through the Church Amendment, adopted in 1973 immediately following the decision in *Roe v. Wade*. This amendment ensured that the federal government could not force an individual or health facility to participate in abortion or other abortion-related services if it is a violation of their religious faith.

© The Editor(s) (if applicable) and The Author(s) 2016   141
A. Von Hagel, D. Mansbach, *Reproductive Rights in the Age of Human Rights*, DOI 10.1057/978-1-137-53952-6_4

Shortly after, the states began adopting similar types of protection for medical professionals and facilities; by 1978, more than 40 states had conscience clause legislation in place, and to date, 46 states have such laws (Duvall 2006; Guttmacher Institute 2015b).

The protection of third-party actors and their rights has not only been one of the first examples of pro-life legislation but also one of the most effective types of legislation; the percentage of third-party legislation enacted into law is higher than that of fetus-centered and women-centered legislation. At the same time, the issue of third-party actors has not received much attention in the pro-life discourse, despite significant scholarly recognition of the issue (Boonstra 2007, 2013; Duvall 2006; Feder 2005; Randall 1994; Salganicoff et al. 2004; Sonfield 2005). However, this gap—between successful legislation and lack of discourse concerning the rights of third-party actors—has been changing; the debate during and following the June 2014 Supreme Court ruling in *Burwell v. Hobby Lobby*, Inc. has been focused almost entirely on the rights of third-party actors'—in this specific case, employers—religious liberty. These rights are framed by the pro-life movement and, more broadly, by organizations fighting for religious liberty, as in opposition to the requirement to provide contraceptives to employees.[1] This framing by the pro-life movement represents a shift in its discourse; for the first time since the controversial ruling in *Roe v. Wade*, the pro-life discourse focuses primarily neither on women's right to control their bodies and reproduction nor on the fetuses' right to life. Instead, the pro-life approach protects the rights of individuals for religious liberty.

This chapter focuses on the legislative protections of the rights of third-party actors beginning in 1973 through 2015, a year following the *Hobby Lobby* ruling. It analyzes the different types of third-party legislation, their success rates at the federal and state levels, as well as their development and change throughout the years. The first section analyzes the legislation since *Roe*, focusing on the two most common types of legislative protections: conscience clauses, which were developed to primarily protect healthcare providers, and limitations on public funding of abortion, which emphasize the protection of taxpayers. The second section introduces the ACA and

---

[1] The arguments concerning third-party actors, in general, and their focus on religious freedom, in particular, are often used not only by the pro-life movement but also by other right-wing groups concerned with religious liberty, from either a conservative or a libertarian perspective. One example is the involvement of the Becket Fund for Religious Liberty in the *Hobby Lobby* case, as well as many of the cases challenging the ACA and the employer mandate.

the religious opposition to the law, which stems primarily from the HHS mandate requiring most employers to provide coverage of all FDA-approved contraceptive devices. The analysis focuses on the legal challenges to this requirement by the for-profit corporations Hobby Lobby and Conestoga Wood Specialties, as well as the challenges to the accommodation process from nonprofit religious organizations exempt from this requirement. The third section analyzes the primary legislative developments following the passage of the ACA as well as the *Hobby Lobby* case, revealing that despite changes in content, pro-life legislation concerning third-party actors remains focused on taxpayers, on the one hand, and religious liberty of individuals, on the other. At the same time, the data from 2010 to 2015 reveals that despite a significant increase in the use of arguments regarding religious freedom by the pro-life movement—a claim that the requirements imposed on individuals opposed to abortion and other related services represents a growing threat to religious freedom—the most successful form of state intervention nevertheless is one that focuses on restricting public funds for use in abortion and abortion-related services.

2   PROTECTING THE RIGHTS OF THIRD-PARTY ACTORS AFTER *ROE*

The discourse on abortion—by both pro-choice and pro-life activists—has primarily focused on the rights of the fetus and the rights of women, with very limited attention to rights or interests of third-party actors. For example, between 1973 and 2015, 473 pieces in *The New York Times* and *The Washington Post* included some references to conscience clauses, to the right to refuse, or to the funding of abortion.[2] The overwhelming majority of these pieces included only brief descriptions of these issues, and almost none of them included detailed statements or references made by pro-life supporters other than legislators. Also, the discourse found in the websites does not focus on the rights of third-party actors in the abortion debate. Even among the 21 websites surveyed that address other issues such as traditional family values and religious liberty, there is very little discussion of the rights of others in the abortion debate. While this is not surprising—the websites often address pregnant women, their partners and families, all with the intended aim to prevent abortion—it nevertheless represents

---

[2] These items were found using the search term "abortion" together with "right to refuse," "conscious clause," "Medicaid," "Affordable Care Act," "ACA," or "Obamacare."

the limited public discussion on the issue of third-party actors involvement (and need for protection) up until the last few years. In light of these data, the analysis of third-party actors offered in this chapter focuses on public policy rather than discourse.[3]

However, in opposition to the discourse, the interests of third-party actors have been the primary locus of pro-life government activity since *Roe*, and the most common form of enacted legislation at the federal and state levels. The two different types of legislation include conscience clauses for healthcare providers, and funding restrictions on abortion services. Conscience clauses were developed primarily to protect the rights of individual healthcare professionals such as doctors, nurses, pharmacists, and researchers as well as healthcare facilities or institutions to refuse to participate in morally or religiously objectionable practices. These protections emphasize the right of individuals to maintain their own religious and moral beliefs, and the responsibility of the government to respect these decisions, not forcing individuals to act in ways that violate their deeply held religious beliefs. Over the years, these protections have been extended to other actors. The other type of legislation protecting third-party actors focuses on the interests of taxpayers, which are most commonly represented in policies that restrict the use of public funds for abortion or abortion-related services. These policies have also become much more extensive over time, including a greater number of funding restrictions at both the federal and state levels. Both conscience clauses and funding restrictions have proven to be the most effective method to limit or impede access to abortion, this despite the emphasis by most of the pro-life movements' activists and organizations on the rights of the fetus or women in the abortion debate.

Conscience Clauses

Immediately following the ruling in *Roe*, concern over the rights of healthcare professionals opposed to abortion, and in particular Catholic practitioners, became part of the larger debate and controversy over the Supreme Court's ruling. Shortly after, this tension was exacerbated as a religious hospital was required to perform a sterilization, denying the right of the hospital and hospital personnel to refuse to participate in a pro-

---

[3] The analysis of the discourse of religious liberty, which became central after the passage of the ACA and the *Hobby Lobby* ruling and has been shaping the current pro-life strategy, is the focus of Chap. 5.

cedure objectionable to Catholic beliefs (Section 401(b) of the Health Programs Exchange Act 1975). While the order to provide this service was based upon the absence of any other medical facilities in the area that provided maternity services, this requirement was seen as unconscionable for Catholics and non-Catholics alike. Thus, soon after, Congress moved to restrict the government from requiring certain healthcare professionals and individuals to perform religiously objectionable acts and procedures. The Church Amendment, enacted shortly after the decision in *Roe v. Wade*, was the first conscience clause passed by the Congress (Health Programs Extension Act, Pub. L. No. 93-45, 1973). The court's ruling prompted significant controversy, yet members of Congress on both sides of the aisle came together to add this amendment to the Health Programs Extension Act. This protection of the right to refuse was seen by many as purely a matter of protecting civil rights and religious freedom, rather than a referendum or restriction on abortion; other pro-life supporters saw this as a protection that would limit access to abortion (Dubow 2015).

This amendment to the Health Programs Extension Act prohibits the courts and government agencies from requiring individuals or facilities that receive federal funding to perform abortions or sterilizations, or to be available for such procedures, if they have moral or religious objections to these procedures (Health Programs Extension Act, Pub. L. No. 93-45, 1973). This amendment has been reauthorized every year, and its protections have been extended to individuals or entities that receive federal financial assistance under the Public Health Service Act, the Community Mental Health Centers Act, or the Developmental Disabilities Services and Facilities Construction Act (Feder 2005). While the Church Amendment was controversial, the debate over it was not overtly partisan in nature as Democrats and Republicans were not sharply divided on the issue, reflecting the lack of polarization between the parties and the nonpartisan nature of abortion during this time.

While conscience clauses offer protection for medical professionals' personal beliefs and conduct, the protection of religious freedom can come into direct conflict with their responsibilities as medical providers. For health professionals, values such as beneficence and nonmaleficence require providers to act in the best interest of the patient as well as to do no harm (Sonfield 2005). Thus, conscience clauses conflict with the rights of patients, as they allow providers to deny services that are necessary for the health and well-being of patients. Further, depending upon the geographical location in which an individual resides, these religious exemptions may also restrict the ability of patients to obtain certain medical treatments or procedures altogether. Thus, the debate over conscience clauses—in the case of abortion, but also for a broader array of treatments—is based on the tension between the right of the provider to enjoy religious liberty and the right of patients to enjoy access to required health services.

In the case of abortion and abortion-related services, conscience clauses have been justified as a type of religious exemption that protects healthcare providers' religious freedom without significantly limiting women's access to reproductive services. Originally, conscience clauses were designed to protect individuals and facilities from governmental requirements to perform abortion in cases of a religious objection. Later, this protection expanded in scope to protect individuals from being required by their employers to participate in abortion or abortion-related services (Feder 2005). Finally, by the 1990s, many states have expanded conscience clauses to include also protections for pharmacists who object to filling prescriptions for birth control or emergency contraception (EC) (Duvall 2006). Further, some insurance companies and HMOs have received such protections, allowing certain facilities to deny coverage of abortion or abortion-related services based upon moral objections on the part of the program or company. Further, conscience clause protections have been extended to different types of practices, including assisted suicide, the withdrawing of feeding tubes, blood transfusions, organ donation, and stem cell research (Duvall 2006; NeJaime and Siegel 2015; Wardle 2010). Despite the existence of these religious exemptions, and their expansion in the last two decades, until recently the issue of religious freedom received little attention in the public discourse and by the pro-life movement.

In the decades following the Church Amendment, the continued controversy over the morality of abortion led to the increased adoption of conscience clause legislation, at both the federal and state levels. By 1978, almost all of the states had passed some form of conscience clause legislation to protect health professionals' right to refuse to participate in abortion or other abortion-related services. A total of 45 states ensured the right to refuse for individual healthcare professionals, with 43 states extending this protection to healthcare entities. Of the states that extend the right to refuse to healthcare entities, in 13 states, this protection is granted only to private healthcare institutions, while one state limits this protection even further to only religious healthcare entities. At the same time, Congress has continued to adopt additional measures protecting individuals or facilities from having to participate in abortion procedures.

A 1988 amendment to Title IX of the 1972 Education Amendments—which prohibits sex discrimination in education programs receiving federal funds—clarified that the act cannot be used to construe either a prohibition or requirement that any individual or institution pay for or participate in abortion (20 U.S.C. § 1681). Further, in a 1996 appropriations act, Congress prohibited discrimination against healthcare facilities that refuse to undergo abortion training, to provide trainings, or to perform abortions (42 U.S.C. §238n(a)(1)).

From the 1970s through the 1990s, conscience clause legislation at the federal level was centered primarily on the protection of healthcare professionals or entities from government coercion to perform abortion as well as from discrimination for such refusal. The 1996 Balanced Budget Act, however, increased the scope of conscience clause legislation by prohibiting any entity that receives federal funding—including state and local governments—from requiring healthcare professionals to provide information on abortion and related services. This requirement also includes companies that pay for abortion and related services within Medicaid and Medicare programing. In addition, the act also allowed Medicaid and Medicare health plans to refuse to pay for abortion counseling or referral (42 U.S.C. § 1396d(a)(4)(C)). This provision is much broader than previous forms of conscience clause legislation; while previously these policies protected providers from being compelled to participate in the procedure, this measure expands the freedom of conscience of providers allowing them also to refuse to refer women to abortion services or to counsel them on this potential form of treatment. Following this expansion, the Medicaid program was adjusted to allow managed care providers to refuse to pay for abortion counseling and referrals if it is in violation of their religious beliefs (Feder 2005).

In 2005, the Weldon Amendment—added to the Consolidated Appropriations Act—further expanded the entities that are protected under this right of refusal. This amendment does not allow federal funds to be provided to any agency or program, local or state government that discriminates against a healthcare entity that refuses to refer, pay, or provide counseling for abortions (P.L. 108-447, Division F, § 508(d)). The Weldon Amendment, together with the 1996 Balanced Budget Act, represents a shift from previous conscience clause legislation; while previous legislation was designed to protect individual health professionals and healthcare facilities' right to refuse, the amendment opens the door for healthcare payers such as insurance companies and Medicare/Medicaid programs to refuse to cover abortion referrals as well as the procedure itself (Feder 2005). The provision of such protections for providers in Medicare/Medicaid programs as well as HMOs may require out-of-pocket spending for women desiring this treatment, and for low-income or poor women, delaying the procedure, which impacts both women's health and safety as well as the costs. These measures also limit the availability of this service; 10 of the largest 25 healthcare networks in the USA are Catholic, largely a result of hospital mergers that have increased since the healthcare reform. Further, one in six hospital patients receive care in Catholic facilities, facilities that do not provide elective abortions, sterilization, or provide certain forms of birth control (Uttley et al. 2013).

Pharmacists, another group of healthcare professionals involved in abortion-related services, have been the focus of conscience clause legislation, particularly in the last decade. This issue of pharmacist's right to refuse gained greater awareness following a number of incidents involving pharmacists not filling a prescription or refusing to refer women to another pharmacist or local pharmacy upon refusal to provide the prescription in question (Smearman 2006; Sax 2010). Pharmacist conscience clauses were first introduced in a handful of states in the years following *Roe*. However, since most oral contraceptives were not covered by the vast majority of insurance plans in the USA prior to the late 1990s, there was no major push for the protection of pharmacists through conscience clause laws for some time. This changed in the late 1990s, as more states required prescription equity, or insurance coverage of all FDA-approved contraceptive devices. Since the pharmacist's primary responsibility is to ensure patient safety and well-being, in the absence of conscience clause protections, a pharmacist may be held liable for refusing to fill a prescription because of a religious objection.

The introduction and FDA approval of EC raised significant controversy among pro-life supporters as well as Catholic medical professionals and institutions (Duvall 2006; Stein 2005). EC can be effective in preventing pregnancy up to five days after unprotected sexual intercourse, although EC is most effective the sooner it is administered. While it is accepted within the medical community that EC cannot disrupt an established pregnancy, defined as the implantation of an embryo on the uterine lining (Armstrong 2010; Mayo Clinic Staff 2015; WHO 2012), it is believed by some that the use of EC may result in an abortion through the destruction of an embryo. In particular, the Catholic Church, as well as some evangelical Christians, opposes the use of EC based on the belief that life begins at the moment of fertilization, and thus needs to be protected from that moment. The FDA, however, as well as others in the medical community, maintains that EC is similar to other forms of birth control, preventing ovulation but not affecting the embryo following implantation (Barot 2013).

The FDA approval of four types of EC, and its 2013 approval of one form of EC—Plan B—for over-the-counter sales, has led to a wide response by state legislatures; it has provoked legislators in over half of the states and the District of Columbia to devise policies either contracting or expanding access to EC. On one end of the spectrum are those states that worked to increase access to EC, with 17 states and the District of Columbia requiring all emergency rooms to provide information about EC to sexual assault victims and 13 states and the District of Columbia requiring these same facilities to dispense EC upon request. Ten states have attempted to increase accessibility to EC by allowing pharmacists to dispense it without a prescription. Finally, there are a handful of states that require either pharmacies (Illinois, New Jersey, Washington, and Wisconsin) or pharmacists (California) to fill all valid prescriptions (Guttmacher Institute 2015d). In total, 23 states and the District of Columbia have some measures in place to promote the accessibility of EC, either through requirements for its availability in emergency rooms or by lessening the restrictions on pharmacists to distribute.

On the other end of the spectrum are those states that have restricted access to EC through the establishment of conscience clause protections for objecting medical professionals or entities. Nine states have established the right to refuse the filling of EC by pharmacists or pharmacies, based upon a moral or religious objection. Six other states have passed some vaguely worded conscience clause protections, which establish the right to refuse for medical professionals. While these protections may include pharmacists or pharmacies, these entities are not specifically identified within the legislation that protects healthcare professionals' right to refuse EC for moral or religious reasons. Finally, two states—Arkansas and North Carolina—exclude EC from the ACA birth control coverage mandate. Thus, while EC has resulted in different type of legislation at the state level, the majority of the states have been working to increase the awareness and availability of EC, particularly for sexual assault victims.

The legislative approach to EC has varied from the approach to other forms of birth control. Fewer states have legislated conscience clause protections for pharmacists' religious objections to other forms of birth control. Only eight states require pharmacists and pharmacies to fill all valid prescriptions, including also all birth control devices. Conversely, six states have established protections for pharmacists' right to refuse filling birth control prescriptions if it violates the moral or religious beliefs of the pharmacist. Seven state laws protect the pharmacist's right to refuse prescribing morally objectionable medications, but prohibit the interference or obstruction of a patient's right to obtain the medication in question. Therefore, these policies require the meaningful transfer of the prescription to another pharmacist or pharmacy that will provide the patient's prescription. Finally, there are seven states that do not explicitly identify pharmacists or pharmacies within the state statute that protects the right to refuse the provision of birth control. However, they use a broadly worded clause, which may apply to pharmacists or pharmacies (Guttmacher Institute 2015b, 2015d). For example, in the state of Kansas, the statute permits the right of healthcare professionals to refuse to provide contraceptive services if it is believed that the service in question may result in an abortion (Kansas Stat. Ann. 65-443, 2012).

Since *Roe*, conscience clause legislation, at the federal and state levels, has proven to be relatively successful, particularly as compared to the legislation that reflects the fetus-centered strategy. Healthcare professionals have been able to secure federal protections from government or employer requirements to perform abortion or abortion-related services, as well as protection from discrimination for the refusal to perform abortion. In addition, 90 % of all states include conscience clause protections for medical professionals involved in abortion, and 26 % of all states have protection for pharmacists and health professionals who object to the provision of contraceptives. While conscience clause measures have received significant attention from scholars (Collins 2006; Dubow 2015; Duvall 2006; Feder 2005; Lipton-Lubet 2014; Sobel and Salganicoff 2015; Sonfield 2005; Wardle 2010), it is funding restrictions, the second type of legislation protecting the rights of third-party actors, which have become the most common—and most effective—means to limit access to abortion. The following section examines the development and increased use of funding restrictions on abortion, which are justified as protections for taxpayers who may be opposed to abortion and object to paying for this service.

Funding Restrictions: Protecting Taxpayers in the Abortion Debate

While pro-life organizations and activists most often emphasize the need to establish protections for the fetus, it is funding restrictions that have proven to be the most palatable and effective means of restricting access to this procedure. As the general public has consistently supported some access to abortion, outright bans on the procedure would be unlikely to pass at either the federal or state level. Restrictions on government funding, however, do not completely prohibit access to the procedure. Rather, they create an impediment for accessing the procedure, primarily for low-income and poor women, while still maintaining a women's right to make their own reproductive choices. These measures include both restrictions on government spending—achieved through limits on the use of state facilities, equipment, and employees for the performance of an abortion—and limitations placed on the private marketplace.

The Hyde Amendment represents the first, and in some respects the most powerful, prohibition on domestic abortion funding by the federal government. The Hyde Amendment, introduced by Representative Henry Hyde, was a rider attached to the 1976 Department of Health, Education, and Welfare appropriations bill, prohibiting federal spending on abortion. While some exceptions for this prohibition are currently in place, in 1976, the only exception to this spending restriction was for the life of the mother. Primarily impacting women on Medicaid, the Hyde Amendment continues to be added to appropriations bills annually since 1976. Despite its continued passage by members of Congress, the Amendment still provokes controversy.

While the focus of the Hyde Amendment is funding, its purpose is clearly to limit access to abortion. Representative Hyde stated as such during the debates over his amendment, declaring that "I would certainly like to prevent, if I could legally, all women from obtaining an abortion, a rich woman, a middle-class woman, or a poor woman. Unfortunately, the only available vehicle is the [Medicaid] bill" (Boonstra 2013). Soon after its adoption, the Amendment prompted similar riders on bills that provide any type of healthcare coverage. In general, the riders now are routinely adopted for Department of Defense appropriations bills—denying coverage of abortion to those in the armed services, their dependents, and Peace Corp volunteers—limiting abortion coverage to those receiving medical coverage under the Indian Health Services Act, and bills that limit the funding of abortion services in federal prisoners (Boonstra 2007).

The constitutionality of the Hyde Amendment, specifically the question whether the restriction represents an undue burden on women's access to abortion, was addressed in the court case, *Harris v. McRae*. In the final ruling, the court maintained that under the decision in *Roe*, the court cannot erect barriers to prevent women from accessing abortion, but the government has no obligation to provide access for those unable to afford the procedure (448 U.S. 297, 1980). This argument is in line with the approach that understands abortion, as well as the right to health, as a negative right; while the government needs to protect women's access to the service—thus, first trimester abortions cannot be prohibited—the government has no obligation to provide or facilitate women's access to this service.[4] To date, 32 states and the District of Columbia provide funding for abortion for women on Medicaid only in cases of rape, incest, and when the life of the mother is at stake, as required under federal law. South Dakota reimburses Medicaid expenditures for abortion only in cases involving risk to the life of the mother, a violation of federal law (South Dakota Codified Law 28-6-4.5, 1978). A total of 17 states provide funding for all or most medically necessary abortions for women on Medicaid with state funds, beyond what is required under federal law.

In addition to the passage of federal policies restricting the domestic funding of abortion, legislators have also limited international aid to organizations that provide abortion and abortion-related services. The Helms Amendment, the first restriction on abortion funding, passed by Congress in 1973, prohibited aid to international organizations that counsel for, refer, or provide abortions (Barot 2013). This amendment was attached to the Foreign Assistance Act, an annual appropriations bill that provides nonmilitary economic aid primarily through the United States Agency for International Development (USAID), and has been attached to its annual reauthorization. While this legislative action restricts US funds from being used for abortion or abortion counseling, executive action taken in the mid-1980s was even more restrictive with regard to the organizations eligible for funding through USAID (Barot 2013).

The Mexico City Policy—often referred to as the Global Gag Rule—was first established by President Reagan in 1984, prohibiting funding for nonprofit and international organizations that use segregated, non-US funds to provide any abortion-related service, including counseling, referral, or the procedure itself. President Clinton rescinded this executive order, in place from 1984 until 1992, shortly after he first came to office (Cincotta and Crane 2001). During this period, the Foreign Assistance Act continued to restrict the use of US funds for the performance of abortion

[4]This type of argument is libertarian in nature, conceptualizing abortion as a private matter that should be addressed as such. This framing, and its place within right-wing politics more generally, will be discussed in Chap. 5.

abroad, and in 2000, President George W. Bush reinstated the Mexico City Policy. This policy was in place until President Obama's election in 2008. Although the Policy was in place from 1984 to 1992 and 2000 to 2008, congressional efforts restricted funding to international organizations that provide abortion or abortion-related services, even if these services are funded by segregated, non-US funds. This legislation continues to be the most effective means to limit access to abortion without prohibiting the practice outright. At the same time, funding restrictions have not stimulated much attention and awareness in the general public, especially as compared to issues that have not been enjoying legislative success such as fetal personhood.

Pre-ACA Status of Federal Abortion Funding Restrictions
From 1973 to 1994, there were 212 measures introduced in Congress to restrict public funding of abortion or related services. This number represents approximately 27 % of proposed bills concerning abortion at the federal level during this time period. Although there was an overall decline in abortion-related proposals at the federal level after 1994 (from 794 proposals to 524), the proportion of abortion-related laws that restricted public funding increased to 30 % of all abortion-related proposals from 1994 to 2014. During the 1970s, 31 proposals to restrict funding were introduced, accounting for 9 % of all abortion-related legislation. Most of these proposals focused primarily on limits to services provided through federally funded family planning programs (8) and limits attached to annual appropriations bills (14).

Between 1981 and 1994, there were 181 proposals addressing the public funding of abortion and abortion-related services, representing 41 % of all abortion-related legislation during these years. A total of 67 proposals restricting abortion funding were amendments or riders attached to appropriations bills; the most common appropriations measures include restrictions on abortion funding for Washington, DC (16), the Department of Labor, Health and Human Services, and Education (10), the commerce and treasury department appropriations (8), and the Department of Defense (4). Further, 18 tax-related proposals included revisions to the US tax code, most of which attempted to deny tax-exempt status to organizations that provide abortion or finance abortions, directly or indirectly (10). Four proposals deny medical expense claims that are a result of abortion, and four deny tax exemptions for children born from a botched abortion.

With the exception of riders and amendments to spending bills, the most common type of funding restriction are general measures that prohibit any federal involvement in or funding of abortion or abortion-related services (36). Another common form of restriction concerns foreign assistance and international aid; 28 proposals would restrict funds for international family planning programs that also provide abortions with segregated, non-US funds. Some of these proposals were introduced during the 1990s, after Clinton rescinded the Mexico City Policy, thus aiming to ensure that the limitations originally established by this policy will remain in effect. Of the 28 proposals, 13 of the bills and amendments to foreign assistance appropriations focused on limiting United Nations Population Fund (UNFPA) funds to China, as a response to the emergence of the one-child policy there. This policy, seen as a form of coercive family planning, which at times required abortion for those in violation of the policy, was heavily criticized by members of Congress during the 1980s and 1990s, and in particular, Representative Chris Smith. Smith, a member of the House since 1981, remains one of the strongest opponents of abortion. He has been especially active in promoting human rights and working to stop abortions abroad (Gray 1997; Gruson 1991).

In the second era examined, 1995–2014,[5] many of the same trends regarding the type of abortion funding restrictions proposed by Congress continue. Of these 154 proposed bills, 67 are similar to the appropriations bills identified above, prohibiting or limiting domestic or international funding of abortion. Also, 22 of the proposed measures would place restrictions on foreign assistance bills, providing such funding only to organizations that do not provide abortions or any abortion-related services. While there was a substantial decline in proposals to change the Internal Revenue Service (IRS) code, disqualifying medical expenses or tax exemptions for abortion or abortion-related expenses, which dropped from 18 proposals in the previous era to 3.

Limits on the use of taxpayer dollars for federally funded family planning programs also continued during this time period, constituting 21 of all proposed taxpayer funding bans. One of the more restrictive proposals,

[5] The legislative proposals introduced at the federal and state levels between 2010 and 2014 are analyzed from two perspectives; the first examination took place in the discussion over public policy between 1995 and 2014, and the second when analyzing post-ACA legislation (2010–2015). While the analysis of the last two decades is used to highlight general trends and changes in pro-life strategy, the latter account focuses in the implication of the ACA, and particularly the *Hobby Lobby* ruling, on this strategy.

the Taxpayer's Freedom of Conscience Act (H.R. 777, 2005), prohibits the use of federal funds for any population control or family planning activity, foreign or domestic. This bill was introduced six times during this time period, yet the measure has never made it out of committee. Other family planning measures, such as the Title X Family Planning Act and the Title X Abortion Provider Prohibition Act (S. 85, 2009; H.R. 4133, 2007), are less restrictive, limiting the use of federal funds granted to family planning programs and organizations for any abortion-related activity.

When considering legislation that passed at the federal level between 1974 and 1994, 31 % (66) of all proposals restricting funding of abortion were enacted. This number is significantly higher than other pro-life legislative attempts; during the same period, only five non-taxpayer funding-related bills passed, none of which were fetus-centered proposals. From 1995 to 2014, the passage rate of taxpayer restrictions on abortion was 29 %, as compared to a passage rate of 9 % overall. Appropriations bills constitute the vast majority of funding restrictions which were enacted into law, some of which have little to do with the regulation of abortion overall as it is only one of the many issues addressed within the bill. Regardless of this issue, funding restrictions represent a fairly powerful tool to regulate access to the procedure, particularly for low-income and poor women, the population most likely to have unplanned pregnancies. Furthermore, poorer women are twice as likely to delay the procedure due to limited financial means and, thus, they may require a more expensive abortion procedure later on in the pregnancy (Finer et al. 2006; Jones and Jarman 2011). Therefore, federal restrictions on taxpayer dollars going to fund abortion or abortion-related services are not only the most likely to pass into law, but they also are effective tools to delay or limit access to abortion.

Pre-ACA Status of State-Level Restrictions on Abortion Funding
Also at the state level, policies involving the funding of abortion and abortion-related services are the most common type of abortion-related legislation. Restrictions on the funding of abortion come in many different forms, including, but not limited to, education appropriations, family planning funds, and the use of state facilities or public employees for the procedure itself. Between 1973 and 1994, 24 laws passed restricting the use of state funds for abortion or abortion-related services. Examples of these laws include limits on the use of funds for abortion or abortion-related services by women's health or family planning programs (Ariz. Rev. Stat. Ann. § A 36-2907, 1988), restrictions on the performance of abortion in

state-run hospitals (N.D. Cent. Code § 14-02.3-01, 1979), and prohibitions on school nurses counseling or referring students for abortion (Miss. Code Ann. § 41-79-5, 1987).

Under the Hyde Amendment, first passed in 1976 and reauthorized every year since, federal funds granted to Medicaid programs can only be used for abortions that are necessary to save the life of the mother.[6] By 1994, three states had laws to reimburse expenses for an abortion through Medicaid for abortions that are necessary to save the life of the mother, with 28 additional states reimbursing expenses for abortions necessary for the life of the mother as well as cases of rape and incest. On the other hand, 16 states use state funds to pay for all medically necessary abortions, which are not covered by federal funds. Finally, three states reimburse expenses for abortions that are necessary for a limited number of health circumstances (Guttmacher Institute 2015b).

In addition to restrictions imposed through Medicaid funding, a handful of states have also imposed restrictions on insurance coverage of abortion. Six states (Idaho, Kentucky, Missouri, North Dakota, Rhode Island, and Pennsylvania) have prohibited health insurance coverage of abortions with the exception of cases involving the life of the mother. Two of these six laws, however, were found to be unconstitutional and later reenacted; in the case of Rhode Island, the legislature reenacted a similar version of the law previously ruled unconstitutional, while legislators in Pennsylvania rewrote the law to require that health insurers provide some policies that explicitly do not cover abortion (R.I. Gen. Laws § 27-18-28, 1989; 18 PA. Cons. Stat. Ann. § 3215(e), 1993). Finally, nine states have restricted abortion coverage for state employees; these nine states include the six

[6] The restrictions on the type of abortions reimbursed through Medicaid—as legislated through the Hyde Amendment—have changed over time; originally, the amendment restricted Medicaid funding of abortion only in cases threatening the life of the mother. In 1978 and 1979, the Hyde Amendment included language that allowed for funding of abortions in cases of rape and incest, as well as in instances that threaten the physical health of the mother (Hyde Amendment, Pub. L. No. 95-205, § 101, 91 Stat. 1460, 1978; Hyde Amendment, Pub. L. No. 95-480, § 210, 92 Stat. 1586, 1979). In 1994, the restrictions on federal funding for abortions were tightened to include coverage only in instances in which the mother's life—rather than the physical health—is threatened, and in cases of rape and incest (Department of Health and Human Services Appropriations Act for fiscal year 1994, Pub. L. No. 103-112, § 509, 107 Stat. 1113, 1994). Today, the Hyde Amendment allows for funding of abortions through Medicaid for cases involving the life of the mother, and instances of rape and incest (Department of Labor, Health and Human Services, and Education Appropriations Act, Pub L. No. 113-76, § 128 Stat. 5, 2014).

states that have restricted all insurance coverage of abortion and three other states that have more narrowly tailored limitations on state employees (Illinois, Massachusetts, and Nebraska).

During the second era examined in this project, 1995–2014, the number of state laws concerning abortion increased dramatically. The number of laws specific to public funding also increased, in particular, policies limiting insurance coverage in the private marketplace and in the healthcare exchanges. During this period, 21 states passed legislation prohibiting all state employees from counseling or giving referrals for abortion, which includes all public school teachers and nurses, as well as personnel at all state-run facilities.[7] With regard to Medicaid reimbursement of abortion, 32 states and the District of Columbia follow federal guidelines, only paying for abortions necessary to save the life of the mother, and instances of rape and incest, while 17 states reimburse for all medically necessary abortions (Guttmacher Institute 2015b). Thus, little change occurred with respect to Medicaid coverage of abortion at the state level despite the increase in state laws addressing insurance coverage of abortion.

Nine states have prohibited all health insurance plans from covering abortion, a slight increase from the previous era in which six states prohibited coverage in the private marketplace. A total of 15 states prohibit insurance coverage of abortion for all state employees, also increasing from the previous era. Five of these restrictions on insurance coverage permit insurance companies to offer riders, which offer extra coverage for employees, thus requiring out-of-pocket expenditures for coverage for abortion (Guttmacher Institute 2015b).

This review of the two types of legislation that focus on securing the rights of third-party actors highlights the success of this type of legislation. Funding restrictions, especially at the federal level, are especially successful in limiting access to abortion and abortion-related services as compared to measures designed to secure fetal rights and even those purported to protect women's health. In light of the relatively limited attention third-party legislation receives in the media as compared to issues such as partial-birth abortion and fetal personhood as well as the limited focus on third-party rights by pro-life organizations and activists, the relatively high rates of legislative success are unexpected. Pro-life organizations are, by their very

---

[7] North Dakota's ban on the use of public funds for abortion counseling or referral was found invalid in *Valley Family Planning v. State of N.D.*, No. 80-1471, Eighth Circuit Court of Appeals, October 12, 1981.

nature, focused on the rights of the fetus and thus place much of their focus or efforts on banning the procedure itself and work toward convincing the general public of the sanctity of life. Thus, this type of legislative success, found in policies that establish small, incremental barriers and limitations on the procedure, has created a divide within the movement itself. Some organizations and activists remain "purists," who believe it necessary to work toward banning the procedure to protect the fetus, never deviating from the position that life begins at conception and must be afforded all of the legal protections under the US Constitution (Eckholm 2011). Others, such as the Americans United for Life, have adopted a more pragmatic and opportunistic approach, acknowledging that most Americans are not comfortable with outright bans on the procedure, but are accepting of limited restrictions, including funding limits at the federal and state levels (Khazan 2014, 2015).

This analysis also reveals the libertarian nature of most of the third-party restrictions, both at the federal and state levels up until 2010. This approach is distinct from the more conservative version of religious freedom, which emphasizes the importance of maintaining tradition and respect for religious values and practices. Although conscience clause protections are designed to secure religious liberty, an issue of central concern to conservatives, these laws largely reflect a libertarian of religion and religiosity, which are framed as a personal, individual matter that should be protected from state interference. This is most clearly manifested in policies that prohibit discrimination against medical professionals and facilities that either participate or refuse to participate in abortion by governmental officials.

This type of legislation is also based on a libertarian understanding of reproductive rights, arguing that respecting the religious rights of individuals to refuse to participate does not substantially limit women's reproductive rights or choice. As long as the state does not ban the procedure altogether, women's rights are respected and effectively secured by the state. In this context, religious liberty and women's reproductive rights are both understood as negative rights, as the role of the state is limited to protecting the freedom of citizens to believe or act as they wish, rather than imposing regulations to shape individual's behavior or promote a particular type of action.

This libertarian tendency also shapes legislation concerning funding restrictions of abortion or abortion-related services. Some have made the case that funding restrictions will assist in lowering the abortion rate, as in the case of the congressional debate over insurance coverage of abortion through the ACA, in which Congresswoman Bachmann declared that insurance coverage would facilitate a higher abortion rate (Boonstra 2013). However, in general, the majority of these proposals that place limits on state funding are predicated on the assertion that the public should not pay for services—such as abortion—to which they are opposed (Boonstra 2007). The result of these restrictions is a decrease in governmental intervention in the reproductive decision of individuals, which is now framed as a personal issue that should be decided—and paid for—by the individual. In addition, the issue of reproductive choices is now transferred to the market; women are free to make their own decisions regarding abortion, and a free and unregulated market will be able to create services to answer such a demand. The result of funding restrictions is thus the framing of abortion as a personal matter, which should be decided by the individual, who has the right to demand certain services in the open market but not to require state intervention or assistance in the matter.

The passage of the ACA, and later the ruling in *Hobby Lobby*, brought the issue of third-party actors, and especially the issue of religious liberty, to the forefront of the public debate over reproductive rights. While this attention changed the pro-life discourse as well as the public's perception on the issue, in general, the type of legislation at the federal and state levels, as well as the rates of legislative success, remained similar to what was found in earlier decades. The renewed debate over religious liberty has brought increased public awareness and support for protecting individual rights of religious liberty, which has crossed over into other issue areas such as LGBTQ rights (Lipka 2015). Regardless of this increased focus on the protection of individual rights, third-party legislation such as restrictions on the use of public funds remains the most effective type of legislation that limits access to abortion and abortion-related services, particularly at the federal level.

3 ACA AND HOBBY LOBBY

The passage of the ACA created a federal health exchange marketplace where individuals and families, who do not have coverage through an employer, and are not enrolled in Medicaid, Medicare, or any Children's Health Insurance Program (CHIP), can purchase insurance plans. Under the ACA, states have the freedom to create their own state-run healthcare exchange, or to remain under the federally run healthcare exchange. As of 2015, 13 states and Washington, DC, have established their own marketplace, three have federally supported state-based marketplaces, and seven have state partnership marketplaces, the remaining 27 states relying on a federally facilitated marketplace (The Kaiser Family Foundation 2013).[8] Further, the law expanded Medicaid for those at 133 % of the federal poverty level, although states have the option to decline the federal aid provided for Medicaid expansion. In 2012, the Congressional Budget Office (CBO) projected that by 2018, 20 million Americans will be covered through government subsidies; further, it was projected that in 2014, 7 million will enroll in the healthcare exchange, with 6 million of these new enrollees receiving tax credits to subsidize their enrollment (The Kaiser Family Foundation 2013). So far, the HHS reported that 8 million signed up in the federal health exchange marketplace in the 2014 open enrollment period, with an additional 4.8 million enrolling in Medicaid and CHIP (HHS 2014).

In June 2015, the Supreme Court ruled on the case *King v. Burwell*. This case involved federal subsidies and, specifically, the meaning of the ACA's establishment of subsidies through the healthcare exchange. The plaintiffs in the case argued that the plain reading of the text, "enrolled in through an Exchange established by the State under 131," means that the IRS did not have the authority to establish tax credits for those purchasing an insurance plan in the federal marketplace. This claim, if accepted by the court, would lead to the elimination of subsidies for states with federal exchanges, affecting millions of Americans, and potentially could lead to the elimination of the individual and employer mandates in states with federal exchanges (Jost 2014). The court ruled against the plaintiffs, determining that eligibility for tax credits extends to individuals in states operating on the federal exchange. The ruling ended one of the most significant challenges to the ACA to date, preserving the law's general structure and primary intent (576 U.S.__, at 5, 9).

---

[8] States with a state-based marketplace are responsible for all marketplace functions. Consumers in these states apply for and enroll in coverage through marketplace websites established and maintained by the states. States with federally supported state-based marketplace are responsible for performing all marketplace functions, except the federally facilitated marketplace IT platform. Consumers in these states apply for and enroll in coverage through healthcare.gov. States in a partnership marketplace may administer in-person consumer assistance and HHS performs the remaining marketplace functions, including enrollment through healthcare.gov. In a federally facilitated marketplace, HHS performs all marketplace functions, including enrollment through healthcare.gov (The Kaiser Family Foundation 2015b).

Regarding reproductive services, the ACA includes a ban on the use of public subsidies for plans that include coverage of elective abortion, which is in line with the restrictions imposed under the Hyde Amendment. This ban, however, varies based upon the different types of healthcare market-places and plans that are established in each state; subsidies received for the federal healthcare exchange cannot be used for plans that cover abortion beyond the need to save the life of the mother or in cases of rape or incest. In case an individual purchases a plan that does cover nontherapeutic abortions, this coverage must come from an account that is segregated from the government funds provided. For states entering into a multi-state exchange, at least one plan must not provide coverage for abortion beyond what is permitted by the federal law. The law also permits states that have established their own state health exchange to prohibit coverage of abortion in all plans provided through the exchange. Further, similar to the federal exchange, those states that allow for coverage of nontherapeutic abortions must establish segregated accounts for coverage of this particular service (The Patient Protection and Affordable Care Act, P.L. 111-148, 2010).

Finally, abortion coverage is prohibited in the essential benefits plan, which serves as the basis for the most basic health plan that individuals are required to have. For those low- and middle-income individuals and families that qualify for government subsidies on the federal health exchange, it is expected that few insurance companies will provide riders for the additional coverage of nontherapeutic abortions given the limited number of such riders currently available (Salganicoff et al. 2004). Further, plans that offer this additional rider requires consumers to pay out of pocket for extra coverage in addition to the general costs for insurance coverage. It is expected that few women would purchase such additional coverage, as unintended pregnancies are by their very nature unplanned (Boonstra 2013; National Women's Law Center 2013).

One part of the ACA that has been the focus of much controversy concerns the mandate requiring employers to provide insurance that covers contraceptive services. In 2012, the administration published the list of preventive services that must be provided at no cost by all insurance plans in order to comply with the ACA, a list that included all FDA-approved forms of contraception (Sobel and Salganicoff 2015). According to the guidelines, all businesses with 50 or more employees are required to provide insurance coverage of all forms of contraception, with the exception of those plans that have been grandfathered into the program.[9] If said insurance plans includes coverage for prescription drugs, all FDA-approved contraceptive devices—considered preventative services—must also be made available without cost sharing (42 U.S.C. § 300gg-13(a) (4), 2010; Federal Register 2013). Specifically, the law now requires coverage of 20 FDA-approved contraceptive devices, four of which are of concern for some religious institutions and employers (The Kaiser Family Foundation 2015a).

The four contraceptive devices that are the most controversial, and which become the focus of the *Hobby Lobby* case, include two forms of hormonal EC—Ella and Plan B—and two types of intrauterine devices (IUD). All types of hormonal contraceptive devices are labeled by the FDA as preventing the implantation of a fertilized egg on the uterine lining, preventing pregnancy rather than ending one (Grossman 2014). For some religious authorities, these contraceptive devices are thought to act as abortifacients, as they believe that the fertilization of the egg—even if not yet implanted—represents the start of life. Therefore, any interference with this process is understood as aborting a human life. Most medical professionals, including the American College of Obstetricians and Gynecologists (ACOG), do not share this definition of abortion, rather maintaining that fertilization is distinct from conception. Thus, most in the medical community do not share the position that these emergency contraceptives stop a viable pregnancy, but rather prevent the fertilization of the egg (ACOG 2015; Brief of Amici Curiae of Physicians for Reproductive Health, et al., *Burwell v Hobby Lobby*, No. 13-354, 10th Cir. October 21, 2013). Nevertheless, the requirement under the ACA to cover these forms of contraception has been seen by some religious organizations as forcing employers to provide insurance coverage of abortion against their religious belief.

In 2012, when the mandate requiring all FDA-approved contraceptive devices be covered at no cost was supposed to take effect, several hearings were scheduled with respect to the birth control requirement. One of the hearings at the House Oversight and Government Committee received notable attention because of the battle over who was allowed to speak; this hearing consisted of an all-male panel of theologians and

[9] Grandfathered health plans include those in existence prior to March 23, 2010, that have not substantially changed the benefits offered or increased costs since passage of the ACA. These plans are exempt from many of the requirements imposed under the ACA.

clergy members, who challenged imposing this mandate on religious universities, hospitals, and charities. At the same time, Sandra Fluke, a law student from Georgetown University invited by Representative Elijah Cummings, a ranking committee member, was prevented from testifying. Fluke intended to discuss the importance of the contraception mandate for women's health, yet was prevented from participating in this hearing, prompting even more controversy surrounding this issue (Lipton-Lubet 2014).

At the time the bill was first passed, the ACA included exemptions from this mandate for religious institutions registered as a nonprofit entity. This category includes houses of worship, churches, and conventions or associations of churches, which are exempt from coverage of contraceptive devices within their insurance plans (45 C.F.R. § 147.131(a) 2014). Limiting the exemptions to houses of worship and churches, and excluding other nonprofit religious institutions such as universities and church-run service agencies, has been controversial, leading some to challenge the ACA's mandate.

In the wake of this battle over the birth control mandate in the ACA, the administration came out with new guidelines, introducing a compromise for nonprofit religious organizations that were not previously exempt from the coverage mandate—such as private religious universities and church-run health centers—while ensuring women's access to birth control at no cost. The new accommodation for religious nonprofits required such organizations to complete and submit a two-page form to a third-party administrator who will work with insurance companies to provide no-cost contraception as per the ACA requirements (Pear 2012). Despite this change, offered by the HHS as a compromise, the ACA's mandate remains controversial and, thus, has been challenged numerous times in court. Specifically, religious leaders argue that the accommodation is part of the continued "assault on faith and values" by the Obama administration. This position, used by Republican leaders as political fodder for the November 2012 elections, further exacerbated the conflict over the HHS policy (Eckholm 2011).

Opposition to the HHS mandate has focused on the two different requirements, one for nonexempt and the other for exempt organizations. The first type of opposition, of which one visible example is the case of *Hobby Lobby*, focuses on the exclusion of for-profit organizations from the contraception mandate exemption. Requiring for-profit employees who are religious to provide these types of contraceptive services, it is argued, constitutes a violation of religious liberty. The second type of opposition, which has also been challenged in court but so far has failed to gain traction, is the accommodation process, which is argued to also constitute a violation of religious liberty. Through the act of notifying the government or a third-party administrator, the employer becomes complicit in an act that violates their religious beliefs. According to the Kaiser Family Foundation, since the implementation of the contraceptive mandate under the ACA, over 200 corporations have challenged both the government mandate and the accommodation process, maintaining that both represent a violation of religious liberty. To date, 71 lawsuits have been filed against HHS, with the Becket Fund representing the plaintiffs in 50 of these cases (Sobel and Salganicoff 2015). The Becket Fund is also representing 140 religious, nonprofit institutions challenging the coverage or accommodation requirement in 56 cases against the federal government.

The challenges to the ACA contraception mandate from for-profit corporations center on the lack of religious exemptions from this requirement. Of the numerous lawsuits filed by for-profit corporations, the suits brought by the Green family, owners of the craft-store chain, Hobby Lobby, and the Hahn family, owners of Conestoga Wood Specialties, a cabinetry company, made it to the Supreme Court during the 2013 term, and were represented by the Becket Fund. Both corporations challenged the HHS guidelines requiring coverage of all FDA-approved devices because of their religious belief that these particular contraceptive devices act as abortifacients. Their suit alleged that the birth control mandate represented a violation of the first amendment's free exercise clause and the protections established in the 1993 RFRA. Specifically, their claim is that the required insurance coverage for these devices or medications makes the business complicit in abortion, a violation of their religious faith (Liptak 2014).

The RFRA, the basis for the plaintiffs' suit, prohibits the federal government from establishing a "substantial burden" on a person's free exercise of religion unless the government can demonstrate that this burden represents a "compelling government interest" or is the least restrictive means of furthering the government's interest (42 U.S. Code § 2000bb–1, 2009). The RFRA was passed after controversy arose concerning the Supreme Court's decisions on a number of Native American issues; in *Lyng v. Northwest Indian Cemetery Protective Association* (1988), the court allowed the US Forest Service to build on sacred land, while in the case *Employment Division v. Smith* (1990), the court upheld the denial of unemployment benefits to two individuals fired for testing positive for mescaline. Outrage among the general public and political officials to these rulings led to the introduction and swift passage of the RFRA, ostensibly with the intention to protect persons of minority faiths. The Act has since been modified, yet the courts have upheld its primary intent, requiring a substantial burden of proof for any government intervention in the free exercise of religion (Luchenitser 2015). While the claimants in *Hobby Lobby* also raised the free exercise clause of the First Amendment in their suit against HHS, the court relied solely on the RFRA in reviewing the merits of the case.

In light of the RFRA, the owners of Hobby Lobby and Conestoga Wood Specialties claim they are entitled to an exemption from the ACA requirement, since the requirement to supply certain forms of birth control is a violation of their faith. A number of legal questions derive from this claim, including whether religious exemptions extend to for-profit corporations and, in particular, whether for-profit corporations can bring suit based upon the RFRA. Media coverage and public discussion, prior to and after the ruling, focused on the application of the protections established in the RFRA to corporations, often using the phrase "corporate personhood" and similar iterations in discussions of the case (Blow 2015; Cerf et al. 2014; Crouch 2014; Epps 2014; Keller 2013; Sekulow 2014). This term—corporate personhood—was brought into the public lexicon following the 2010 ruling in *Citizens United v. Federal Election Commission*, and became more frequently invoked during the 2012 presidential elections. This, in conjunction with the polarizing effect of the *Citizens United* ruling, ignited a contentious debate, still continuing today, over the application of constitutional protections to corporate entities (Denniston 2014; Schiff 2012; Totenberg 2014).[10]

While the plaintiffs in the *Hobby Lobby* case argued that individual rights of religious liberty extended to their corporate entity, and in particular, the protections of the RFRA, their focus was not on corporate

---

[10] The ruling in *Citizens United*, addressing campaign spending and the Bipartisan Campaign Reform Act, did not include the phrase "corporations are people" or other similar variation. Nevertheless, the case was largely discussed in the media as one in which corporations were being granted the rights given to persons in the 1st and 14th Amendments. This particular phrase became a phenomenon following its use by Republican presidential candidate Mitt Romney in his stump speech in Iowa during the 2012 presidential election, further stoking the controversy surrounding the ruling in *Citizens United* (Parker 2011; Rucker 2011).

personhood. Instead, the arguments in court emphasized the values and religious beliefs of the individuals who run the corporation; in closely held corporations such as *Hobby Lobby*, it is the owners who are required to participate in the provision of insurance. Thus, it is the religious faith of the owners—and its reflection within the corporation—that deserves the same protection under the law. In this account, the focus is on the faith of the owners, which is not lost or put on hold when they go to work or when they incorporate a business. Thus, this faith confers statutory protection to the corporate entity, which serves to protect the owners (Weber 2014).

A second set of claims regarding the application of constitutional or statutory protections to corporations concerns the previous legal precedents that have established this as a practice. It is often noted that this practice has occurred throughout US history; while recently the focus has centered on *Citizens United*, the granting of such protections has occurred many times in the past, in cases ranging from the right to enter into and make contracts (*Trustees of Dartmouth College v. Woodward*), equal protection under the law (*Santa Clara County v. Southern Pacific Railroad* and *Pembina Consolidated Silver Mining Co. v Pennsylvania*), and protection from warrantless search and seizure (*See v. City of Seattle*). Another issue before the court concerned the RFRA's "substantial burden" clause, which prohibits the government from imposing a substantial burden on individuals' free exercise of religion. In the public discussion of the Green and Hahn families' challenge to the ACA mandate, many conservative commentators have noted that the administration had already granted nonprofit entities such as churches and houses of worship an exemption from the law. This exemption, they argued, illustrates the acknowledgement that coverage of contraceptive devices does impose a substantial burden upon some individuals' religious beliefs and values (Plaintiff's Motion for Preliminary Injunction, *Hobby Lobby v. Sebelius*, No. CIV-12-1000-HE, U.S. District Court of Appeals, September 9, 2012). If a substantial burden on one's religious beliefs is demonstrated by the plaintiffs, the final questions are whether the government has a compelling interest in burdening some individuals' religious beliefs, and whether this compelling interest is achieved in the least restrictive means possible (Sobel and Salganicoff 2015).

Numerous critiques have arisen in response to the *Hobby Lobby* lawsuit, ranging from challenges to the standing of companies to sue HHS for this purported violation of the RFRA to the substantial burden imposed on these corporations. Some critics have maintained that a corporate entity lacks the capacity to perform many religious practices and traditions, thus it should not be understood as an entity whose religious rights need protection by the state; a corporation "doesn't have knees to pray on or a soul to save" (Shapiro 2014), and it cannot attend worship services or participate in any activities which are protected under the First Amendment's free exercise clause, which are quintessentially human activities. In addition, some have raised challenges to the characterization of the four contraceptive devices in question, contending that these objections center on the misclassification of certain contraceptive devices as abortifacients (Abcarian 2015). As the medical community maintains these drugs and devices do not end existing pregnancies and serve only a preventative function, the argument that their provision constitutes a violation of their religious liberty to oppose abortion does not stand to reason.

Further, many opponents have focused on the potential harm that the ruling in support of Hobby Lobby will cause for women, especially women who use these devices for particular health conditions such as endometriosis, polycystic ovarian syndrome, and amenorrhea (C.H. 2014; Cohen et al. 2014; Eichelberger and Redden 2014). More generally, many see this case as having detrimental effects on women's equality and equal participation in economic and social life. Finally, despite claims by supporters of the Hobby Lobby plaintiffs that birth control is easily accessible and available at a low cost, the Guttmacher Institute's supporting brief illustrates the significant burden this ruling may have for women. In shifting the responsibility to cover all FDA-approved contraceptive devices from the employer to women, cost may be the overriding factor that determines the type of birth control used. The most reliable forms of birth control, however, are the most expensive, and many surveys have indicated that women would choose other forms of birth control if cost was not a factor (Brief of the Guttmacher Institute and Professor Sara Rosenbaum, Nos. 13-354 & 13-356, U.S. Court of Appeals 10th & 3rd Circuits).

The court announced its decision in *Burwell v. Hobby Lobby* on June 30, 2014. First, the court accepted the argument that Hobby Lobby, as well as Conestoga Wood Specialties, has standing to file suit under the RFRA. In this determination, the opinion, authored by Justice Samuel Alito, noted that while "corporate personhood is a legal fiction," corporations are made up of human beings and thus it remains essential to ensure the protection of the individuals who make up that corporation (573 U.S.__, at 18). Further, the opinion states that "[a] corporation is simply a form of organization used by human beings to achieve desired ends" and, "separate and apart from the human beings who own, run, and are employed by them, [corporations] cannot do anything at all" (573 U.S.__, at 19). The ruling cited the Dictionary Act, which governs the interpretation of US Code, and states that the word "persons" includes corporations, companies, associations, firms, partnerships, societies, as well as individuals (1 U.S.C. § 1, 2012). The decision to extend the protections of religious liberty through the RFRA was also shaped by the nature of the corporations in question. Both corporations are closely held, run by a single family with shared religious beliefs. Classifying these companies as "closely-held corporations," the decision emphasized the family structure and values of the people who own the corporation. As the ruling opinion noted, there have been no similar claims offered by publicly traded corporations requesting the same exemption. Thus, in the case at hand, it is clear the sincerity of the owners' religious beliefs in this particular matter, and thus the ruling, applies only to similarly organized, closely held corporations (573 U.S.__, at 29).[11]

The ruling opinion did not engage in an extensive discussion of the question regarding the substantial burden imposed by the ACA mandate, the second primary question before the court. Nevertheless, the ruling opinion noted that HHS had not disputed the veracity or sincerity of these families' religious beliefs. Justice Alito also writes that the stated intent of the families not to pay for this contraceptive coverage, which would result in penalties of just under half a million dollars, demonstrates the substantial burden the mandate would create (573 U.S.__, at 32). Justice Ginsburg, authoring one of the dissents in the case, addresses the substantial burden question in greater detail, focusing on the nature of the mandate and what it requires of employers. As she outlines in the dissent, the law does not require the employer to purchase or provide the contraceptive device in question, rather the employer must "direct money into undifferentiated funds that finance a wide variety of benefits under comprehensive health plans" (573 U.S.__, at 23). Further, if the employee shares the same

---

[11] Justice Ginsburg's dissent rejects the claim that corporations should receive protection under the RFRA. She notes that no court decision prior to this has created a religious exemption for a for-profit corporation. Specifically, churches and houses of worship are created for the express purpose of uniting individuals with a shared purpose and intent with regard to their religious faith; for-profit corporations are not created for such a purpose. Corporations are commonly composed of individuals of varying faiths and they are not, in their nature, designed to "perpetuate the values shared by the community of believers" (573 U.S.__, at 18-19).

religious beliefs as the employer, the individual does not have to use the contraceptive device in question. Thus, Ginsburg concludes that the relationship between the families' religious objections and the ACA mandate is too weak to compel the court to accept the claim of a substantial burden on religious liberty (573 U.S.__, at 23).

The ruling opinion accepts the HHS' argument that the contraceptive mandate serves a compelling government interest, concluding that the mandate follows the RFRA requirement that any substantial burden on an individual's religious beliefs or values by the government needs to be justified by such an interest. However, the ruling opinion disputes the claim that the mandate represents the least restrictive means of achieving this interest. This claim was reinforced in the concurrence, authored by Justice Kennedy, who also asserted that the government did not demonstrate that the current HHS mandate is the least restrictive means to carry out the objective found within the ACA. In examining the least restrictive means test, Justice Alito brought into light numerous alternatives that could be used to achieve this interest of the state. Specifically, the opinion notes that the government could assume the costs of providing contraception to prevent such a burden; the costs of folding contraception costs into the overall costs of the ACA would not be a significant encumbrance for the federal government (573 U.S.__, at 41). Further, the government could also create an accommodation process for the for-profit religious organizations, using the process that has already been put into place and utilized by some nonprofit organizations (573 U.S.__, at 43-44). Thus, the government did not meet the RFRA's least restrictive means test that is required for imposing a substantial burden on another's religious liberty.

Ginsburg's dissent also examines the question of compelling interest that is before the court, addressing the reasoning behind the contraceptive mandate, and detailing the HHS' argument concerning the necessity of this coverage for women's health and well-being. She cites studies documenting the costs of contraceptives, focusing on IUDs, which are the most effective yet one of the most costly forms of birth control. Ginsburg states that for many women, particularly low-income and poor women, reliable birth control is not available. The cost of an IUD is roughly the equivalent of a month's salary for a woman earning minimum wage. Ginsburg also includes data from a 2004 study that found that almost a third of women would change their current form of contraception if cost was not an issue. In her dissent, she notes the necessity of such coverage for women, including discussion of the negative health and emotional effects of an unplanned pregnancy as well as the medical indications for which birth control is often prescribed (573 U.S.__, at 24-25). Ginsberg addresses the question whether the mandate is the least restrictive means to secure the government's interest, rejecting the ruling opinion's argument that there are more viable—and less restrictive—means to achieve the objections of the ACA. The ACA was intended to ensure that all citizens have access to healthcare coverage and, in particular, access to preventative services. Ruling in favor of Hobby Lobby raises the potential for religious objections, based upon a variety of religious belief systems, to be raised regarding other services or procedures covered under the ACA, such as vaccinations, antidepressants, blood transfusions, and medications derived from pig tissue.

One issue not discussed in the court's decision is the assumption that stands at the center of this case; that contraceptive devices—specifically, two forms of hormonal EC and two types of IUD—act as abortifacients. The absence of any discussion regarding this issue, especially in light of the assertion by the mainstream medical community—including the American Medical Association (AMA) and the ACOG—that they do not act as such, is meaningful for the framing of the debate. In accepting the claims of the Green and Hahn families regarding the abortifacient nature of these contraceptives, without addressing the scientific merit of this claim, the court framed the ruling as one concerning an individual's religious belief, determining that scientific debate or findings are irrelevant to the issue of freedom of religion. This type of framing, which emphasizes personal beliefs and ideologies rather than moral convictions or scientific evidence, is now playing a central role in the pro-life strategy and, in general, in right-wing debates over social issues such as same-sex marriage.

The decision, rather than resolving or diminishing the controversy surrounding the issue, only served to further ignite conflict in the ACA birth control provisions (Cohen et al. 2014). Many of those opposed to the court's ruling focused on its potential impact for women's health and well-being, and the failure of the court to consider the harm imposed on women in their final decision (Davidson 2014; Hamilton 2014; NWLC 2015b). In addition to the concerns for women's interests, others have focused on the court's expansion of rights for corporations (Wydra 2014). This expansion of rights, while limited in this case to closely held for-profit companies' provision of birth control under the ACA, may allow for discrimination in other instances. Concerns have been raised regarding the rights of corporations to discriminate against the LGBTQ population and single mothers in particular, as a number of states have recently pursued or adopted religious liberty laws that would protect individuals and companies from legal proceedings alleging discrimination based upon sexual orientation or activity (Parvini and Duara 2015; Stern 2015). While the full extent of these legislative developments will be examined in Chap. 6, shortly following the ruling in *Hobby Lobby*, speculation over the expansion of this protection of religious liberty was widespread (Denniston 2014; Toobin 2014).

In addition to the lawsuits brought forward by for-profit corporations such as Hobby Lobby and Conestoga Wood Specialties, another type of legal challenge was introduced by nonprofit religious organizations that were not exempt by the HHS from the required mandate. The lawsuits filed by these nonprofits, including Little Sisters of the Poor (a Catholic-run nursing home) and Wheaton College (a religious college), targeted the HHS accommodation process and forms. These religious nonprofits are not exempt from the contraception mandate, as are churches and houses of worship. The accommodation process requires religious entities, which oppose providing contraceptives within their insurance coverage and are not exempt from the HHS mandate, to notify the federal government of their request for accommodation, by filling Employee Benefits Security Administration (EBSA) form 700. The accommodation process will ensure that coverage for contraceptive services for female employees, students, and dependents will still take place, while the government would cover the costs. Thus, these employers would not have to include contraceptives under their insurance coverage, and also would not be required to directly notify the insurance company, which was argued to be a violation of religious liberty (Denniston 2014). This accommodation process was originally designed only for religious nonprofits, but, following the *Hobby Lobby* ruling, was expanded by the HHS in July 2015 to include for-profit "closely-held" corporations. Some of these organizations, however, fight against the accommodation process itself, arguing that the requirement to notify the government of their objection to providing birth control. To date, the courts have heard over 40 challenges to the accommodation, and there is speculation that the Supreme Court may hear at least one of these cases in the next term (Sobel and Salganicoff 2015).

The accommodation process, these organizations argue, does not relieve them from participation in a morally objectionable act. It is the notification itself that triggers coverage of birth control, thus the process of accommodation renders them complicit in the sinful action; as a result of signing the form, "the organization's employees receive the covered services. If this is not 'facilitating,' in a morally complicit fashion, the exact result to which the organizations object, then the word 'facilitating' has no meaning...The employees will get just what their employer wishes, for reasons of a sincere religious objection, they were not getting; they will get it by virtue of their employment with that organization; and they will get it because that employer told HHS who they were, what kind of plan they have, and who the insurance provider is. This is facilitation all the way down. The employer's actions from beginning to end are the sine qua non of the mandated coverage" (Franck 2015).

Therefore, the accommodation process is morally problematic because of the concept of complicity-based sin; in addition to engaging in the practice itself, participating in actions that lead to sinful behavior is also considered a sin. In addition to Catholics, Evangelicals and other Protestants have begun to rely on complicity-based religious objections in the provision of healthcare, increasingly using this argument to refuse compliance with certain federal and state antidiscrimination laws (Eckholm 2011; Healy 2015). The argument regarding religious opposition to complicity in the sinful acts of others, which has lately been used also in other issues such as gay marriage and adoption by same-sex couples, signifies a shift from the free exercise claims usually raised under the RFRA Act (NeJaime and Siegel 2015).

As of summer 2015, the plaintiffs' claims have been rejected in circuit courts hearing these cases. In the case of *Wheaton College v. Burwell*, the Seventh Circuit Court of Appeals determined that the college is not being "forced to allow use of its healthcare plan for emergency contraception." Rather, they are being "forced only to notify insurers (including third-party administrators), that it will not use its health plans to cover emergency contraception" (*Wheaton College v. Burwell*, No. 14-2396, 10th circuit court, July 1, 2015, at 6-7). Similarly, the Seventh Circuit Court of Appeals ruled against Notre Dame, rejecting the argument that the university was being forced to serve as a conduit for women to obtain contraceptive coverage (*Notre Dame v. Burwell*, No. 13-3853, 7th circuit court, May 19, 2015). The Tenth Circuit Court of Appeals also ruled for the government on similar grounds, in the suit brought by Little Sisters of the Poor and a number of additional Christian, nonprofit organizations. Circuit appeals courts' have also ruled against similar suits brought by East Texas Baptist University, the Archdiocese of Washington, and College of the Ozarks; further, a number of cases have been dismissed on procedural grounds, including lawsuits brought forward by Liberty University,

Franciscan University, and the American Family Association. Several appeals have been made to the Supreme Court, and it is speculated that the Supreme Court may hear a case on this issue in the next term (Sobel and Salganicoff 2015). As a number of cases remain under appeal, the issue of the accommodation process, and especially the question of what requirements are considered a violation of religious freedom, remains unsettled.

The ACA, in general, and the employer mandate, in particular, has been facing much opposition, mainly by right-wing and pro-life supporters; this opposition has led to efforts to create public policy at both the federal and state levels. This legislation is similar in nature to much of the third-party legislation introduced and enacted prior to the ACA, which focused primarily on funding restrictions for abortion and exemptions for individuals and entities that perform abortion. While the *Hobby Lobby* ruling has been considered a victory for the rights of individuals not directly involved in abortion to secure protections for their religious liberty in objecting to the practice, public policy following this ruling continues to appear similar to that which was found prior to the passage of the ACA and the court's ruling in *Hobby Lobby*. The two types of legislation—religious liberty arguments and funding restrictions—are examined below.

Religious Liberty After Hobby Lobby

Following the *Hobby Lobby* ruling, the pro-life movement began a more systematic integration of religious liberty as part of their mission. This trend, however, has yet to be manifested in legislation. In general, at both the federal and state levels, the subject of religious liberty is mentioned primarily in legislation that introduces funding restrictions to abortion or abortion-related services. At the federal level, the type of legislation introduced following the ruling in *Hobby Lobby*, during the second half of the 113th and through the 114th sessions of Congress, is similar to that found in earlier congressional sessions. These measures included fetal rights proposals (9) and women's rights (13). Of the 31 tax provisions introduced during this time period, a number of proposals included some reference to religious liberty; these include objections to the ACA based upon its failure to protect the religious or moral objections of individuals or entities, which, for example, includes insurance companies' coverage of abortion. Many of these funding bills identify the ACA as infringing upon the moral convictions of those opposed to abortion yet are forced to buy or offer policies that cover abortion. Further, one measure establishes that no individual or company would be required to purchase policies that include abortion coverage (H.R. 3020, 2015).

One resolution, H. Res. 399 introduced by Walter Jones during the 114th session of Congress, expresses support for a number of bills before the House, including H.R. 802, the First Amendment Defense Act, and H.R. 3197, the Protecting Life and Taxpayers Act of 2015. Specifically, H. Res. 399 declares that the USA was founded on Judeo-Christian values, with the Declaration of Independence acknowledging that our rights are expressly given to us by our Creator, thus taxpayer-funded abortions must be prevented as should same-sex marriage. Another example of funding restrictions on abortion is the Protecting Life and Taxpayers Act; despite the inclusion of the phrase "protecting life" in the bill's title, there is no mention of fetal rights or the sanctity of life, and the bill's content focuses only on the prohibition of federal funds from going to any entity that performs abortion (H.R. 3197, 2015).

In the years after the passage of the ACA and the *Hobby Lobby* ruling, despite the increase in state laws concerning abortion, few of these laws invoke the claims of religious liberty that have become so prominent in the public sphere. The policies that have been introduced and passed in state legislatures around the country share some traits, particularly in southern states. These policies, which often include funding restrictions, do not expressly identify religious liberty as the primary purpose or intent behind the law, as was found in several bills before Congress. While some bills concerning religious liberty were introduced, these measures primarily addressed LGBTQ rights, including same-sex marriage, adoption rights for single and same-sex couples, and employment practices involving same-sex individuals. Thus, although religious liberty is a primary component of many state laws previously enacted, and has increasingly been playing a central role in the strategy of the pro-life movement, there has not yet been a significant increase in proposals that invoke these claims. Even in the proposals that mention religious freedom—at the federal and state levels—the focus and intent is on funding restrictions, thus defining religious liberty as the freedom to not pay for these services.

Funding Restrictions Following the ACA

At the federal level, the debate over and passage of the ACA prompted a significant amount of proposals concerning insurance coverage of abortion; 50 % of all proposals between 2010 and 2015—and 58 % since the ruling in *Hobby Lobby*—focus on the protection of taxpayers through funding restrictions. A total of 25 of the 99 proposed bills dealing with federal spending and abortion concerned the ACA. Of these 25, almost all measures would impose some type of limitation—or most often, a complete restriction—on federal funding of abortion through the health exchange. Two measures—the Abortion Insurance Full Disclosure Act (H.R. 3279, 2013; S. 1848, 2013), proposed twice, and the Health Plan Notice Requirement Act (H.R. 3953, 2013)—would require the disclosure of abortion coverage in advertisements and information materials on health insurance plans.

Among the other ACA-related measures introduced during this time period, most are intended to prohibit taxpayer funds from going toward payment for abortion or any abortion-related service. These restrictions would either prohibit all multistate exchanges from including abortion in insurance coverage (2) or repeal the ACA (3) and prohibit any federal spending on abortion or related services (12). Further, all of these policies reiterate the position that no federal funds will be used for abortion, this despite the Hyde Amendment and other federal restrictions, which already prohibit federal funds from going toward abortion, in either domestic or foreign expenditures. None of these bills—to date—have been enacted.

One of the proposed bills not dealing directly with the ACA is the No Taxpayer Funding of Abortion Act, which proposes restrictions on abortion funding by the federal government. This act was introduced five times from 2010 to 2014, and received a fair amount of media coverage in the lead up to the adoption of the ACA as well as after the act was passed by the House. This law would impose many restrictions on the funding of abortion, and would alter the tax code to adjust the claims that can be made after an abortion. One clause of this measure prohibits deductions for medical expenses related to abortion unless the abortion was due to rape, incest, or in the case to save the life of the mother (H.R. 7, 2013). In one of the first iterations of this bill, there was significant controversy over the use of the term "forcible rape"; this term was heavily criticized by many women's groups, as well as female members of Congress, both Republican and Democrat. The use of this term, it has been argued, at best would create confusion and at worst, exclude some forms of rape from this legal definition, including statutory rape. The word "forcible" was removed from the bill, particularly as it was Republican women who provided the most vociferous objections to the term.

Another controversial aspect of the No Taxpayer Funding of Abortion Act concerns the restrictions on medical exemptions for expenses incurred related to abortion. In one of the hearings related to this provision of the law, it became clear that the intent of the bill is to grant authority to the IRS to determine the authenticity of claims for such deductions. Thus, under the provisions of this bill, it is the IRS that will have to decide whether there was rape, incest, and risk to the life of the mother, before determining whether the woman is eligible for tax exemption. The support for this provision of the law by many Republicans (and four Democrats) is unique given their simultaneous aversion to granting the IRS any authority to implement the ACA in the first place (Weiner 2014). In 2011, the House passed the No Taxpayer Funding of Abortion and it was then placed on the Senate calendar. To date, the bill has been referred to the Senate Finance Committee but will most likely not pass in the Senate (Peters 2014).

At the state level, legislative attempts following the passage of the ACA have been successful in passing funding restrictions for the coverage of non-therapeutic abortion services. These restrictions have been complemented by a number of prohibitions that were already in place prior to the ACA, restricting funding for abortions at the state level. These existing restrictions include limits on private insurance coverage of abortion and Medicaid spending. Prior to passage of the ACA, four states prohibited private insurance coverage of abortion, and had limits on Medicaid funding for abortion, allowing Medicaid funding for abortions only in cases of rape, incest, and when the life of the mother is at risk. An additional 29 states plus Washington DC had limits on Medicaid funding of abortion, providing funds only for those cases in which the state is legally required to provide coverage. These laws continue to be implemented after the passage of the ACA, maintaining the same restrictions on Medicaid funding. In addition, following the passage of the ACA, 6 states adopted restrictions on private insurance coverage of nontherapeutic abortions and 25 states banned coverage by insurance companies in the state exchange. To date, there are 16 states that have no limits on coverage of abortion; prior to passage of the ACA, 17 states had no limits on coverage. While there is a significant increase in the number of funding restrictions, they are largely the same states that continue to adopt more limitations and prohibitions on funding.

4   Conclusion

The ACA was and remains a controversial piece of legislation, particularly for conservatives. While there were numerous facets of the bill that contributed to this disagreement over the legislation, the contraception mandate was one of the primary issues of concern for conservatives. The case of *Hobby Lobby* has brought the debate over the rights of third-party actors to the forefront of the public debate over abortion. While the rights of third-party actors have been addressed through public policy since 1973, this case brought attention to an actor that has rarely been the focus of pro-life activists and organizations' strategy to limit or restrict access to abortion.

In general, pro-life third-party legislation follows libertarian principles; it is based on the conceptualization of rights—including religious liberty and reproductive rights—as negative rights. The role of the government, according to this legislation, is to protect the freedom of individuals to exercise their rights, but without significant intervention or regulation that imposes requirements on others. This libertarian nature of the third-party legislation is evident even in the few cases when the justification for the legislation includes more conservative language. While this language, which includes arguments against certain values and behaviors that legitimize abortion, may be conservative, the legislation is nevertheless libertarian in nature; it emphasizes the rights of individuals—as taxpayers—to limit their financial support of the practices they oppose. In addition, and despite the moral opposition included in the legislation in some cases, the measures neither prevent others from having an abortion nor call for an increase in regulation that will limit abortions. Instead, the legislation is based on the idea of personal decision and independence, ideas that are very different from the legislation—as well as discourse—that characterizes the fetus-centered and women-centered strategy.

The relative success of funding restrictions explains the continuous use—and even increase—in the number of measures addressing this type of legislation. At the same time, however, in light of the success of third-party legislation, including conscience clauses, it is surprising to find that in the last few years, there has been little legislative focus on religious liberty. This dearth of public policy attempts also seems to conflict with the increase in public support for the need to respect religious liberty arguments when they contradict right claims by some groups (Lipka 2015). Nevertheless, despite the limited legislation addressing religious freedom, the years since the ACA and the *Hobby Lobby* ruling are characterized by a shift in pro-life discourse, which has been increasingly focusing on arguments of religious liberty, emphasizing this right as natural right of individuals, who have the right to be protected by the government from coercion. The analysis of this shift, and its accordance with the legislation, is the focus of Chap. 5.

References

Abcarian R. The craziest thing about the Supreme Court's hobby lobby decision. Los Angeles Times. 2015 Sept 1.

American College of Obstetricians and Gynecologists (ACOG). Committee opinion: access to contraception. Committee on Healthcare for Underserved Women no. 615. Jan 2015.

Armstrong C. ACOG recommendations on emergency contraception. Am Fam Physician. 2010;82(10):1278.

Barot S. Abortion restrictions in U.S. foreign aid: the history and harms of the helms amendment. Guttmacher Policy Rev. 2013;16(3).

Blow CM. Religious freedom vs. individual equality. The New York Times. 2015 April 1.

Boonstra H. The heart of the matter: public funding of abortion for poor women in the United States. Guttmacher Policy Rev. 2007;10(1).

Boonstra H. Insurance coverage of abortion: beyond the exceptions for life endangerment, rape and incest. Guttmacher Policy Rev. 2013;16(3).

Cerf M, Huq A, Mentovich A. Do Americans think corporations have the right to religious freedom? Slate. 2014 July 1. http://www.slate.com/articles/news_and_politics/jurisprudence/2014/07/do_americans_think_corporations_have_the_right_to_religious_freedom.html. Accessed 22 July 2015.

C.H. Aborted, once more. The Economist. 2014 Jun 30.

Cincotta R, Crane B. Public health—the Mexico City policy and US family planning assistance. Science. 2001;294:525–6.

Cohen IG, Lynch HF, Curfman GD. When religious freedom clashes with access to care. N Engl J Med. 2014;371(7):596–9.

Collins M. Conscience clauses and oral contraceptives: conscientious objection or calculated obstruction? Annals of Health Law 2006;15(1): 37-60.

Crouch A. Life together, again: after hobby lobby, vibrant corporate life is needed more than ever. Christianity Today. 2014 Sept 2.

Davidson R. Hobby lobby decision jeopardizes women's right to equal health care. League of Women Voters. 2014 Jun 6.

Denniston L. Analysis: the little sisters case and EBSA form 700. SCOTUSblog. 2014 Jan 4. http://www.scotusblog.com/2014/01/analysis-the-little-sisters-case-and-ebsa-form-700/. Accessed 13 July 2015.

Dubow S. 'A constitutional right rendered utterly meaningless': religious exemptions and reproductive politics, 1973–2014. J Policy Hist. 2015;27(1):1–35.

Duvall M. Pharmacy conscience clause statutes: constitutional religious 'accommodations' or unconstitutional 'substantial burdens' on women? Am Univ Law Rev. 2006;55:1485–522.

Eckholm E. Anti-abortion groups are split on legal tactics. The New York Times. 2011 December 4.

Eichelberger E, Redden M. In hobby lobby, the Supreme Court chooses religious over science. Mother Jones. 2014 June 30.

Epps G. Should corporations have the same religious freedoms as people? The Atlantic. 2014 Mar 25.

Feder, Jennifer. The history and effect of abortion conscience clause laws. Congressional Research Service: The Library of Congress. 2005:CRS 1–CRS 5.

Federal Register. Coverage of certain preventive services under the affordable care act. Final rules. Department of Health and Human Services. 2013;78(127): 39870–99.

Finer L, Frohwirth LF, Dauphinee LA, Singh S, Moore AM. Timing and of steps and reasons for delays in obtaining abortions in the United States. Contraception. 2006;74:334–44.

Franck MJ. Fifth circuit taken in by HHS peek-a-boo. National Review. 2015 June 23.

Gray J. House votes plan to curb international abortion aid. The New York Times. 1997 Sept 5.

Gruson L. Decade of Rep. Smith: fluke to tactician. The New York Times. 1991 Aug 10.

Grossman CL. What's abortifacient? Disputes over birth control fuel obamacare fight. The Washington Post. 2014 Jan 28.

Hamilton M. A federal judge upholds the women's health regulations of the affordable care act against a free exercise of religion challenge. Justia. 2014 Oct 4.

Healy J. States weigh gay marriage, rights and cake. The New York Times. 2015 July 7.

Health and Human Services (HHS). Enrollment in the health insurance marketplace totals over 8 million people. 2014. http://www.hhs.gov/news/press/2014pres/05/20140501a.html. Accessed 18 July 2015.

Jones R, Jarman J. Abortion incidence and service availability in the United States, 2011. Perspectives on Sexual and Reproductive Health. 2014; 46(1): 3-14.

Jost T. Court's won't void the affordable care act over semantics. The Washington Post. 2014 July 9.

Keller B. Conscience of a corporation. The New York Times. 2013 Feb 10.

Khazan O. Can an abortion be undone? The Atlantic. 2015 Mar 27.

Khazan O. Pro-lifers' existential crisis. The Atlantic. 2014 Nov 7.

Lake Research Partners. Catholics and birth control coverage. 2012 Feb 7. http://www.lakeresearch.com/news/Catholics%20and%20birth%20control.Lake%20Research%20Partners.pdf.

Lipka M. Americans split over whether businesses must serve same-sex couples. The Pew Research. 2015 Mar 30.

Liptak A. Birth control order deepens divide among justices. The New York Times. 2014 Jul 3.

Lipton-Lubet S. Contraceptive coverage under the affordable care act: dueling narratives and their policy implications. J Gend Soc Policy Law. 2014;22(2):343–85.

Luchenitser AJ. A new era of inequality? Hobby Lobby and religious exemptions from anti-discrimination laws. Harv Law Policy Rev. 2015;9(1):63–88.

Mayo Clinic Staff. Morning-after pill. The Mayo Clinic. 2015 Apr 14. http://www.mayoclinic.org/tests-procedures/morning-after-pill/basics/definition/prc-20012891. Accessed 18 July 2015.

National Women's Law Center (NWLC). Supplemental insurance coverage of abortion only further encourages the end of all private insurance coverage of abortion. 2013 Dec. http://www.nwlc.org/sites/default/files/pdfs/supp_ins_covg_abortion_factsheet_12-6-13.pdf. Accessed 9 Aug 2015.

NeJaime D, Siegel R. Conscience wars: complicity-based conscience claims in religion and politics. Yale Law J. 2015;124:2516–91.

Parker A. 'Corporations are people,' Romney tells Iowa hecklers angry over his tax policy. The New York Times. 2011 Aug 11.

Parvini S, Nigel Duara. In conservative Indiana, bemusement over amid boycotts over religious freedom law. Los Angeles Times. 2015 Apr 1.

Pear R. Obama administration says birth control mandate applies to religious groups that insure themselves. The New York Times. 2012 Mar 16.

Peters JW. House votes to restrict payments for abortions. The New York Times. 2014 Jan 28.

Randall S. *Health Care Reform and Abortion*, Berkeley Women's L.J. 1994;9(1): 58-76.L

Rucker P. Mitt Romney says 'corporations are people.' The Washington Post. 2011 Aug 11.

Salganicoff A, Barbara W, Usha R. Emergency contraception in California. The Henry J. Kaiser Family Foundation. 2004 Feb.

Sax JK. Access to prescription drugs: a normative economic approach to pharmacist conscience clause legislation. Me Law Rev. 2010;63(1):82–122.

Schiff A. The supreme court still thinks corporations are people. The Atlantic. 2012 July 18.

Section 401(b) of the health programs extension act. An abortive attempt by congress to solve a constitutional dilemma. 1975;17(2): 303-31.

Sekulow J. Hobby Lobby case—three reasons why corporations must have religious freedom. FoxNews.com. 2014 Mar 25. http://www.foxnews.com/opinion/2014/03/25/hobby-lobby-case-three-reasons-why-corporations-must-have-religious-freedom.html. Accessed 29 Jun 2015.

Shapiro I. Symposium: mandates make martyrs out of corporate owners. SCOTUSblog. 2014 Feb 24. http://www.scotusblog.com/2014/02/symposium-mandates-make-martyrs-out-of-corporate-owners/. Accessed 20 July 2015.

Smearman C. Drawing the line: the legal, ethical and public policy implications of refusal clauses for pharmacists. Ariz Law Rev. 2006;48:469–540.

Sobel L, Salganicoff A. Round 2 on the legal challenges to contraceptive coverage: are nonprofits 'substantially burdened' by the 'accommodation'? The Kaiser Family Foundation. 22 July 2015

Sonfield A. Rights vs responsibilities: professional standards and provider refusals. Guttmacher Rep Public Policy. 2005;8(3).

Stein R. Pharmacists' rights at front of new debate: because of beliefs, some refuse to fill birth control prescriptions. The Washington Post. 2005 Mar 28.

Stern MJ. Immoral convictions. Slate. 2015 July 23.

Taub JS. Is Hobby Lobby a tool for limiting corporate constitutional rights? Const Comment. 2015;30:403–63.

The Guttmacher Institute. An overview of minor's consent law. State policies in brief. 2015a. Accessed 1 Aug 2015.

The Guttmacher Institute. An overview of state abortion laws. State Policies in Brief. 2015b. Accessed 1 Aug 2015.

The Guttmacher Institute. Emergency contraception. State Policies in Brief. 2015c. Accessed 1 Aug 2015.

The Guttmacher Institute. Requirements for ultrasound. State Policies in Brief. 2015d. Accessed 1 Aug 2015.

The Kaiser Family Foundation. State-by-state estimates of the number of people eligible for premium tax credits under the affordable care act. 2013 Nov 5. http://kff.org/health-reform/issue-brief/state-by-state-estimates-of-the-number-of-people-eligible-for-premium-tax-credits-under-the-affordable-care-act/.

The Kaiser Family Foundation. State health insurance marketplace types, 2015. 2015b. http://kff.org/health-reform/state-indicator/state-health-insurance-marketplace-types/.

The Kaiser Family Foundation. Preventive services covered by private health plans under the affordable care act. 2015a June 11. http://kff.org/health-reform/fact sheet/preventive-services-covered-by-private-health-plans/. Accessed 30 July 2015

Toobin J. Supreme court rulings: it's GOP v democrats. CNN. 2014 Jun 30.

Totenberg N. When did companies become people? Excavating the legal evolution. NPRorg. 2014 July 28. http://wwwnprorg/2014/07/28/335288388/when-did-companies-become-people-excavating-the-legal-evolution. Accessed 23 July 2015.

Uttley L, Sheila R, Lorraine K, Louise M. Miscarriage of medicine: the growth of catholic hospitals and threat to reproductive care. American Civil Liberties Union and Merger Watch. 2013 Dec. https://www.acluorg/sites/default/files/field_document/growth-of-catholic-hospitals-2013pdf. Accessed 30 July 2015.

Wardle L. Protection of healthcare providers' rights of conscience in American law: present, past, and future. Ave Maria Law Rev. 2010;9(1):1–46.

Weber T. Hobby Lobby symposium: the exercise of religion is inseparable from human activity—including supporting one's family. SCOTUSblog. 2014 Jun 30. http://www.scotusblogcom/2014/06/hobby-lobby-symposium-the-exercise-of-religion-is-inseparable-from-human-activity-including-supporting-ones-family/. Accessed 20 July 2015.

Weiner J. Should the IRS decide whether a woman has been raped? The Washington Post. 2014 Jan 22.

World Health Organization (WHO). Emergency contraception. Fact Sheet No. 244. July 2012. http://www.who.int/mediacentre/factsheets/fs244/en.

Wydra E. Playing politics with the supreme court over Obamacare. The Huffington Post. 2014 Oct 23.

CHAPTER 5

Between Conservatism and Libertarianism: Pro-life Strategy After the ACA

1 INTRODUCTION

The passage of the ACA, and in particular the debate over the employer mandate as examined in the *Hobby Lobby* case, has influenced both the right-wing arguments over religious liberty and the strategy of the pro-life movement. The current strategy of the movement emphasizes not only the importance of protecting the life of the fetus and the rights of the mother but also the protection of an individual's liberty and autonomy, specifically the right to remain free from government interference. Contraceptive services, pro-life activists argue, are a private matter and not a social good. Thus, the HHS mandate represents a violation of an individual's freedom and religious liberty, requiring employers to pay for reproductive services that should be the responsibility of the individuals themselves. While the ruling focuses specifically on religious liberty, the discourse extends this claim beyond the individuals with a religious objection to contraception. Instead, this framing is used today by conservatives and libertarians to claim that every American should be fearful of a usurpation of individual rights and religious liberty by government forces.[1]

Although the topic of religious liberty may seem conservative in nature, the framing of religion in this case is not as a compass of social norms

---

[1] For example, similar arguments that classify religious liberty as a private matter appear in the right-wing arguments against same-sex marriage, discussed further in Chap. 6.

© The Editor(s) (if applicable) and The Author(s) 2016
A. Von Hagel, D. Mansbach, *Reproductive Rights in the Age of Human Rights*, DOI 10.1057/978-1-137-53952-6_5

and morality—as the conservative approach believes—but, rather, as an individual decision and belief, which should not be compromised by government intervention. This approach to religion, which better fits libertarian conceptualization of religious liberty, allows the pro-life movement to argue that it is protecting everyone—not only those who are religious or support pro-life policy—from government actions that interfere with citizens' beliefs and ideologies. As such, this strategy does not emphasize moral or scientific claims, which can easily be challenged by nonbelievers or new scientific research. Also, it does not explicitly call on individuals to change or rethink their moral positions regarding abortion. Instead, this strategy emphasizes the need to respect and protect other people's beliefs, regardless of your own opinion about the practice or its morality. Thus, this latest iteration of the pro-life strategy sees government intervention in supporting women's access to abortion as deeply problematic, especially as the marketplace should remain free from excessive government entanglement.

While these arguments appear in both the pro-life discourse and legislation, the manifestation of the religious argument in these two categories differs. With regard to the pro-life discourse, the focus on third-party actors and their right to religious liberty in the debate over reproductive rights represents a significant shift as compared to previous eras in which the focus centered only on the fetus and mothers. While arguments of religious liberty are now employed more often in the discourse, and have been increasingly accepted within the general public, bills addressing moral or religious objections to abortion remain similar in nature to those introduced and enacted in earlier time periods. For example, the Taxpayer Conscience Protection Act is intended to require each state to publish an online report as well as report to the Secretary of HHS the number of abortions performed in the state with the use of federal funds. This report must provide a "specification of the purpose for which the payment was made" and how much money was expended on each procedure (H.R. 489, 2015). This bill is similar in nature to other reporting requirements imposed on abortion providers, which are most commonly found at the state level. Further, the Health Care Conscience Rights Act would permit any individual or insurance company opposed to abortion for religious or moral reasons to not purchase or offer coverage that includes abortion (H.R. 940, 2015). This bill, while specific to the insurance mandate under the ACA passed in 2010, is similar in nature to many other proposals that seek to limit public funding of abortion. Although the pro-life discourse has shifted substantially since the *Hobby Lobby* ruling, thus far the legislative strategy among pro-life public officials remains similar to previous years. With the shift in discourse, it is the pro-life discourse and public policy outcomes that have both increasingly become more libertarian in nature.

This chapter analyzes the most recent developments in the pro-life strategy, focusing mainly on its manifestation in the discourse. The first section introduces the framing of the discourse following the *Hobby Lobby* case, based on the legal and public discussion of the ruling. This framing defines the debate as centered on the need to protect individual liberties, with specific emphasis on religious liberty. The second section examines the use of this discourse by the pro-life movement, analyzing the characteristics of this new discourse, as well as the way in which the argument of religious liberty has been used by the movement to expand its base of support. The final section examines the implications of this new strategy, arguing that it transforms the concept of religious liberty, and challenges the separation between contraceptive services and abortion. Regarding right-wing politics, this new strategy turns away from the interventionist approach of the women-centered strategy, instead focusing on legislation and discourse that are almost completely libertarian.

The first two sections in this chapter are based mainly on an analysis of the discourse of pro-life activists as well as organizations and leaders involved in the fight over religious liberty. This data covers a short period; while Hobby Lobby filed suit in US district court in September 2012, the public attention to this case increased after November 2013, when the Supreme Court agreed to hear the case. However, only in the spring and summer of 2014, before and after the ruling in the case, the public discourse, as well as attention of pro-life and religious freedom activists, turned to this case. Due to the limited period covered, the analysis of the pro-life discourse is not based on quantitative data, but rather on analyses of newspaper items (including *The New York Times*, *The Washington Post*, and *Touchstone*), blogs (pro-life blogs as well as some that focus on the Supreme Court), pro-life websites, and other forms of online communication and networking such as Twitter. These sources, while unable to provide exact numbers or concretely demonstrate shifts within the discourse, are nevertheless able to highlight the main trends and arguments that appear within the pro-life discourse, as well as scholarly research on the topic.

2   RELIGIOUS LIBERTY IN THE AFTERMATH OF HOBBY LOBBY

The *Hobby Lobby* case has been conceptualized by supporters of the ruling as a struggle over the right to religious liberty, which should not be controlled or limited by the government. The discourse surrounding the case, and to a lesser extent also the legislation, framed the ruling as a triumph not only for those who support protecting individual's religious freedom but also to any person who aims to ensure the freedom of individuals to follow their own beliefs and values. This framing has largely superseded the legal facts of the case, in which this freedom is granted only to "closely-held" corporations. The result of this account of the ruling is that the religious liberty discourse expands the number of subjects whose rights are in need of protection, allowing the pro-life movement to define themselves as protectors of rights of conscience of all Americans. As in the case of the previous discourses, this new discourse complements, rather than replaces, the fetus-centered and women-centered strategies.

Following the ruling, Barbara Green, the cofounder of Hobby Lobby, stated,

> Our family is overjoyed by the Supreme Court's decision. Today the nation's highest court has re-affirmed the vital importance of religious liberty as one of our country's founding principles. The Court's decision is a victory, not just for our family business, but for all who seek to live out their faith. We are grateful to God and to those who have supported us on this difficult journey (Berry 2014).

This quote includes some of the arguments that have become central in the framing of the *Hobby Lobby* case by its supporters. In her statement, Green frames the case as a struggle between religious liberty, which is a natural right of individuals and one of the most important human rights, and the aim of institutions—specifically the government—to control and limit this right. The ruling, according to this account, should be understood as a victory for individuals and families—rather than corporations—whose religious beliefs are central to their everyday lives, thus shaping all their interactions, including the economic ones. In the statement sent to the HHS by the Family Research Council in 2011, as part of their opposition to the draft for the employer mandate, Monahan and Gacek also argue that the mandate "will deny many Americans a most basic right: freedom from government interference in religious and moral matters" (2011).

The Becket Fund for Religious Liberty, and the role that it has played in the case, has influenced the conceptualization of the lawsuit as a struggle over religious liberty and against governmental control. The Becket Fund, which represented Hobby Lobby as well as other organizations in similar lawsuits, was established in the 1990s as a legal and educational institute aiming to preserve religion as a natural right. The Fund has been paramount in the fight against the HHS requirement that nonexempt organizations comply with the employer mandate, as well as against the accommodation process for organizations exempt from the mandate. These legal cases, while focusing on the requirement to provide certain contraceptives, are not about any specific contraceptive device or even abortion. Instead, as William Thierfelder, who was involved in the first lawsuit against the federal government over the HHS mandate, states, "as much as we're focused on contraception, that's just a detail in a fundamental problem, which is about religious liberty. This is about First Amendment rights, rights of conscience" (Kliff 2012).

The understanding of this case as a struggle for religious liberty and against the attempt of the government to limit religious freedom of individuals has been evident also by demonstrators and pro-life activists during the months of the trial. The signs held up by pro-lifers during these demonstrations included slogans such as "Stand Up for Religious Freedom" and "Women for Religious Freedom."[2] The rallies during this period were meant "to get people to wake up, to really pay attention to what's going on in this country because we are losing our religious freedom" (Henshaw 2013). While the legal case focuses on corporations, groups for religious liberty emphasized that all Americans are facing the same threats; the mandate

> will deny many Americans a most basic right: freedom from government interference in religious and moral matters. As a result many religious businesses or non-profit organizations, as well as Americans with insurance in the individual market, will be forced to violate their consciences on the issues they hold most profoundly...Individuals will be unable to purchase health plans without contraceptive and sterilization procedures (Monahan and Gacek 2011).

---

[2] While some activists focused on religious freedom, others continued to argue for the fetus-centered and women-centered arguments, using signs such as "Life Counts" and "Pro-Life is Pro-Woman."

The demonstrations, one activist clarified during a rally, are crucial since people must wake up and realize that "we are losing our religious freedom" (Henshaw 2013), which is "one of our most cherished rights" (Berry 2014).

In this discourse, the ruling, while examining the rights of closely held corporations, defined individuals as the bearers of the right to religious freedom; the employer mandate, according to this account, violates the religious liberties of individuals who own the corporation in question. The framing of the case as an attempt to protect the rights of individuals and their families to exercise their right to religious freedom also appears in the case; the ruling referred specifically to the Green family (31 times), and the Hahn family (36 times). It also included a discussion of the implication of limiting religious freedom for "family businesses," "family-run" and "family-owned" businesses. The framing of this case may seem different from the legal question, which focuses on the applicability of the RFRA toward for-profit organizations. However, a corporation, according to this account, is merely "a form of organization used by human beings to achieve desired ends," and the extension of rights to corporations allows us "to protect the rights of these people" (576 U.S. ___, at 18). It is thus impossible to separate the rights of corporations from the rights of the people who won them, at least in the case of closely held corporations. As a result, the rights of corporations are not limited only to economic rights or to freedoms regarding the operation of the market. Instead, like persons, corporations are eligible for all rights of individuals, since imposing requirements and restrictions—such as in the case of the employer mandate—is a violation of the rights of the people who own the business, rather than of some vague business entity without religious beliefs or other rights. Thus, the ruling "is a victory for common-sense as pro-life Americans do not lose their First Amendment freedoms when they open a family business or when they value unborn life" (Americans United for Life 2014).

The rights of individuals, according to this account, are violated by governmental restrictions on businesses, which in practice limit the freedom of individuals to work and provide for their families. The employer mandate, according to this account, requires individuals to separate between their work and faith. However, as Justice Kennedy states, "religious exercise includes 'the right to express those beliefs and to establish one's religious (or nonreligious) self-definition in the political, civic, and economic life of our larger community,' including how one makes a living" (Weber 2014). This means that it is impossible to "leave your faith at home." Since this separation is impossible, the result of the employer mandate, or any other type of regulation that determines what people need to do as employers or workers, is that people of faith are required to choose between their work and their belief. And if they want to continue operating their businesses and providing for their families, they are in practice forced to compromise their religious and ideological beliefs. Within this context, John Seago, Texas Right to Life Legislative Director, stated, the Supreme Court ruling is a victory for the right to work and provide for your family; the court "has protected Pro-Life business owners from being forced to violate their moral convictions" (Texas Right to Life 2014). The ruling thus should not be seen as ensuring the right of religious freedom for corporations but, instead, as protecting the right of all Americans. No one—including job creators who, according to Alliance Defending Freedom, are often targeted by this administration—should "lose their religious freedom simply because they choose to organize a business" (Berry 2014).

The argument that corporations are built around a group of individuals, and that they include within them their beliefs and values, is promoted by the claim that corporations—and especially those that are closely held—are not merely tools for profit making. Instead, supporters of the *Hobby Lobby* ruling argue, companies reflect the values and beliefs of their owners, thus defining limitations on their operation as limitations on their owners. This violation is particularly evident in the operation of the Hobby Lobby chain; since its founding, "the Greens have managed their company in accordance with their Christian principles. For example, Hobby Lobby closes on Sunday, doesn't sell shot glasses, takes out ads suggesting that readers seek Jesus, and refuses to 'back-haul' beer on its trucks, foregoing considerable profits" (Shapiro 2014). The way their company is managed is part of who they are, and

> it is impossible for the Greens and the Hahns to simply shut down beliefs which have long guided their lives from the very core of their being. To ask them to deny these beliefs simply denies their humanity. In holding that closely held for-profit corporations can exercise religion, the Court simply recognizes the inseparable nature of religion from informing all areas of a person's life (Weber 2014).

Therefore, the case for religious freedom of corporations "does not start with, 'Does the corporation pray?' or 'Does the corporation go to heaven?' said Kyle Duncan, general counsel of the Becket Fund for

Religious Liberty…'It starts with the owner.' For owners who have woven religious practice into their operations, he told me, 'an exercise of religion in the context of a business' is still an exercise of religion, and thus constitutionally protected" (Keller 2013). It is thus impossible—and undesirable—to attempt and separate between the owners and their companies.[3]

Since these businesses act in a way that reflects the moral and religious beliefs of their owners, the intervention of the government should be understood as an attempt to impose liberal and secular values on religious people, in particular, and the American public, in general. This argument, which is more conservative in nature than other arguments found in the discourse, is that the employer mandate is based on the assumption that "contraceptives must be provided, especially to young people, who are expected to 'explore their sexuality'; and abortion must be provided for those who are insufficiently cautious" (Hitchcock 2011). That means that, "Obamacare isn't only about guaranteeing access to insurance. Obamacarians want to use the centralized regulatory control imposed by Obamacare as a cudgel to impose their cultural values" (Smith 2015). In order to promote these values, "religious freedom—our first and oldest liberty—is being 'balanced' against a 'right' created, historically speaking, mere moments ago, a 'right' to free contraceptives" (Sekulow 2014). This debate is thus framed as between two conflicting systems of values and beliefs, in which the aim of one side is to impose their ideology on the other side, while the other side is interested in living their lives according to their own values of freedom and liberty. In this context, it is clear that "the battle to preserve religious liberty 'in all areas of life' may be 'the civil rights movement of this decade,'" comparing the *Hobby Lobby* case to the Birmingham bus boycott (Keller 2013). As Rick Warren, an evangelical pastor, argues, "every American who loves freedom should shudder at the precedent the government is trying to establish by denying Hobby Lobby the full protection of the First Amendment. This case is nothing less than a landmark battle for America's FIRST freedom, the freedom of religion

---

[3] While the argument about the link between the individual and the business is central to the discourse, the legal aspect of this link is more complex; "Perhaps the most significant problem with this 'look to the people behind the corporation' argument is that it is in some tension with corporate law. One of the purposes of the formal, separate entity in corporate law is precisely to permit courts to disregard those human beings behind the corporate form" (Piety 2015: 113).

and the freedom from government intervention in matters of conscience" (The Becket Fund 2013).[4]

Following this account, supporters of the *Hobby Lobby* ruling argue that the government's attempt to control and limit people's religious liberty should concern all Americans who believe in this right; "This is not just a Catholic issue...This issue should matter to anyone who believes there is room in the public square for people of all faiths—not just those faiths that pass some government test" (Wuerl 2012). Furthermore, these actions reflect a general tendency of the government to intervene in personal issues, and limit liberties—not only religious liberties—through regulations and requirements. The employer mandate is just a reflection of the larger problem; "The notion that the government can decide which religious beliefs are important enough to protect exemplifies the dangers of 'big government'" (Sligh and Rocklin 2015). Therefore, even individuals who do not support the pro-life mission, or have no religious affiliation, need to worry about the employer mandate, and the type of intervention that this requirement signals; "In America, the rightness and legality of government control has become the default position, from which people now must try to find refuge in some provision of the Bill of Rights. The owners of Hobby Lobby were like Dickens' Oliver Twist, in effect begging, 'Please sir, may I have an exception?'" (Leef 2014).

While the case represents the risk in big government, in particular it highlights the danger in a government that tries to intervene and control the market; "If the United States government can force the people running a corporation to use corporate resources to provide free abortion-pills to employees (especially when contraceptives are cheap and widely available on the open market), it is difficult to imagine the meaningful limits on government power in the marketplace" (Sekulow 2014). The intervention of the state in the marketplace is dangerous because it limits the ability of the market to operate freely, without regulations and requirements. It also prevents individuals from acting as rational agents, who can make their own decisions regarding their interests and preferences. Following this understanding of the market, not only that requiring employers to provide abortifacients is a

[4] The HHS justifies the employer mandate—the inclusion of all FDA-approved forms of a birth control in the list of basic, preventive services required at no cost—as an attempt to ensure equality for women, through prohibiting the exclusion of these services by employers and insurance plans. Further, the requirement to cover these preventive services is designed to keep costs low as well as promote general health and well-being (HHS Website 2013).

violation of their religious liberty, but also this requirement does not make sense; as long as there is a market for abortifacients, and people who are willing to sell them, there is no need for government regulations to provide them. These employers do not prevent women from using contraceptives, thus "employees of these corporations who want access to contraception are free to pay for it on their own, or they can find other employers who cover contraception" ("Faith and Rights: A Test for the Justices" 2014). Since the employer mandate is meant to provide something that is available in the open market, it is not designed to ensure a right. Instead, the ACA and the employer mandate are "the high-water mark of an outdated liberalism, the latest attempt to impose upon Americans a Euro-style bureaucracy to manage all aspects of their lives" (Berg 2015: 104).

This case thus positions the rights of individuals—who happen to own businesses and employ other people—as in opposition to government control and intervention, which is meant to impose certain sets of values and ideas and to restrict freedom. Ensuring the rights of employers, according to this account, can be done without harming women, who can access contraceptives through other means (Berg 2015; Gedicks 2015; Sepper 2015). Working, as an employee or an employer, is not merely a tool for providing for your family. Instead, it is a sphere of freedom and self-expression, which must be free from regulations and requirements in order to respect the rights of people. In this context, the mission of the pro-life movement is to defend rights—religious liberty, but also any other attempt on threat to freedom and self-expression—and to protect individuals from government actions meant to violate these rights. These arguments are now central in the pro-life strategy, changing and expanding the debate over reproductive rights.

3   Pro-life Discourse and Strategy

The ruling in *Hobby Lobby*, and more generally the passage of the ACA, has transformed the pro-life strategy in several ways. Following the framing of the ruling as a triumph of individual rights against government intervention, the pro-life discourse started focusing more on the rights of third-party actors that are defended by the pro-life mission. This shift introduces three main changes to the previous pro-life strategies. First, the focus on religious liberty introduces the interests of third-party actors into the abortion debate. As shown in Chap. 4, pro-life legislation has been protecting the rights of health-care providers and taxpayers for decades.

However, and despite the relative success of this legislation, the pro-life discourse rarely focused on these subjects or arguments. Instead, it emphasized the rights of the subjects directly involved in this process—the fetus, the mother, and sometimes the father—focusing not only on changing public opinion on abortion but also on women themselves.

In addition to the introduction of third-party actors into the pro-life discourse, the strategy following *Hobby Lobby* also expands the number—as well as the type—of actors who are considered to be part of the debate. So far the legislation of religious exemptions focused on third-party actors who are considered to be active participants in the process of abortion, such as physicians, pharmacists, and some insurance providers. While the scope and requirements for exemptions depend on the state, in all cases the exemption is to address the problem; that is, as part of their work, these professionals may be required to be involved in the act of performing or facilitating others to have an abortion, by performing the surgery, and providing medications, counseling, or referrals. In case this involvement violates their religious beliefs, they are eligible for these exemptions, freeing them from the need to choose between their profession and their religion. In the case of institutions such as HMOs, the requirement for religious exemptions is even more limited; in addition to their focus on health-care services, in order to be eligible for exemptions, these institutions have usually been expected to have an institutional religious affiliation.

Employers, however, are neither directly involved in the abortion procedure, nor are they in the health-care profession. While employers might be more similar to taxpayers, the justification for funding restrictions is often different; although these restrictions aim to protect taxpayers who might oppose abortion, the legislation is rarely framed in religious terms, and it is not based on an examination of the individual's objection. Instead, it is justified more as a personal matter that the public should not be involved in funding. Thus, the current third-party discourse merges these two different actors and their arguments; it is based on the argument for religious protections, emphasizing exemptions for individuals who have religious objection to abortion. At the same time, it focuses on employers who do not directly participate in the abortion procedure, or in the decision-making process. Therefore, it moves assertions of complicity from a first-person to a third-person perspective.

By merging these two types of arguments, the discourse is expanded, and it now includes employers as a group that deserves to have the right to refuse, this in order to protect them from the requirement to provide insurance policies that cover contraceptive services. This expansion is justified on the grounds that employers play a role in the process of abortion; by providing an insurance that covers these services, they are "complying in sin."[5] This account, which argues that the employer participates in some way in the abortion process by providing such insurance, is based on a positive concept of money. While a negative concept of money refers to the transferring merely as an economic transaction, a positive concept is based on the idea that the transferor of money has some responsibility to the way it is being used, as in the case of boycott (Stolzenberg 2014).[6] Therefore, it is the transfer of money, which may indirectly result in women receiving contraceptive services that the employer deems abortifacients that makes the employer eligible for religious exemption. One result of this expansion is the increase in the number of individuals whose rights and preferences should be considered before allowing, or providing, an abortion. The inclusion of a more diverse array of individuals in the process of decision-making affects the centrality of women's interests in this discourse over rights and access.

The second change in this pro-life discourse is the broadening of the type of rights that are at the center of pro-life concern; the pro-life mission is protecting religious liberty and, more generally, all individual rights and freedoms that are threatened by the government. The discourse on the religious liberty of employers frames their operation in the market as a personal issue, which should not be regulated by the government. Women, however, are not harmed by this approach since reproductive decisions are also a private matter, which should be neither regulated nor paid for by the state or by any other actors besides the subject herself. Therefore, the ruling, as well as any exemptions given to people based on religious belief, does not harm women:

> For all the 'war on women' rhetoric and venom spewing over the recent *Burwell v. Hobby Lobby* ruling, it's prudent to examine what this week's ruling doesn't do. It does not: 1. restrict women's access to contraceptives;

---

[5] Another issue that is raised by some authors but not fully developed here is the argument that complicity-based claims are not well developed or explained, thus making it difficult to distinguish between legitimate and illegitimate arguments on this issue (Sepinwall 2015).

[6] Stolzenberg argues that positive concept of money is linked with positive concepts of rights. In this case, however, the positive concept of money is accompanied by a negative concept of rights, framing liberty as the freedom from, and the responsibility of the government to protect—rather than provide—this freedom (2014).

2. restrict women's access to miscarriage-inducing abortifacient drugs; 3. restrict women's access to abortions. The only thing being restricted is the federal government's power to force some employers, morally opposed to certain types of birth control, from having to pay for that birth control under Obamacare. That's all (*Augusta Chronicle* Editorial Staff 2014).

The argument that women are not harmed—and even benefit—from this regulation appears within the pro-life discourse, although less frequently than the argument of religious liberty as applied to third-party actors. Women, according to this account, benefit since defining reproductive rights as a personal matter protects their liberty and freedom through the limitation on government to regulate or limit their reproductive options;

> For many feminists, mandatory birth control coverage is probably less about money than about principle: establishing that a woman's right to control her fertility is so fundamental that its exercise should be fully guaranteed by the government. But there is another, libertarian feminist way to look at this issue: the view that it's hypocritical for women to tell the state, 'Keep your laws off my body!' and then demand laws that make the state underwrite your reproductive choices (Young 2014).

Therefore, women also benefit from this libertarian appeal, which limits public intervention in reproductive choices altogether. Following this argument, pro-life activists argue that the *Hobby Lobby* ruling, and more generally, legislation that limits the control of government on reproductive decisions, should be embraced by pro-choice supporters.

While the pro-choice movement objects to the validity and veracity of these claims, as well as to the legislative actions that emanate from this line of reasoning, this pro-life argument nevertheless makes the distinction between these two sides of the abortion debate more complex than ever. The pro-choice movement has always emphasized the importance of personal choice and autonomy over reproductive choices. This claim was also at the center of their opposition to the *Hobby Lobby* case, which led to the 2014 NARAL campaign on social media arguing "Not My Bosses Business." In addition to a Twitter hashtag with the same name, pro-choice demonstrations during that time included signs such as "Mind Your Own Business," "No Bosses in my Bedroom," "Birth Control Not My Boss's Business," and "Contraception is MY Business." The proposed legislation to restore the contraceptive coverage under the ACA, which was offered by Senate Democrats in July 2014 and blocked by Republicans, was also nicknamed "Not My Boss's Business" by pro-choice activists as well as Democratic legislators. According to this approach, the way to protect women's reproductive freedom is by granting them autonomy and independence, rather than restricting their options, as done by the pro-life women-centered strategy.

The ruling in *Hobby Lobby*, some pro-life activists argue, promotes exactly these values; it limits the ability of employers to intervene in personal reproductive choices, as well as the ability of the government to intervene or regulate them. As a result, it leaves the responsibility for reproductive choices to the woman herself. This pro-life argument was evident in the demonstrations during the *Hobby Lobby* case, with slogans that included "Women in Control: Don't Want Bosses' Handouts" and "Women in Control: Can Manage their Fertility."[7] Further, the Twitter hashtag #WomenInControl has been used extensively following the June 2014 ruling, with messages such as "Let women make their own health care decisions" and "If I want birth control, I will put on my big girl pants and get it myself." The message behind these statements is that reproductive decisions—including the method of payment for birth control—are personal, and should be made only by the woman, without any intervention or assistance by the state. One manifestation of this argument, and the way it corresponds with the pro-choice argument, is a cartoon created by Chip Bok in July 2014, which since has appeared in numerous publications (Fig. 5.1).

The cartoon demonstrates the link between the pro-choice argument that reproductive choices should not be in the hands of bosses and the pro-life argument against the federal requirement to cover contraception. These arguments, pro-life activists argue, complement each other; they both call for the right of individuals to make their own choices, and thus they can both be seen as promoting a libertarian vision of minimal control and intervention, by the government as well as society. For pro-choice supporters, however, this link between the pro-choice and pro-life claims for autonomy in decision-making is based on the misrepresentation of their argument. The requirement to provide coverage of contraceptive services, they believe, is not a limitation on liberty. Instead, for pro-choice activists, whose ideology is often closer to "new" or "progressive" liberalism, the

---

[7] In general, slogans emphasizing religious liberty received more attention in the media, and seemed to appear more often in demonstrations.

Fig. 5.1 Chip Bok Editorial Cartoon used with the permission of Chip Bok and Creators Syndicate. All rights reserved.

role of government is to ensure equality and justice through laws and regulations. These laws should also target the private sphere—as in the case of domestic violence or marital rape—as well as the behavior of individuals in the marketplace, a space that often fails to provide equal access and opportunity to certain individuals. In light of this account, pro-choice supporters understand the employer mandate not as a violation of women's freedom and autonomy but, rather, as a requirement that grants them reproductive choices and promotes equality in the marketplace and within society.

While the different interpretations of the same requirement are based on numerous differences between the pro-choice and pro-life worldview, one central distinction lies in their approach to liberty; the pro-life account is based on a conceptualization of liberty as a negative right, thus understanding the actions of the government as meant only to ensure that no one—as well as the government itself—violates another's person liberty. The employer mandate, according to this account, is such a violation. The pro-choice account is based on conceptualization of liberty as a positive right, which requires others to provide it in order to be fully accessible to people. In light of this account, the employer mandate is needed in order to make contraceptive services accessible to women, thus granting them the right to choose their reproductive services.

Despite the clear distinctions between the two approaches, the focus of the pro-life movement on ensuring freedom means that now, more than ever, both sides in the abortion debate are using similar terms and concepts to arrive at opposite conclusions. At the heart of the pro-choice movement is the argument that women have the right to make their own decisions over their reproductive choices. The argument of religious freedom used by the pro-life movement is based on a similar claim; it emphasizes the importance for an individual to follow his or her own belief regarding contraception and abortion. Of course, the idea that no one besides the woman has a right to influence and limit women's access to their reproductive choices is at the heart of the pro-choice argument. What the two movements share is the argument that individuals should be able to make decisions that are right for them regarding this issue.[8] The result of this similarity in their arguments is that the pro-life movement may now define itself not only as protecting women's concerns, like the pro-choice movement, but also as promoting values of liberty, choice, and autonomy, just like the pro-choice movement does. As such, the pro-life discourse is able to once again offer an answer to the arguments raised by the pro-choice movement.

The third change introduced by the focus on liberty, and particularly religious liberty, is in the type of discourse that is used; the pro-life approach is now justified as defending personal opinions, rather than being based on morality or scientific facts. As discussed in Chap. 4, the *Hobby Lobby* case focuses on four contraceptive devices—Plan B, Ella, the copper IUD, and the IUD with progestin—which are seen by the plaintiffs and some pro-life supporters as abortifacients. However, the ruling, as well as the public discourse on the matter, rarely addresses the question whether these devices actually cause an abortion or not. Ignoring this topic altogether results in a discourse that is centered on beliefs; what matters

---

[8] While the focus of the pro-life movement on religious freedom—of employers as well as anyone else—may lead to limiting access of women to contraception and abortion, this outcome is not an explicit part of the discourse, and may be framed as an unintended result of a situation in which many people exercise their freedom of religion, thus making access to these services more difficult.

is what the employer believes this device or medication can do, and not what science or other experts claim. As Ginsburg states in the dissent to the ruling, "courts are not to question where an individual 'draws the line' in defining which practices run afoul of her religious belief."[9] Thus, it is the belief of some employers that certain actions or services violate their religion belief that needs to be respected by legislators and society.

This argument differs from those used previously by the pro-life movement; both the fetus-centered and the women-centered strategies aim to change people's perceptions and ideas about abortion, and not only about access to abortion services. In the case of the fetus-centered strategy, the pro-life movement aims to convince people that the fetus is a human being by using moral, religious, and scientific arguments. If successful, this strategy would lead people to think about abortion as murder, and thus to criminalize it. In the case of the women-centered strategy, the pro-life movement uses scientific data and research to argue that abortion causes harm to women, because of its emotional and physical harm, as well as feelings of regret and the need to act against their maternal tendencies. If successful, this strategy would lead people to see abortion as dangerous and undesired solution for women, thus criminalizing it, or at least making the process highly regulated and controlled. In both cases, the strategy is meant to expand the number of people who oppose abortions, by changing their opinion about the act itself, or the damage it causes.

The argument for the need to protect the rights of third-party actors, however, is based on a different type of justification; it emphasizes respect for the opinions of others, and their freedom not to be coerced to act against their beliefs. Thus, the argument moves away from trying to convince people to change their opinion about abortion. Instead, it defines the abortion debate as a disagreement between two sides—women seeking abortion, on the one hand, and some employers, on the other—who have different beliefs and understanding of what is the desired act in this situation. This discourse frames the disagreement as not being about facts—what is scientifically or religiously true—but, rather, about what people believe to be true. Even in the ruling, the court did not address "the question whether the companies' religious beliefs are actually reasonable," but instead aimed "to figure out whether the companies' convictions are

---

[9] At the same time, Ginsburg argues that the majority ruling "elides entirely the distinction between the sincerity of a challenger's religious belief and the substantiality of the burden placed on the challenger" (573 U.S. ___, at 22).

sincere—not whether their beliefs are 'mistaken or insubstantial'" (Howe 2014). This discourse does not include calls for the criminalization of abortion or contraceptives. Instead, it is based on the idea that abortion is legal and, particularly, that contraceptives are easily available to women who are interested in them.

The result of this discourse is that the pro-life movement is now able to frame the abortion debate as between two actors—or individuals—who feel that their rights are being violated. On the one side, there are some women who want the right to make their own reproductive choices but believe they should not be required to pay for them, while on the other side, there are some religious employers who feel that providing certain contraceptives violates their religious beliefs. Following this account, the pro-life strategy structures this debate as between two sides, which disagree but nevertheless have equally valid claims; individuals on both sides want to have autonomy and the freedom to act as they choose, whether it is about making reproductive decisions or about exercising religious freedom. While the needs of these two sides may seem to contradict one another—one side wants access, while the other side does not want to provide it—there is a simple way to fulfill both sides' requests: women who are interested in contraceptives should just buy them in the free market, or get them in any other way which does not involve their employers or forces others to act against their own personal beliefs. According to this account, what violates the religious freedom of employers is the requirement by the government to pay for something they disagree with, not the existence of contraceptives and abortion. Within this context, canceling the employer mandate will secure the religious freedom of job creators, without limiting women's ability to access contraceptives.[10] The conflict between the two sides, pro-life supporters argue, is thus not a real conflict, since both the woman and her employer can win.

[10] Despite this framing of the issue, there have been some attempts of legislators to limit the ability of women to use certain contraceptives. For example, a number of states restrict minors from accessing contraception without parental notification or consent (26 states and the District of Columbia) (Guttmacher 2015a). Further, personhood bills and initiatives were considered in seven states, measures that would recognize zygotes (a fertilized ovum, which is not yet an embryo) as legal persons. This recognition would prohibit IUDs and most hormonal forms of birth control, in effect criminalizing some of the most common and effective forms of birth control used by women in the USA today (Guttmacher 2015b). These cases of course do not correspond with this claim, a tension that can be explained as between the more libertarian argument of limited regulations and free market, and the conservative aim to limit the use of abortifacients and to require certain moral behavior from employees.

One of the results of emphasizing values of liberty and nonintervention is that this discourse is able to target groups that are not necessarily pro-life supporters. Since this strategy does not aim to change people's opinions on abortion in order to support this pro-life mission, it is enough to believe in the right of individuals to practice their religion—or any other right—freely. Instead of having to agree on a specific set of values or ideas, this discourse emphasizes the need to respect the beliefs of those who are different from you. By doing so, this third-party discourse is able to expand the base of support of the pro-life movement; you can support it without believing in the pro-life mission regarding abortion, and without being religious yourself. In addition, while many in the pro-life movement use the argument of religious freedom to demand exemptions from certain requirements—such as equality of gays in employment (Park 2014) and same-sex marriage—a few in the pro-life movement see the discourse of religious liberty as an opportunity to expand the base of support to include other marginalized groups. Religious individuals, according to this account, can create a coalition with other groups that are marginalized and oppressed because of their identity, like gays and lesbians. This type of shared mission is evident in the pledge of some Mormon leaders to support antidiscrimination laws for LGBTQ, as long as they include religious protections;

'When religious people are publicly intimidated, retaliated against, forced from employment or made to suffer personal loss because they have raised their voice in the public square, donated to a cause or participated in an election, our democracy is the loser,' said Elder Dallin Oaks, a member of the church's Quorum of Twelve Apostles. 'Such tactics are every bit as wrong as denying access to employment, housing or public services because of race or gender' (Burke 2015).

Thus, the third-party discourse represents a significant shift in the pro-life strategy, one which fully adopts libertarian values and arguments, calling for the support of the mission by every American who believes in freedom. This transformation shows, again, that the pro-life movement is able to adopt different strategies based on current developments and public opinion, a fact that is especially striking in light of the relative stagnation of the pro-choice movement. Since this type of strategy is so new, it is too early to know exactly how it will develop and what alliances it will create. For example, it is yet to be seen whether the discourse on liberty and freedom expands the base of support to groups that have traditionally opposed the pro-life mission, like LGBTQ activists. However, what seems to be clear already is that the arguments for religious freedom are supported by some who are not necessarily supporters of the pro-life mission or conservative regarding social issues. For example, while a majority of Americans (55 %)—including 62 % of mainline Protestants and 57 % of Catholics—are in support of same-sex marriage, when asked if businesses such as florists, bakers, caterers, and photographers should be allowed to refuse to provide their services for same-sex marriages because of religious objections, 47 % sided with the religious objectors (Lipka 2015). Regardless of this success, the pro-life mission is now able to position itself as protecting the fetus, the mother, and the freedom of all individuals.

4   ANALYSIS

The focus on religious liberty as part of the pro-life debate, and the specific understanding of the concept of liberty that is developed in this strategy, influences our understanding of the concepts of human rights and reproductive rights, while also solving—even if only temporarily—some of the tension within right-wing politics concerning the abortion issue. Regarding human rights, the right to religious liberty is framed in a way that expands the definition of what constitutes a violation of this right, thus increasing the number of people who can claim to have their religious rights violated. With regard to reproductive rights, this strategy challenges the distinction between contraceptives and abortion, while also redefining the issue of reproductive rights as a personal matter. The third-party strategy also plays a role in resolving the tension between libertarian and conservative tendencies within right-wing politics; the focus on religious liberty seems to solve the debate, since it is clearly an embracement of libertarian values and practices, with little—if at all—reflection of conservative ideas.

Human Rights

The framing of the pro-life debate as between women's right to control their reproductive choices and the right of others to follow their religious beliefs signifies a new stage in the use of human rights arguments by the pro-life movement. Specifically, the pro-life movement introduces a new conceptualization of the right to religious liberty, which expands what constitutes this right, as well as what are the acts that violate it. As a result, the new framing of religious liberty also expands the definition of the players whose religious rights are being violated.

Until now, religious exemptions were provided primarily to health-care providers, with a limited number of exceptions.[11] This type of exemption introduces a relatively limited concept of religious freedom; in addition to the requirement for religious affiliation, what constitutes an act that violates your religious freedom is the direct involvement in abortion, by providing or facilitating this act. According to this account, the act that violates someone's religious freedom is not whether a woman has an abortion, but whether you are forced to actively be involved in this act. Freedom of religion thus includes the right not to personally participate in the process of abortion, focusing on first-person involvement as the basis for granting religious liberty protections. These criteria also appear in the few religious exemptions that are granted to institutions or entities; they are required to be defined as religious institutions, and to provide health-care service broadly defined.

The ruling in *Hobby Lobby*, and specifically the pro-life and religious discourse that followed, introduces a new definition of what is a violation of religious freedom. According to this account, providing insurance that covers certain contraceptives that are believed to cause abortion—namely, potentially paying for an abortion—is a violation of religious freedom. Within this context, religious liberty is violated by another persons' use of contraceptives, even when the person claiming this violation is not directly involved in the process of performing an abortion. Furthermore, the violation of religious liberty is an outcome of the insurance coverage, regardless of whether the person covered is interested in, or will ever use, these contraceptives. Thus, what violates the religious freedom of the employer is the fact that such a medication is available to the employees under the employer-based insurance.

This type of understanding of religious liberty introduces a possible tension regarding the nature of this right; until now, the pro-life discourse addressed religious liberty as a negative right, which is protected as long as the government does not put any restrictions or requirements that violate it. However, the concept of "complicity-based sin" promotes a broad definition of acts that violate other people's liberties. Such acts resemble

---

[11] Legal protections for individuals have been extended to pharmacists (NCSL 2012), physicians (Guttmacher 2015b; HHS 2012), and, in some cases, granted to "healthcare professionals" generally construed (Guttmacher 2015b).

violations of religious liberty, since complicity claims "are faith claims about how to live in community with others who do not share the claimant's beliefs, and whose lawful conduct the person of faith believes to be sinful" (NeJaime and Siegel 2015: 2519), they may result in calls for certain values or behaviors to be promoted—or even required—within a business and, more generally, within society. For example, can a case of an employee who has an abortion using her salary be understood as a violation of religious belief? While this option might sound significantly different from the *Hobby Lobby* ruling with its emphasis on nonintervention, this possible development resembles Arizona's H.B. 2625, which would repeal the current law requiring contraception coverage if it is used for contraception, abortifacient, or sterilization purposes. Further, if the woman desires contraception coverage, she would be required to submit a claim to the employer documenting the medical necessity of the contraceptive device in question. If it was found out that the contraception was used for preventing pregnancy, the woman could be fired (H.B. 2625, 2012). The purpose of the law, protecting religious liberty, is most clearly illuminated in a statement from the sponsor, Majority Whip Debbie Lesko, who declared, "I believe we live in America. We don't live in the Soviet Union. So, government should not be telling the organizations or mom-and-pop employers to do something against their moral beliefs" (Bassett 2012).[12]

This argument, while framed around libertarian arguments regarding the limited role of government, in practice expands the concept of religious liberty, as well as the acts of others that are considered to offend our beliefs. The result is that while the government is prevented from requiring employers or anyone else from covering or providing certain services, society—through employers—is able to intervene in the decision-making process of individuals. While limiting reproductive rights, this conceptualization also expands the concept of religious liberty, and may eventually lead to the definition of religious liberty as a positive right. For human

---

[12] Another example of the expansion of the concept of religious liberty, including the acts that are considered to violate this freedom, is the dozens of lawsuits against the accommodation form for exempt religious organizations. The plaintiffs in these cases oppose the requirement to notify the government of that their employers are not covered for contraceptive services, this in order to initiate the process in which they get covered by the federal government. The claim that this notification is already a violation of religious liberty introduces a broad definition of this right, since any type of action that may result on coverage of contraceptives is "complicity-based sin."

rights activists, in theory, this shift is not problematic, because of the general tendency to prefer the concept of human rights as positive, thus attaching them to the responsibility of the government not only to protect but also to provide these rights (Donnelly 2013; Fredman 2008). At the same time, however, the emphasis on religious liberty as the first—and often most important—right may lead to the prioritization of this right over all other rights, as is already the case with reproductive rights.

Therefore, the conceptualization of the right to religious liberty following *Hobby Lobby* expands the scope of actions that constitute a violation of religious liberty; from an active involvement in the conscious clauses to a complicity-based approach, under which being linked in some way—even in theory rather than in practice—to abortifacients is already a violation of religious beliefs. As a result of this expansion, the definition of who is a third-party actor with interests and need for protection in the abortion debate also changes. Instead of limiting this category to healthcare professionals and religious institutions, the category may now include other actors who feel that their actions make them involved in providing abortion against their will.

Reproductive Rights

The third-party strategy influences the understanding of the concept of reproductive rights in two different ways. First, it conflates abortion and contraceptives in a way that allows the pro-life movement to delegitimatize the latter. In the debates during and following the *Hobby Lobby* case, there was little discussion of the nature of the four contraceptive devices in question and the claim of the plaintiffs that they are abortifacients in nature. While these four contraceptives have been evaluated and classified by the FDA as contraception, as they prevent pregnancy, the courts and, to a certain extent, the public discussion of the case do not address the implications of accepting the plaintiff's line of reasoning. Although a number of journalists and commentators identified and called into question the classification of these contraceptive devices as abortifacients as problematic in nature, there was minimal discussion of the conflation of these two distinct medical services (Posner 2012). The unquestioned acceptance of the claim that these devices are abortifacients in effect allowed a single employer to define the nature of this medical treatment, regardless of the scientific validity of the claim.

This conflation of the two services raises several implications for the future of reproductive rights in the USA. This conflation serves a practical purpose for the pro-life movement. As was demonstrated in previous chapters, fetal rights legislation, and specifically the move to establish personhood, has proven to be uniformly unsuccessful since it was initiated in 1973. Even at present, voters still remain uncomfortable and unwilling to establish a complete ban on abortion; this at a time when more abortion restrictions have been enacted than at any time since 1973, limiting access of women to abortion services. Particularly with respect to personhood, voters have rejected approximately 20 ballot initiatives across the country in the past few election cycles. However, the conflation of abortion and contraception is based on the acceptance of the idea that pregnancy begins at fertilization, rather than implantation (Dreweke 2014). Thus, while this does not necessarily make the passage of personhood legislation more likely, it does legitimize restrictions on contraceptive devices today, the same ones that may be restricted or completely prohibited under personhood laws. The decision in *Hobby Lobby* and, more importantly, the fairly widespread acceptance of the religious liberty claims made by the plaintiffs, legitimate some restrictions on services—even if only based on personal religious beliefs—which previously the pro-life movement had been unable to secure.

The pro-life movement, highly aware of voter preferences, has been utilizing the rhetoric surrounding this case, including the conflation of abortion and contraceptives. For example, the Susan B. Anthony List has recently declared its support for the Health Care Conscience Act, introduced in both the 113th and 114th sessions of Congress, stating that the law would protect the rights of taxpayers and health professionals' conscience, which are under assault in the ACA, and in particular the "abortion pill mandate." The bill proposed by Representative Diane Black and Senator Tom Coburn[13] would ensure that no individual is required to purchase insurance coverage nor is any sponsor or institution required to offer health plans that include abortion or any other item that the individual, sponsor, or institution has a religious objection to (H.B. 940 and S. 1204, 2014). Although the SBA List's webpage emphasizes the HHS abortion-pill mandate as the basis of their opposition, the bill explicitly

---

[13] S. 1204 was introduced in the 113th session by Senator Tom Coburn, although the Susan B. Anthony List's Website lists Senator Deb Fischer—with Representative Diane Black—as leaders on this bill. Fischer is listed as one of 21 cosponsors on the bill (S. 1204, 2014).

identifies abortion as the service that violates the rights of freedom of conscience of taxpayers and health professionals. By focusing on the rights of conscience, and framing this as an abortion mandate, the SBA List is able to promote the Health Care Conscience Rights Act.

Another way activists are attempting to attract voters to the pro-life cause has been initiated by the United States Conference of Catholic Bishops (USCCB), a group that is responding to the lack of interest or support of restrictions on birth control. The conflation of contraceptives and abortion serves to attract a specific demographic that has largely been opposed to the USCCB's work to restrict access to birth control through their opposition to the HHS mandate. Catholic women support and use contraception at approximately the same rate as other women; further, Catholics have expressed one of the highest rates of approval of the HHS mandate under the ACA. Further, the disapproval of this mandate by the USCCB has no measurable impact on Catholic support or approval of the ACA with the inclusion of the mandate for contraception coverage at no cost (Lake Research Partners 2012). With Catholic supporters unable to back the bishops' attempt to restrict coverage of birth control at no cost under the ACA, creating such an indelible connection between contraception, abortion, and religious liberty may prove to be more influential among those who are less religious, disaffected Catholics or Evangelical Protestants, or even those who are unaffiliated with a religious sect.

The second influence of the third-party discourse is the way it frames reproductive rights as a personal matter. While so far the result of this ruling is that contraceptives continue to be provided publicly—in some cases by the federal government rather than employers and states—the ruling nevertheless reflects the traditional dichotomy between "the family-wage model for men and government-welfare model for women" (Sepper 2015: 219). This separation between the needs of men—which are covered by the employer-based insurance—and the needs of women—which are provided by the government, and later maybe by the free market—reinforces the traditional concept of citizenship. Citizens, according to this account, are eligible for entitlements and benefits—such as unemployment benefits or social security—which are a result of the contract between them and the state. As part of the contract, these rights cannot be taken away. Some other benefits, however, are understood as charity—as in the case of welfare and "handouts"—and are seen as a favor that is given by the state to nondeserving citizens (Fraser and Gordon 1992). The distinction between these two types of benefits is often gendered, as women are referred to the private sphere, where their needs are provided by themselves, by other individuals, or by charities.

This framing of reproductive rights as a personal matter is part of the shift in the pro-life discourse from arguments that are based on universal concepts of human rights to arguments that emphasize relativism as well as individual's beliefs and ideologies. The fetus-centered strategy emphasizes universal moral arguments as the basis of the claim regarding the sanctity of the life of the fetus; the fetus, according to pro-life activists, is a human being and, as such, eligible for exactly the same rights as other human beings. The universalistic nature of human rights means that the specific assumption of society about the nature of the fetus, or that of the mother, is irrelevant to the discussion. Instead, all human beings have the right to enjoy the same human rights, and in a similar manner. The third-party strategy, however, is based on a different conceptualization of human rights, emphasizing the need to respect a wide array of rights, as well as the personal conceptualization of rights that is offered by the people themselves. This approach is more relativist in nature, emphasizing the way people perceive their rights and identity as the basis for granting them human rights. According to this account, the way in which people perceive their rights and protections is central to the definition of human rights, as well as human rights violation. Thus, the attempt to grant human rights needs to focus on people's own beliefs and perceptions, rather than establishing universal common rights.

Right-Wing Politics

The *Hobby Lobby* ruling and the pro-life discourse that follows appear to overcome the tension between conservative and libertarian tendencies within right-wing politics. The focus on religious freedom, and especially the assumption that religious beliefs are one of the most cherished and basic natural rights, follows conservative ideas about the importance of religion; religion, according to traditional conservative thinking, provides the moral compass for people's actions, thus it needs to be respected in the public sphere. However, while the topic is conservative in nature, the pro-life discourse and policy that follow are generally libertarian; they do not stake their claim on the need to preserve traditional values and beliefs, which would have resulted in them calling for the criminalization of abortion, as social conservatives often argue. Instead, the conceptualization of religious freedom as the freedom to not participate directly or indirectly in abortion aligns with a libertarian understanding of the concept of religious liberty as a negative right.[14]

This discourse defines religion as central to individuals, but as a personal and private preference, which is not, or should not be, necessarily shared by all. Thus, religious beliefs should be respected as part of the rights of individuals to enjoy liberty in the public sphere. In light of this approach, the right of employers to not pay for contraceptives is a reflection of their personal—rather than their company's or society's—beliefs, and preventing them from exercising their belief is a violation of their freedom. Since the emphasis of this account is on individual liberty rather than social values, it does not promote—at least not directly—a public sphere that is religious or conservative in nature, as desired by social conservatives. Instead, the emphasis is on the need to protect individuals—rather than communities—from government intervention and control.

According to this account, it appears that this conceptualization of religious liberty bridges the gap between conservative and libertarian ideas, both in discourse and in policy. As such, it may be seen as solving the tension that has been characterizing the GOP for the last two decades. Following the ruling in *Hobby Lobby*, the discourse focused primarily on religious liberty, and a libertarian conception of religious liberty at that. Particularly with respect to discussion of the case, there is no desire to restrict or ban access to contraception and, to a limited extent, abortion. Rather, the focus remains centered on the protection of individuals' right to religious liberty. The only government controls or intervention desired is the protection of one's right to oppose and thus not pay for or support the availability or accessibility of birth control. This libertarian conception of rights can also be found, to a certain extent, in public policies from this time period. For example, the Protecting Human Life and Taxpayers Act of 2015, introduced by Representative Diane Black, does not contain a ban on birth control or abortion, rather it is designed "To prohibit Federal funding to entities that do not certify the entities will not perform, or provide any funding to any other entity that performs, an abortion" (H.R. 3197, 2015). There were eight other similar bills introduced at the federal level in the previous year (June 2014–July 2015) that included restrictions on taxpayer funding of some aspect of abortion while clarify-

---

[14] A challenge to this claim has been raised by Gedicks (2015), who calls attention to the fact that in practice, the ruling promotes a government-funded option as a less restrictive option.

ing the imposition of these restrictions is justified based upon taxpayer conscience rights. It has yet to be seen if this type of restriction or limit on funding will be successful, or experience greater success as compared to previous types of funding restrictions. However, the use of these types of claims, as found in the discourse and public policy, illustrates a clear libertarian influence on the pro-life movement and its supporters.

REFERENCES

Americans United for Life. AUL calls landmark U.S. Supreme Court decision upholding First Amendment conscience rights "a victory for common-sense." 2014 June 30. http://www.aul.org/2014/06/aul-calls-landmark-u-s-supreme-court-decision-upholding-first-amendment-conscience-rights-a-victory-for-common-sense/. Accessed 23 June 2015.
Augusta Chronicle Editorial Staff. This is not a war. The Augusta Chronicle 2014 July 2. http://chronicle.augusta.com/opinion/editorials/2014-07-02/not-war. Accessed 20 May 2015.
Bassett L. Arizona birth control bill penalizes women for using contraception for non-medical reasons. The Huffington Post. 2012 Mar 13.
Berg T. Religious accommodation and the welfare state. Harvard Journal of Law and Gender. 2015;38: 103-151.
Berry S. Pro-life community celebrates SCOTUS hobby lobby decision. Breitbart. 2014 June 30. http://www.breitbart.com/big-government/2014/06/30/pro-life-community-celebrates-scotus-decision-for-religious-freedom-against-obamacare-hhs-abortion-pill-mandate/. Accessed 19 Jun 2015.
Burke D. Mormon church backs LGBT rights- with one condition. CNN. 2015 Jan 28. http://www.cnn.com/2015/01/27/us/mormon-church-lgbt-laws/. Accessed 28 July 2015.
Donnelly J. Universal human rights in theory and practice. Ithaca: Cornell University Press; 2013.
Dreweke J. Contraception is not abortion: the strategic campaign of antiabortion groups to persuade the public otherwise. Guttmacher Policy Rev. 2014;17(4).
Faith and rights: a test for the justices. The New York Times. 2014 March 24.
Fraser N, Gordon L. Contract versus charity. Socialist Rev. 1992;22(3):45–67.
Fredman S. Human rights transformed: positive rights and positive duties. Oxford: Oxford University Press; 2008.
Gedicks FM. One cheer for hobby lobby: improbable alternatives, truly strict scrutiny, and third-party employee burdens. Harvard J Law Gender. 2015;38: 153-76.
Health and Human Services (HHS). Affordable care act rules on expanding access to preventive services for women. 2013. http://www.hhs.gov/healthcare/facts/fact-sheets/2011/08/womensprevention08012011a.html. Accessed 18 July 2015.

Health and Human Services (HHS). Your rights under the federal health care provider conscience protection laws. 2012. http://www.hhs.gov/ocr/civil-rights/provider_conscience_factsheet.pdf. Accessed 19 July 2015.

Henshaw S. Ralliers protest obamacare mandate. Reading Eagle (PA) 2013 July 28.

Hitchcock J. The French connection. Touchstone. 2011.

Howe A. Court rules in favor of for-profit corporations, but how broadly? In plain english. SCOTUSblog. 2014 June 30. http://www.scotusblog.com/2014/06/court-rules-in-favor-of-for-profit-corporations-but-how-broadly-in-plain-english/. Accessed 20 July 2015.

Keller B. Conscience of a corporation. The New York Times. 2013 Feb 10.

Kliff S. Interview: the legal case against the contraceptives mandate. The Washington Post. 2012 Feb 15.

Lake Research Partners. Catholics and birth control coverage. 2012 Feb 7. http://www.lakeresearch.com/news/Catholics%20and%20birth%20control.Lake%20Research%20Partners.pdf.

Leef G. Hobby Lobby and Harris v. Quinn- a pretty good day for the first amendment. Forbes. 2014 July 1. http://www.forbes.com/sites/georgeleef/2014/07/01/hobby-lobby-and-harris-v-quinn-a-pretty-good-day-for-the-first-amendment/. Accessed 30 July 2015.

Lipka M. Americans split over whether businesses must serve same-sex couples. The Pew Research. 2015 Mar 30.

Monahan J, Gacek C. FRC submission on HHS contraceptive mandate. 2011 Sept 30. http://downloads.frc.org/EF/EF11I58.pdf. Accessed 29 Jun 2015.

National Conference of State Legislatures (NCSL). Pharmacist conscience clauses: law and information. 2012 May. http://www.ncsl.org/research/health/pharmacist-conscience-clauses-laws-and-information.aspx. Accessed 3 Jun 2015.

NeJaime D, Siegel R. Conscience wars: complicity-based conscience claims in religion and politics. Yale Law J. 2015;124:2516–91.

Park A. The legacy of the Hobby Lobby case: protecting anti-gay discrimination? Mother Jones. 2014 July 9. http://www.motherjones.com/mojo/2014/07/hobby-lobby-anti-gay-discrimination. Accessed 20 July 2015.

Piety TR. Why personhood matters. Const Comment. 2015;30:101–28.

Posner S. OB/GYN corrects bishop's false claim about how contraceptives work. Religion Dispatches. 2012 Mar 7. http://religiondispatches.org/obgyn-corrects-bishops-false-claim-about-how-contraceptives-work/. Accessed 21 July 2015.

Sekulow J. Hobby lobby case—three reasons why corporations must have religious freedom. FoxNews.com. 2014 Mar 25. http://www.foxnews.com/opinion/2014/03/25/hobby-lobby-case-three-reasons-why-corporations-must-have-religious-freedom.html. Accessed 29 Jun 2015.

Sepinwall AJ. Conscience and complicity: assessing pleas for religious exemptions in Hobby Lobby's wake. U Chi Law Rev. 2015;82(4).

Sepper E. Gendering corporate conscience. Harv J Law Gender. Winter 2015;38:193–233.

Shapiro I. Symposium: mandates make martyrs out of corporate owners. SCOTUSblog. 2014 Feb 24. http://www.scotusblog.com/2014/02/symposium-mandates-make-martyrs-out-of-corporate-owners/. Accessed 20 July 2015.

Sligh H, Mitchell R. Which religious practices should be protected? National Review Online. 2015 Apr 24. http://www.nationalreview.com/article/417391/which-religious-practices-should-be-protected-howard-slugh-mitchell-rocklin. Accessed 30 Jun 2015.

Smith WJ. Hobby Lobby protects another company. National Review Online. 2015 Jan 13. http://www.nationalreview.com/human-exceptionalism/396297/hobby-lobby-protects-another-company-wesley-j-smith. Accessed 30 Jun 2015.

Stolzenberg NM. It's about money: the fundamental contradiction of Hobby Lobby. S Cal Law Rev. 2014;88:727–68.

Texas Right to Life. Supreme Court's Hobby lobby decision protects pro-life Americans, upholds religious freedom. 2014 june 30. http://site.texasright-tolife.com/a/1237/Supreme-Courts-Hobby-Lobby-decision-protects-ProLife-Americans-upholds-religious-freedom#.VtMqevF_hGQ. Accessed 23 June 2015.

The Becket Fund. Pastor Rick Warren on hobby lobby lawsuit. 2013 Jan. 4. http://www.becketfund.org/pastor-rick-warrens-on-hobby-lobby-lawsuit/. Accessed 2015 June 30.

The Guttmacher Institute. An overview of minor's consent law. State policies in brief. 2015a. Accessed 1 Aug 2015.

The Guttmacher Institute. An overview of state abortion laws. State Policies in Brief. 2015b. Accessed 1 Aug 2015.

Weber T. Hobby Lobby symposium: the exercise of religion is inseparable from human activity—including supporting one's family. SCOTUSblog. 2014 Jun 30. http://www.scotusblogcom/2014/06/hobby-lobby-symposium-the-exercise-of-religion-is-inseparable-from-human-activity-including-supporting-ones-family/. Accessed 20 July 2015.

Wuerl D. Protecting our catholic conscience in the public square. The Washington Post. 2012 May 23.

Young C. Hobby Lobby ruling is not a 'war on women'. Newsday. 2014 July 1. http://www.newsdaycom/opinion/columnists/cathy-young/hobby-lobby-ruling-is-not-a-war-on-women-cathy-young-18618862. Accessed 26 Jun 2015.

CHAPTER 6

The Future of Reproductive Rights in the Age of Human Rights

It has now been a year since the *Hobby Lobby* ruling. During this short period, the case has transformed the pro-life discourse and, to a limited extent, public policy regarding reproductive rights and religious freedom. It is too soon to know the precise influence this strategy will have on religious rights in the future. In addition, the exact direction this discourse will take and the impact it may have on other contentious social and political issues are not yet clear. However, the amount and volume of the discourse surrounding the ruling, as well as the increase in public policy efforts responding to religious liberty claims, clarify that these issues will continue to dominate the public sphere, as well as structure movement and policy efforts in the coming years. Therefore, this chapter aims to examine the legal, social, and political changes that have been taking place in the past year, articulating possible directions in which the third-party strategy and ruling will impact human rights, reproductive rights, and right-wing politics.

1   THE FUTURE OF HUMAN RIGHTS: CORPORATIONS

The *Hobby Lobby* ruling, as well as the public framing of the discussion surrounding the case, focused on the rights of individuals to practice their religion without intervention by the state. Shifting attention from corporations to individuals is, in some way, the cause of the success of this discourse, and, despite Romney's claim, the public is not convinced that

© The Editor(s) (if applicable) and The Author(s) 2016
A. Von Hagel, D. Mansbach, *Reproductive Rights in the Age
of Human Rights*, DOI 10.1057/978-1-137-53952-6_6

"corporations are people." Much of the public opposes the 2010 ruling in *Citizens United*, which was understood as granting corporations the same rights as individuals. Polls show that the overwhelming majority of Americans, Democrats and Republicans alike, oppose the ruling and have expressed their desire to limit corporate spending in elections, emphasizing the difference in value between corporate and individual contributions to campaigns (Fein 2015). This framing of the *Hobby Lobby* case in the public discussion, however, overlooks to a great extent the legal impact of the ruling, which granted religious freedom to closely-held corporations. The ruling determined that these types of corporations are a reflection of their owners' ideology and, therefore, the requirements on the business are a violation of the religious liberty of the owners. Thus, despite the general public's belief that the ruling as granting religious liberty to individuals (Lupu 2015), in practice, the ruling establishes corporations as bearers of human rights.

The idea of corporate personhood, as well as the argument that private economic actors are bearers of human rights, is not new (Pollman 2011; Ripken 2009). However, the ruling in *Citizens United* brought renewed attention to this concept. The scholarly discussions that followed this ruling focus on, among other things, the effect of corporate personhood on corporate constitutional rights, campaign finance, and corporate religious exemptions (Greenfield 2015; Joo 2015; Piety 2015; Taub 2015). In general, studies on the implications of corporate personhood have often centered on the economic protections conferred to corporations, arguing that this concept promotes a corporate capitalist order and the definition of property rights as human rights (Alvarez 2011; Douzinas 2007; Sklar 1988).

One example of such an account is found in the literature examining corporate personhood in the international sphere, where transnational corporations may have more rights and access to tribunals and courts than individuals. The protections granted to transnational corporations are often used "to challenge the policies pursued by investors or states under international economic agreements," thus limiting the ability of the state to apply regulations or promote interests that are not shared by the transnational corporation (Isiksel 2015: 20–21). The need to consider the rights of transnational corporations when making domestic decisions often limits the ability of states to pursue the policies that will benefit their population. At the same time, some governments use their human rights obligations toward transnational corporations as a way to justify their actions (and inactions), defending "certain government actions or measures that may have had negative impacts on foreign investors" (Peterson 2009: 22). The result of these obligations may be the exemption of transnational corporations from economic and employment regulations, thus granting them economic benefits and advantages at the cost of protections to the local population. The case of *Hobby Lobby*, however, seems to raise different implications for corporate rights; while the *Citizens United* ruling, as well as much of the discussion on corporate personhood, is perceived by the public as granting corporations rights concerning economic activity and spending, the *Hobby Lobby* ruling is not framed around such issues. Instead, it focuses on the right to religious freedom. Thus, corporations are granted human rights that are neither economic in nature nor necessarily relevant to their operation as a business, such as in the case of the right to enter contracts or the right to sue and be sued.

As a response to claims that corporate personhood grants businesses the same rights as the rights granted to people, some legal scholars emphasize the legalistic differences between the two. For example, in the case of *Hobby Lobby*, religious freedom was not granted to corporations but only to closely-held corporations. Another example is that while corporations have been granted the right to corporate speech in the past, this type of speech is not identical to individual's freedom of speech (Piety 2015). These distinctions, however, while crucial for the legal implications of the ruling, may not be so relevant when examining the public's perception of the case. In addition, while the actual ruling in *Hobby Lobby* did award religious protections only to closely-held corporations—a category that is clearly distinguished from corporation—the ruling did not investigate whether the actual operation of these corporations follows the definition of closely held, or whether they are more closely related in their operation to the corporate form, thus raising the possibility of future legal challenges to this limited application (Cismas and Cammarano 2016).

The discourse of religious liberty, together with the lack of specific guidelines regarding the precise application of the ruling, may open the floodgates for the use of similar justifications for other entities, which are not necessarily closely-held, and whose owners are not following religious practices as closely as the Green family. This type of expansion has been taking place in some states, which introduced legislation to significantly expand these protections. In Indiana, S.B. 101 (2015) broadens the definition of "person" within the state's RFRA to include different legal entities such as partnership, corporation, and LLC. The law passed and went into effect in July 2015. In 2014, Arizona also proposed and enacted a similar law (S.B. 1062), which expands the RFRA to include for-profit corporations, trust, associations, LLC, estate foundations, and any other legal entities. Other measures include South Dakota's law protecting businesses and citizens' speech on sexual orientation (S.B. 128, 2014), as well as measures that are designed to protect individuals from the requirement to provide services, thus defining business owners or corporations as individuals with the right to not be forced to act against their beliefs. While all these proposals expand, in some way or another, the *Hobby Lobby* ruling beyond closely-held corporations, they do maintain the framework of the discourse; they grant religious protections to entities that are not human beings, while framing these rights as protecting the individuals within the business.

The legal and technical implications of the ruling—specifically, what rights are granted and what entity can enjoy them—are thus less relevant to the public discourse, which grants religious liberty to corporations, through their owners. The ability to conflate the individual with the business, we argue, is a result not only of the use of vague legal and public language on the matter but also of the focus on religious liberty rather than economic rights. In the ruling, as well as the discourse that follows, the right to religious liberty is framed as disconnected from the economic operation of the business; the owners of Hobby Lobby did not sue based on the monetary burden of the insurance, or even the fee, but instead on the way in which the employer mandate violates their beliefs. The focus on religious liberty further conflates the distinction between individuals and companies, since, of course, companies cannot pray or believe in God, and it will be meaningless to argue that corporations are interested in the right to freely exercise their religion. Human beings, however, do hold such beliefs and values, and those should be respected. In addition, Americans can more easily imagine the way religious protections—or protection of freedom more generally—are relevant to their own lives or the lives of other Americans. This is different from the ruling in *Citizen United*, which focused on limits to campaign contributions, dealing with amounts that are outside of reach for most Americans.

Thus, and despite the focus of the ruling on closely-held corporations, within this context, it is not surprising that the pro-life and religious liberty discourse has framed the debate as over the rights of individuals, who own corporations. The result of expanding the applicability of human rights—and not just property rights—to nonhuman entities is the dehumanization of the concept of human rights (Isiksel 2015). While it is clear why the applicability of the concept of human rights to corporations is debated and challenged, the literature on transnational corporations shows how the concept of human rights has been established to include nonhuman entities. One possible result of this expansion is further devaluing of human rights claims, as well as the ability of institutions—including the state—to protect the rights of human beings through human rights institutions and frameworks.

One of the reasons why nonhuman entities have been able to enjoy human rights protections is the long history of using the concept of human rights as a defense against state actions. According to this account, it is the state that often performs many of the violations. Defining a right as a human right is one way to protect individuals from coercive and exploitative actions by the state, regardless of whether these acts are backed by legislation. Human rights are thus often positioned in opposition to government actions, putting less of an emphasis on the definition of the subject whose rights are being violated, and more on the entity that is violating these rights. In addition, perceiving the state as the main violator of human rights has led the human rights movement to fight against any attempt of the state to define who gets the protections of human rights. Granting this right to the state may lead to the exclusion of certain groups of people, thus legitimizing the state's oppression and human right violation; this has been evident in the past, such as in the case of slavery, but also more recently, as in the case of undocumented migrants. As the main violator of human rights, the state should not be allowed to define who is eligible for these rights.

In addition, human rights supporters argue that personhood is not defined by the state or by any other institution. Instead, it is what defines every human being, and thus already exists within the person herself. This type of argument further limits the legitimacy of any claims against the humanness of another person or, in this case, a company. Within this context, human rights activists and supporters argue that the state also has no right to define human beings, as well as what religious practices are acceptable, and who is eligible to enjoy religious rights. The risk in granting these rights to the state, together with the difficulty in defining what constitutes a violation of religious freedom, leads some courts—for example, the European Court on Human Rights—to often side with the plaintiffs in such lawsuits, adopting their definition of what constitutes a violation of their religious liberty by the government (Cismas and

Cammarano 2016). Defining the state as the main human rights violator thus leads to increased suspicion with regard to both who it defines as a human being eligible for protections and the religious protections the state assumes to be essential to individuals. Within this context, the opposition to the government's granting of rights to corporations is questioned and challenged, as it is the state that often limits the freedom and liberty of actors. It is thus the framing of the debate as over the right to enjoy religious liberty without state intervention that influences the public acceptance to the *Hobby Lobby* ruling.

While it is still too early to fully understand the effects of granting nonhuman entities a broad range of human rights, the current discourse and proposed legislation seem to provide some possible answers regarding these directions, which may in the future affect the way the concept of human rights is understood. Most importantly, the future of human rights seems to include both human subjects and nonhuman entities, granting both equal rights and protections. Following this account, the type of rights that are granted to nonhuman entities seems to be indistinguishable from those granted to humans; this is because of the inability to separate between the individual who is behind the entity and the entity itself. Within this context, the violation of the entity's right is the same as the violation of the individual's right. Any preference to individuals over other entities may be defined as discriminatory, since in practice it prefers someone's right to another's. This would make it difficult for anyone—including the government and the courts—to prioritize individuals over other entities. In addition to expanding the list of subjects who are eligible to human rights, the inclusion of corporations within the human rights discourse may also in the future change the type of rights that are included under the human right regime, defining, for example, only negative rights as human rights.

2   REPRODUCTIVE RIGHTS

The analysis of the pro-life strategy reveals the central role that science has played in the debate over abortion and the right to access birth control. During the past four decades, the pro-life movement has introduced the use of scientific language and data, usually in a way that is not necessarily accepted by the mainstream medical and scientific community. Nevertheless, this use of scientific claims has been shaping the discourse on abortion, as well as the legitimacy of pro-life arguments. For example, the scientific findings concerning the beginning of life have often been touted by conservatives and pro-life supporters as the justification to legally protect the personhood of fetuses; Republican presidential candidate Mike Huckabee stated that "Life begins at conception. This isn't just a Biblical view—its affirmed by modern science and every unique human DNA schedule, which is present at conception" (Huckabee 2015).[1] Similar statements maintain, "the zygote is composed of human DNA and other human molecules, so its nature is undeniably human and not some other species." Thus, "the scientific evidence is quite plain: at the moment of fusion of human sperm and egg, a new entity comes into existence which is distinctly human, alive, and an individual organism—a living, and fully human, being." It becomes clear that the claim that the fetus is not a person is a "decidedly unscientific argument: it has nothing to do with science and everything to do with someone's own moral or political philosophy, though that someone may not readily admit it" (Cleaver Ruse and Schwarzwalder 2015).

Similarly, the organization Life News also frames stories as scientific, including titles such as "Scientific Fact: Human Life Begins at Conception, or Fertilization," "The Los Angeles Times Claims that Ultrasound Photos Aren't 'Objective' Scientific Fact," and "41 Quotes from Medical Texts that Human Life Begins at Conception" (Life News 2013a, 2014, 2015). Fetal pain laws are another example of the use of scientific claims; the argument of scientific findings that the fetus has developed pain receptors that create the feelings of pain serves as the sole basis for laws prohibiting abortion after viability, and most recently at 20 or 24 weeks (Robertson 2013). Other pro-life arguments that are framed as scientific include PAS, the connection between breast cancer and abortion, and the prevalence of infertility, depression, suicidal ideation, and psychosis following abortion (Cohen 2004). Similar to the scientific research concerning the connection between abortion and physical and emotional harm, scientific arguments have been used also to argue for abortion reversal, a term describing the use of progesterone to stop the effects of mifepristone, the first of two medications to abort a fetus during the first 12 weeks of pregnancy. This despite the lack of any research on abortion reversal conducted on humans (Khazan 2015).

[1] "DNA schedule" is not a medical or biological term, so it remains unclear exactly the basis of Huckabee's assertion.

The scientific value of these arguments varies. For example, the argument that the fetus is a living entity is often used to convince the ambivalent or moderate supporters of abortion rights. However, while the assertion that the fetus is a living organism or entity is not in dispute, this explanation conflates a moral argument concerning personhood with a scientific observation that the fetus is a living entity. Of the scientific claims regarding fetal pain, the DNA schedule, or PAS, none have been validated or replicated by researchers utilizing the scientific method. Furthermore, no research regarding these claims has been published in peer-reviewed journals accepted by the mainstream medical or academic community (Bazelon 2012; Belluck 2013; Cohen 2004; Robertson 2013).

While using scientific evidence to assert the personhood of the fetus or the negative health effects of abortion, many in the pro-life movement and its supporters have rejected the scientific evidence used to disqualify or discount their claims. One such example is a statement made by Representative Joe Walsh, who declared that, "With modern technology and science, you can't find one instance [of abortion necessary to save a woman's life]...There is no such exception for the life of the mother, and as far as health of the mother, same thing" (Robillard 2012). Another case of the rejection of some scientific findings concerns the nature of EC as well as other forms of hormonal birth control. Despite medical evidence to the contrary, it is firmly believed by some (including the plaintiffs in the *Hobby Lobby* case) that these contraceptives are abortifacients. Despite the absence of valid data or research, the scientific claims of the pro-life movement have been accepted by some policymakers, and even by the general public. The success of these arguments is evident in the passage of fetal pain laws in at least 12 states, the funding of crisis pregnancy centers (CPCs)—organizations which counsel women on PAS and other supposed negative health effects of abortion—by 15 states, as well as the passage of informed consent laws requiring physicians to detail these problems prior to women obtaining an abortion in 33 states (Benson Gold and Nash 2012). Regardless of the value or nature of the data, the use of scientific discourse seems to be central to the success of the pro-life movement.

This use—as well as the rejection—of scientific discourse by the pro-life movement positions this movement within a larger trend of using scientific discourse in a way that is not accepted by the scientific community to address contemporary social issues. One prominent example of such an issue is the political and public discussions of climate change. Part of the current debate in the USA on the issue focuses on the findings of the scientific community; specifically, forces opposing the argument that climate change has been influenced by human actions have been debating the presence, effects, and implications of research on climate change since the 1980s (Houghton et al. 2001; Orsekes 2004). These forces, often defined as the antienvironmentalist movement, have been working toward discrediting—and in certain instances, rejecting outright—the scientific research on climate change. This movement, driven by conservatives, serves an economic and nationalistic purpose, arguing that climate change science, and, in turn, the proposed responses by environmentalists, threatens American principles and values (Jacques et al. 2008; McCright and Dunlap 2003). Largely motivated by politics and ideology, the denial or rejection of climate change allows policymakers to accept or reject proposals based upon their own convictions or understanding of the issue. For example, numerous studies of Congressional hearings on climate change find that scientists represent a small fraction of those testifying; the largest proportion of those testifying include representatives from the business community and members of Congress or government officials, more generally (Burstein and Hirsch 2007; Fisher et al. 2013; McCright and Dunlap 2003).

Media coverage has also covered this debate, providing roughly equal amounts of airtime and coverage to both sides of the debate. The result is the framing of the issue of climate change as still being debated by the scientific community, this despite the consensus among the overwhelming majority of climatologists regarding the science of climate change. One of the results of this framing is that the avenues for addressing climate change, primarily regulating fossil fuel emissions, provoke considerable political controversy (Fisher et al. 2013). The use of testimony given by political or government officials, rather than scientists, represents this approach to science; these Congressional hearings do not manifest an outright rejection of science altogether. Rather, they are based on the use of claims purported to be scientific in nature from inexpert individuals. Similar to the debate over abortion and, in particular, the discussion of research on PAS and other harmful effects of abortion on women, the development of public policy is largely based on testimony or findings from nonexperts within their respective fields. For example, the South Dakota Task Force Report, used to write the Women's Health and Human Life Protection Act, employed unlicensed counselors, social and political activists, and nongovernmental leaders, in addition to doctors and licensed social workers and counselors. Most of their testimony includes statements regarding the harm experienced by women during and after an abortion procedure, as well as a lack of awareness or misunderstanding of the nature of abortion and the personhood of the fetus (South Dakota Task Force Report 2005).

One stark, if anecdotal, example of the rejection of the existing scientific research while offering instead an alternative scientific argument was seen at the 2014 hearing in the House Committee on Science, Space, and Technology in which the President's Science Advisor John Holdren was questioned on the President's initiative to reduce carbon emissions. Political satirist Jon Stewart presented some of the exchanges that went on between Advisor Holden and House Representative Larry Buschon, from Indiana. Representative Buschon, when questioning Holdren about the science of climate change, declared that the climate change phenomenon had been addressed and rejected by the American public. When further pushed by Holdren, Representative Buschon stated that he did not read the scientific literature on climate change because he did not believe it. Further, Representative Steve Stockman of Texas asked Holdren about the time it will take for sea levels to rise two feet upon the melting of the glaciers; he further posited "I mean think about it, if your ice cube melts in your glass it doesn't overflow, its displacement. This is the thing, some of the things they're talking about, mathematically and scientifically don't make sense" (Stewart 2014). In this exchange, House representatives both discount and offer their own interpretation of climate science, despite the testimony offered by the President's Science Advisor, John Holdren, who is trained in aeronautics, astronautics, and plasma physics, and holds degrees from the Massachusetts Institute of Technology and Stanford University (Wilke and Talcott 2008).

A second example of climate change denial in Congress can be seen in Senator James Inhofe's use of a snowball on the floor of the Senate to call into question the science of climate change. He stated that "It's very, very cold outside. Very unseasonable" while the Senate was in session in February (Bump 2015). Further, he has stated, "I take my religion seriously. [T]his is what a lot of alarmists forget: God is still up there, and He promised to maintain the seasons and that cold and heat would never cease as long as the earth remains." He quoted one of his "favorite Bible verses," Genesis 8:22, to back up his claim. The verse reads, "As long as the earth remains, There will be springtime and harvest, Cold and heat, winter and summer." In a radio interview, he stated that it was ridiculous that scientists continue to address global warming. "The arrogance of people to think that we, human beings, would be able to change what He is doing in the climate is to me outrageous" (Colmes 2015). These two examples are representative of the views of members of Congress, who deny the existing scientific research as legitimate, either based upon faulty scientific inquiry or a rejection of the entire phenomenon of climate change. What is clear is that among a certain segment of the population, the use of scientific claims is effective; this effectiveness is not undermined by the lack of any replicable findings or appropriate methodological approaches, as well as by the rejection of these arguments by most in the medical and academic community.

These examples illustrate how the rejection of scientific evidence on climate change is based on the individual's own understanding of science or personal, religious beliefs. This type of approach to science has been shaping the pro-life strategy regarding the regulation of abortion and contraception. Science, according to this account, is used as a way to legitimize certain arguments, which are not accepted by the scientific community, while also challenging other data and accepted findings. The *Hobby Lobby* case represents the next step in the use of science and scientific arguments as a means to promote pro-life approaches. While the lawsuit is based on the (medically disputed) claim that these four contraceptives act as abortifacients, the court accepted this claim at face value (Sepinwall 2015); not only that this statement was not challenged, but there was not even a demand for the plaintiffs to introduce scientific data or research that proves their belief. Instead, it is the fact that they believe these contraceptives to be abortifacients that led the court to accept this definition in their ruling. Thus, the use of scientific language and methods becomes disconnected from the scientific findings and claims, which are of lesser importance. The beliefs and values of the individuals in question dictate their own personal or religious understanding of the physiological processes that underlie how contraception works. The effectiveness of these arguments implies that the use of these scientific claims will continue, regardless of the acceptance—or lack thereof—of these arguments by the scientific community.[2] This may be the future of reproductive rights; a

---

[2] At the same time, however, the effectiveness of the scientific claim differs, according to the issue area; the analysis of state and federal public policy outcomes indicates that bills designed to protect women from these purported ill-health effects have been much more successful as compared to claims that science establishes that personhood begins at the moment of conception. Thus, while the use of scientific language and terms will continue, its use may vary in different areas.

reality in which beliefs and claims shape scientific understanding of facts, regardless of the data available. The definition of certain contraceptives as abortifacients is one example of such a trend.

3 RIGHT-WING POLITICS

In the public discussion of the ruling in *Burwell v. Hobby Lobby*, much of the focus has centered on religious liberty and the extent to which an individual's freedom and rights supersede federal or state law. Religious liberty, a concept embraced by social conservatives and libertarians, has been capitalized upon to push a number of laws at both levels of government. These laws reflect social conservative as well as libertarian goals, but often in ways that contradict each other. Thus, the use of the concept of religious liberty, while a valuable strategy for the pro-life discourse, has yet to result in any substantive policy change. As such, this issue demonstrates the continued presence of this ideological division within the GOP.

Immediately following the decision in *Hobby Lobby*, a number of Republican leaders issued statements regarding the court's ruling. These statements reflected primarily a libertarian understanding of the ruling, focusing almost solely on the issue of religious liberty. Senator Ted Cruz stated, "The decision affirms that Americans, contrary to what the Obama Administration attempted to impose, have a right to live and work in accordance to their conscience and can't be forced to surrender their religious freedom once they open a business," declaring that "This ruling is a repudiation of the Obama Administration's untenable position that people with sincerely held religious beliefs should be forced to comply with an unconstitutional mandate while a parade of waivers, exemptions, and delays are granted for purely commercial and political interests." Senator Rand Paul also made a statement based on libertarian values when he declared that the ruling means Americans will not have to worry about "big government intervention and punishment for following their religious conscience." Further stating that "Our nation was founded on the principle of freedom, and with this decision, America will continue to serve as a safe haven for those looking to exercise religious liberty" (Al-Faruque 2014).

Reince Priebus, the chairman of the Republican National Party, stated that

This decision protects the religious freedom that is guaranteed to all Americans by the First Amendment, and we're grateful the Court ruled on the side of liberty. The central issue of this case was whether the federal government can coerce Americans to violate their deeply held religious beliefs, and thankfully the Court has upheld the proper limits on the government's power.

Further, he declared,

The fact that Americans had to bring this case in the first place reveals once again just how intrusive Obamacare is. It's a misguided one-size-fits-all policy that not only failed to fix our healthcare system but has trampled on our Constitutional rights. Americans deserve a healthcare system that allows them to make the right choices for themselves, gives them more freedom, and comes nowhere close to encroaching on our First Amendment rights (RNC 2014).

Statements from House Speaker John Boehner and Senate Minority Leader Mitch McConnell also centered on the protection of religious liberty, including references to the need to check the overreach of the federal government (Burke 2014).

A handful of statements reflected a more socially conservative understanding of the ruling, although they have proven to be less common than those focusing on religious liberty claims. For example, Karl Rove declared that the ruling would be supported "in parts of the country where traditional values are strong, and parts of the country where, for example, the Catholic Church is strong," stating also that women would welcome the ruling because "a substantial number" were "pro-life in their outlook." Finally, he concluded, "The country is becoming more pro-life. Should somebody be forced to violate their moral beliefs by having to pay for something that they believe causes an abortion?" Finally, while on a news radio show, Representative Mike Lee was asked if the *Hobby Lobby* case primarily referred to "whether or not a person who runs a business should be forced to provide something that is largely for recreational behavior, if it goes against their religious beliefs?" a description to which Lee positively affirmed as an accurate depiction of the case (Burke 2014).

While these statements include both conservative and libertarian elements, they mostly focus on religious liberty, rather than on birth control, abortion, or corporate rights. The focus on religious liberty has also been shaping some of the legislative proposals during this period, although most of the proposals for promoting religious liberty focus on other issue areas, often related to same-sex marriage. With regard to legislation from Congress concerning abortion and abortion-related issues, few proposals explicitly address religious liberty. The focus of these proposals, as well as their frequency, reflects earlier eras. One exception is H.R. 399 (2015), a resolution submitted to express that Congress should support traditional marriage and the prevention of taxpayer-funded abortion. Representative Jones declared that the USA was founded on Judeo-Christian principles, with the "Creator explicitly mentioned in the Declaration of Independence," as justification for the need to support the end to taxpayer-funded abortions (H.R. 399, 2015).

There has yet to be a significant amount of legislation utilizing claims of religious liberty in proposals regarding contraception and abortion. There has, however, been a substantial rise in such claims attached to proposals addressing other issues besides abortion. In the last few sessions following the ruling in *Hobby Lobby*, the issue of religious liberty featured prominently in a number of proposals addressing same-sex marriage, in general, and the ruling in *Obergefell v. Hodges* (2015), in particular. The ruling in *Obergefell* invalidated the contested state bans on same-sex marriage before the court, declaring that marriage is a fundamental right secured through the due process and equal protection clauses of the 14th Amendment. The reaction to this ruling among conservatives, similarly to the reaction after the *Hobby Lobby* ruling, centers on religious liberty, and in *Obergefell*, the newly created need for increased protections of religious freedom. Charles Donovan of the Charlotte Lozier Institute declared that following this ruling,

> [traditional] marriage advocates must insist on the broadest First Amendment protections possible. We can expect the macro-aggressions against our freedoms of belief, speech, political engagement, and social service work to multiply rapidly. After *Roe* and *Doe* in 1973, bipartisan legislators enacted the Church Amendment and other federal measures to preserve the conscience rights of dissidents against the decisions. The battle for similar protections now will be far more intense—and just as consequential (The Supreme Court has Legalized Same-Sex Marriage: Now What?" 2015).

Further, John Stonestreet, part of the National Review Online Symposium reacting to the *Obergefell* decision, stated that this ruling does not settle the marriage issue just as *Roe v. Wade* did not settle the abortion issue. And similar to *Roe*, the current decision is considered the "fruit of the very bad ideas of the sexual revolution" (The Supreme Court has Legalized Same-Sex Marriage: Now What?" 2015). Finally, the *Obergefell* represents the "the greatest crisis of religious liberty in American history."

The violation of traditional marriage law supported by the court represents a broader transformation, "of something much larger and more dangerous than same-sex, monogamish 'marriages.' Yes, polygamy is just around the corner" (The Supreme Court has Legalized Same-Sex Marriage: Now What?" 2015). The concerns over religious liberty in response to the ruling have also been found in legislative proposals addressing both religious liberty and the role of the courts in deciding issues of marriage.

Fifteen proposals have been introduced concerning same-sex marriage since 2013. Seven of these measures specifically focus on religious liberty, ensuring that an individual's religious freedom regarding their beliefs about traditional marriage is respected. Specifically, the First Amendment Defense Act, introduced twice in the House and once in the Senate, prohibits the federal government from engaging in discriminatory action against an individual who, based upon religious or moral convictions, believes that marriage "should be recognized as the union of one man and one woman" or that "sexual relations are properly reserved for such marriage" (H.R. 2802, 2015). There has been one House Resolution proposed to establish a constitutional amendment that would establish that in the USA, marriage is defined as consisting between one man and one woman (H.J. Res 51, 2013). Finally, the Military Freedom Protection Act would require an accommodation for those with religious or moral convictions concerning the appropriate and inappropriate expression of human sexuality. Further, the bill would protect military chaplains from providing any service that would violate their rights of conscience. This bill is, in part, a reaction to complaints from military chaplains objecting to counseling LGBTQ service members or counseling spouses of same-sex couples. One of the most recent incidents involved a military chaplain who had chastened sailors for homosexuality and premarital sexual activity (Tighman 2015). The Military Freedom Protection Act has been referred to committee and has yet to make to the floor for a vote.

The remaining nine bills concerning same-sex marriage attempt to return the power to regulate marriage to the states. The State Marriage Defense Act was introduced four times from 2014 to 2015, a bill which would restore each state's definition of marriage and, specifically, ensure that marriage "shall not include any relationship which that state does not recognize as a marriage" and that the term spouse "shall not include an individual who is a party to a relationship that is not recognized as a marriage by the State" (S. 435, 2015). The remaining acts would prohibit judicial involvement in hearing questions regarding marriage issues, deferring this authority to the state.

At the state level, a number of Republican leaders also made statements addressing the ruling in *Hobby Lobby*, and initiated legislative proposals based upon the claims of religious liberty substantiated in this case. The response, however, was quite muted, particularly in comparison to the response in *Obergefell*. The governor of Mississippi declared, "I am very pleased the Supreme Court moved to uphold religious freedom today in its opinion in the *Hobby Lobby* case. Its decision confirms my position that our state did the right thing in enacting a state-level Religious Freedom Restoration Act and protecting religious liberty for Mississippians." He continued, stating,

> The federal RFRA requires the government to prove that substantially burdening religious freedom is necessary to achieve a truly compelling government interest. The Obama Administration had other options for implementing its policy, yet it chose to try and force individuals to violate their strongly held religious beliefs. This proves how out of line and self-important this administration is and how out of touch this president is with the basic principles of freedom on which this nation was founded (Mississippi News Now 2014).

Oklahoma governor Mary Fallin stated that affected women have "other alternatives, like Planned Parenthood" to obtain coverage of birth control. She also stated that *Hobby Lobby* only opposed coverage of 4 of the 24 types of FDA-approved contraceptives. "[Women] still will have access, they can still go out and do that legally in the United States" (Cheney 2014).

These reactions, in general, focus on religious liberty and reflect a largely libertarian understanding of the concept. In particular, Fallin's statement illustrates one of the primary libertarian arguments offered in response to *Hobby Lobby*, noting that the individual's choice to obtain contraception is still protected and it is up to individuals to obtain this medication on their own. The focus on religious liberty, found in the discourse over abortion and contraception coverage, is very clearly part of the political approach to attempt a ban on same-sex marriage or at least protect conscientious objectors from participating in any way in this practice.

Similar to what was found at the federal level, a limited number of legislative proposals were initiated in the states in response to the court's ruling. Twenty-one states submitted an amici curiae brief in support of the *Little Sisters of the Poor* appeal to the 10th Circuit Court following the denial of an exemption to the accommodation process. In the brief, it was stated that these states have a substantial interest in ensuring the protection of constituents' religious liberty. Specifically, the courts and federal government must "respect religious beliefs by refusing to second-guess religious adherents' line-drawing about what conduct is prohibited to them as sinful or immoral. The States' commitment to guarding the dignity of religious convictions is reflected in many of the States' own laws," 20 of which statutorily protect religious liberty (Brief of Texas, et al., *Little Sisters of the Poor v. Burwell,* No. 15-105, 10th Circuit Court of Appeals).

Immediately following the ruling in *Hobby Lobby*, Wisconsin governor Scott Walker declared that the state would stop enforcement of the contraceptive equality coverage act for companies with religious objections to the coverage of birth control. Although the ruling does not apply to state law, and it was later clarified by the Office of the Commissioner of Insurance that the state is still enforcing the contraceptive equity law, groups opposed to coverage of birth control welcomed Walker's statement (Vanegeren 2014). Further, three states (Colorado, North Dakota, and Tennessee) had initiatives on the ballot in the 2014 election cycle, with one from South Carolina proposed for the 2016 ballot. Two ballot initiatives in Colorado and North Dakota would establish personhood or legal protections for the fetus, which would also prohibit most hormonal forms of birth control; voters rejected both of these initiatives. Tennessee legislators passed the Legislative Powers Regarding Abortion Act, securing the authority of the state officials to regulate all aspects of abortion. This measure ensures that the states retain the authority to regulate this practice, inhibiting any attempts by the courts or federal officials from overreach.

The ruling in *Obergefell* has led to statements by conservative officials and to legislative proposals concerning same-sex marriage at the state level. Following the ruling, Arkansas governor Asa Hutchinson stated

> I am committed to ensuring the rights of pastors, religious institutions, and private individuals to exercise their freedom of conscience. It is my view that the Religious Freedom Restoration Act passed earlier this year accomplishes this purpose. I will continue to determine what legislative action is needed to address the myriad of legal issues that will result from the ruling and also what legislation is needed to protect the churches, pastors and religious institutions who cannot follow the dictates of the Court (Lanning 2015).

Further, the Republican caucus in Arkansas, in a statement signed by 24 Republican senators, declared that they would be "drafting legislation to ensure the rights of churches, pastors, and religious schools and institutions will not be infringed upon" (Lyon 2015). Alabama's governor was more direct in stating that "I have always believed in the Biblical definition of marriage as being between one man and one woman. That definition has been deeply rooted in our society for thousands of years. Regardless of today's ruling by the Supreme Court, I still believe in a one man and one woman definition of marriage" (Gardner 2015).

Legislators in four states (Florida, Ohio, Tennessee, and Texas) have submitted or expressed their intention to introduce bills addressing pastor protections following *Obergefell*. For example, in Texas, the Pastor Protection Act "protects houses of worship, religious organizations and their employees and clergy or ministers, from being required to participate in a marriage or celebration or a marriage if it would violate a sincerely held religious belief" (Akers 2015). In Tennessee, legislators proposed a similar piece of legislation, upon hearing of the Texas law in response to *Obergefell*. As stated by Representative Holt, one of the bill's sponsors, "To my friends of faith, to those who endear the principles of social conservatism, and to those who ascribe to the original intent of the Tenth Amendment, we must never give up." Further the other sponsor of the bill, Representative Terry, declared,

> I have had multiple constituents concerned with how the ruling may impact their church and their religious beliefs. If the issue is truly about equality of civil liberties and benefits, then this ruling should have minimal legal impact on churches, however, if the issue and the cause is about redefining marriage to require others to change their deeply held religious beliefs, then the concerns of many will be valid (Holt 2015).

Four states (Arkansas, Kentucky, Michigan, and Utah) have proposed bills to protect churches and clergy members from having to perform same-sex marriages or would protect religious practices from government interference more generally. For example, in Utah, a proposed bill would prohibit government officials from issuing marriage licenses, leaving this an entirely religious process to churches and religious organizations, with the state issuing and acknowledging civil contracts. Libertas, a libertarian think tank in Utah, supported this proposal, stating that the government should be kept out of the marriage business (Libertas Institute 2015).

Finally, three states (Arkansas, Indiana, and Michigan) proposed RFRAs, following the lead of 19 states that had previously passed RFRAs. In the Supreme Court case, *City of Boerne v. Flores* (1997), the court ruled that the federal RFRA is not applicable to state or local ordinances. In the wake of this ruling, 8 states had passed state-level RFRAs by 1999, with 11 passing such laws by 2014. Arkansas and Indiana passed state RFRAs in 2015, both of which caused substantial controversy given the absence of any protections for same-sex individuals from employment or housing discrimination.[3] Upon passage of Indiana's RFRA, statements made by business owners regarding the right to deny service to same-sex couples based upon their religious objection further fueled the tension surrounding the bill. The heads of a number of major corporations released statements expressing their opposition to the bill, with a number of states and localities refusing to fund travel to the state of Indiana, and some performers canceling their tour stops in Indiana. A provision was later added to the measure that was designed to prevent discrimination against LGBTQ individuals, although controversy surrounding the state's RFRA remains (Cook 2015).

During the 2015 legislative session, RFRAs were proposed in 16 states; in Arizona, S.B. 1062 was passed into law, which would expand the state's RFRA to include for-profit corporations under the umbrella of the entities receiving such protection. Governor Jan Brewer vetoed the bill. Further, three states (Missouri, Oklahoma, and Texas) also sought to expand their RFRAs; the proposal in Texas would replace the term "substantial burden" with "any burden," thus restricting the state from imposing an act that places a burden on an individual or organizations' religious liberty (Texas H.J. Res. 55, 2015).

The analysis of the discourse and legislative attempts following the *Hobby Lobby* and *Obergefell* rulings reveals a number of political statements as well as federal and state laws, all designed to protect the religious liberty of those opposed to some acts that are now legal—and often socially acceptable—such as abortion and contraception, same-sex marriage, and climate change. While the bulk of these proposals focus on LGBTQ issues, this focus is a result of the understanding by some of the ruling in *Obergefell* as threatening the right of religious liberty. Therefore, these legislative attempts, together with the discourse and public policy on science,

---

[3] Although 19 states had already passed RFRAs, Indiana's proposal produced substantial controversy given the absence of a statewide antidiscrimination order.

Hobby Lobby, and same-sex marriage, represent a broader trend of emphasis on religious protections. Virtually all of the proposals, enacted laws, and public statements during this time period express the need to ensure the right of individuals to religious conscience. In the case of *Obergefell*, some legislators acknowledge that it is unlikely that the government can compel religious institutions to officiate same-sex marriages; these proposals serve to reassure those concerned of a potential requirement in the future, while at the same time further emphasizing the threat in such an interventionist government (Estep 2015; Holt 2015).

If state and federal legislators continue in this fashion, it is clear that a greater number of laws designed to protect religious liberty—pertaining to a vast number of distinct issue areas—will be developed. Reflecting a largely libertarian view, these trends, seen in both discourse and policy, allow greater leeway for individuals and entities to refuse to participate in any activity that violates their religious liberty. At the same time, these laws and statements promote a certain vision of what is moral or acceptable within the public sphere but also as a private decision. If this approach continues, religious objections to same-sex marriage, abortion, and the provision of birth control—or anything at all that offends one's conscience such as evidence of climate change or vaccinations—will be widely accepted, and protected, around the country. Thus, while it is too early to determine how this tension within the GOP will be resolved, the case of *Hobby Lobby*, and, more generally, the discourse over religious liberty, merges a conservative topic with more libertarian discourse and legislation.

REFERENCES

Akers S. Two Florida State lawmakers sponsor version of pastor protection act. Charisma News. 2015 July 21. http://www.charismanews.com/politics/50370-scott-plakon-marriage-law. Accessed 25 July 2015.

Al-Faruque F. Republicans hail Hobby Lobby decision as religious victory. The Hill. 2014. Jun 30.

Alvarez JE. Are corporations subjects of international law. Santa Clara J Int Law. 2011;9(1):1–35.

Bazelon E. Charmaine Yoest's cheerful war on abortion. The New York Times. 2012 Nov 2.

Belluck P. Complex science at issue in politics of fetal pain. The New York Times. 2013 Sept 16.

Benson Gold R, Nash E. Troubling trend: more states hostile to abortion rights as middle ground shrinks. Guttmacher Policy Review 2012;15(1): 14-19.

Bump P. Jim Inhofe's snowball has disproven climate change once and for all. The Washington Post. 2015 Feb 26.

Burke C. GOP: high court Hobby Lobby ruling 'victory for religious freedom.' Newsmax. 2014 Jun 30.

Burstein P, Hirsh E. Interest organizations, information, and policy innovation in the U.S. Congress. Sociological Forum. 2007;22(2): 174-199.

Cheney K. GOP governors see scant Hobby Lobby political fallout. Politico. 2014 Jul 13.

Cismas I. Cammarano SN. Whose right and who's right? The US Supreme Court v. The European Court of human rights on corporate exercise of religion. B U Int Law J. 2016;34(1):00–0.

Cohen J. Minimalism about human rights: the most we can hope for? J Polit Philos. 2004;12(2):190–213.

Colmes A. James inhofe: there is no global warming because god. FOX News Radio. 2015 Mar 7. http://radio.foxnews.com/2015/03/07/james-inhofe-there-is-no-global-warming-because-god/. Accessed 27 July 2015.

Cook T. Gov. mike pence signs 'Religious Freedom' bill in private. Indy Star. 2015 Apr 2.

Douzinas C. Human rights and empire: the political philosophy of cosmopolitanism. London: Routledge; 2007.

Estep B. Kentucky legislator pre-files bill about performing same-sex marriage ceremonies. Kentucky.com. 2015 July 3. http://www.kentucky.com/2015/07/03/3929716/kentucky-legislator-pre-files.html. Accessed 3 July 2015.

Fein RA. Symposium foreword. Const Comment. 2015;30:213–463.

Fisher DR, Waggle J, Leifeld P. Where does political polarization come from? Locating polarization within the US climate change debate. Am Behav Sci. 2013;57(1):70–92.

Gardner M. Alabama politicians and leaders issue statements in response to supreme court same-sex marriage ruling. WHNT19. 2015 June 16. http://whnt.com/2015/06/26/alabama-politicians-and-leaders-issue-statements-in-response-to-supreme-court-same-sex-marriage-ruling/. Accessed 26 Jun 2015.

Greenfield K. In defense of corporate persons. Const Comment. 2015;30: 309–463.

Holt A. Rep. Holt introduces pastor protection act in reaction to gay marriage ruling. State Representative Andy Holt. 2015 June 26. http://www.andy-holt4tn.com/rep-holt-introduces-pastor-protection-act-in-reaction-to-gay-marriage-ruling/. Accessed 27 July 2015.

Houghton JT, Ding Y, Griggs DJ, Noguer M, van der Winden PJ, Dai, X. Climate change 2001: The scientific basis. Cambridge University Press: Cambridge, UK. 2001.

Huckabee M. Values. http://www.mikehuckabee.com/family-values. Accessed 29 July 2015.

Isiksel T. The rights of man and the rights of the man-made: corporations and human rights. Paper presented at Freie Universität Berlin Kolloquium zur Praktischen Philosophie. June 2015.

Jacques PJ, Dunlap RE, Freeman M. The organization of denial: Conservative think tanks and environmental scepticism. Environmental Politics, 2008;17: 349-385.

Joo TW. Corporate speech & the rights of others. Const Comment. 2015;30: 335–463.

Khazan O. Can an abortion be undone? The Atlantic. 2015 Mar 27.

Lanning C. Ark. Senate republicans to propose legislation securing religious freedoms. 5newsonline. 2015 July 2. http://5newsonline.com/2015/07/02/ark-senate-republicans-to-propose-legislation-securing-religious-freedoms/. Accessed 1 Aug 2015.

Libertas Institute. Statement on U.S. Supreme Court ruling legalizing same-sex marriage nationwide. 2015 Jun 26.

Life News. 41 quotes from medical textbooks prove human life begins at conception. 2015 Jan 8. http://www.lifenews.com/2015/01/08/41-quotes-from-medical-textbooks-prove-human-life-begins-at-conception/

Life News. Los Angeles claims ultrasound photos aren't "objective scientific fact." 2014 Dec 29. http://www.lifenews.com/2014/12/29/los-angeles-times-claims-ultrasound-photos-arent-objective-scientific-fact/

Life News. Scientific fact: human life at conception, or fertilization. 2013a Nov 18. http://www.lifenews.com/2013/11/8/undisputed-scientific-fact-human-life-begins-at-conception-or-fertilization/.

Lyon J. Arkansas state GOP lawmakers plan legislation to address gay marriage. Times Record. 2015 July 3.

Lupu IC. Hobby Lobby and the dubious enterprise of religious exemptions. Harv J Law Gend. 2015;38(1).

McCright A, Dunlap R. Defeating Kyoto: the conservative movement's impact on U.S. climate change policy. Soc Probl. 2003;50(3):348–73.

Mississippi News Now. Governor Bryant please with Hobby Lobby ruling. 2014 Jun 30.

Orsekes N. The scientific consensus on climate change. Science 2004; 306(5702).

Peterson LE. Human rights and bilateral investment treaties. rights and democracy: international center for human rights and democratic development. Montreal (2009).

Piety TR. Why personhood matters. Const Comment. 2015;30:101–28.

Pollman E. Reconceiving corporate personhood. Utah Law Rev. 2011;4:1629–75.

Report of the South Dakota task force to study abortion. 2005 Dec.

Ripken SK. Corporations are people too: a multi-dimensional approach to the corporate personhood puzzle. FJCFL. 2009;15:97.

RNC Statement. RNC statement on Burwell v. Hobby Lobby. GOP. 2014 Jun 30. https://www.gop.com/rnc-statement-on-burwell-v-hobby-lobby. Accessed 25 July 2015.

Robertson J. Fetal pain laws: scientific and constitutional controversy. Bill of Health: Petrie-Flow Center. 2013 Jun 26.

Robillard K. Rep. Joe Walsh: abortion never saves mom's life—Kevin Robillard. POLITICO. 2012 Oct 19. http://www.politico.com/news/stories/1012/82620.html. Accessed 26 July 2015.

Sepinwall AJ. Conscience and complicity: assessing pleas for religious exemptions in Hobby Lobby's wake. U Chi Law Rev. 2015;82(4).

Sklar MJ. The corporate reconstruction of American capitalism, 1890–1916: the market, the law, and politics: Cambridge University Press; 1988.

Stewart J. Burn noticed. The Daily Show. 2014 Sept 22.

Taub JS. Is Hobby Lobby a tool for limiting corporate constitutional rights? Const Comment. 2015;30:403–63.

"The Supreme Court has Legalized Same-Sex Marriage: Now What?" National Review Online. 2015 Jun 27.

Tighman A. Chaplain faces possible discharge for being 'intolerant'. Military Times. 2015 Mar 11. http://www.militarytimescom/story/military/2015/03/10/chaplain-fired/24699275.

Vanegeren J. Wisconsin insurance commissioner office clarifies it is still enforcing contraceptive equity law. The Capital Times. 2014 July 25. http://hostmadisoncom/news/local/writers/jessica_vanegeren/wisconsin-insurance-commissioner-office-clarifies-it-is-still-enforcing-contraceptive/article_ceb36140-140f-11e4-a0b4-0019bb2963f4.html. Accessed 26 July 2015.

Wilke S, Talcott S. Harvard Kennedy school's John P. Holdren named Obama's science advisor. Press Release, Harvard, University, Belfer Center for Science and International Affairs. 2008 Dec 20.

Court Cases, Appeals, and Briefs

Brief of Texas, et al, *Little Sisters of the Poor v. Burwell,* No. 15-105, 10th Circuit Court of Appeal.

Burwell v. Hobby Lobby, 573 U.S. ___ (2014).

Citizens United v. Federal Election Commission, 558 U.S. 310 (2010).

City of Boerne v. Flores, 521 U.S. 507 (1997).

Doe v. Bolton, 410 U.S. 179 (1973).

Eisenstadt v. Baird, 405 U.S. 438 (1972).

Employment Division v. Smith, 494 U.S. 872 (1990).

Griswold v. Connecticut, 381 U.S. 479 (1965).

Harris v. McRae, 448 U.S. 297 (1980).

King v. Burwell, (2015).

Lying v. Northwest Indian Cemetery Protective Association, 485 U.S. 439 (1988).

Notre Dame v. Burwell, No. 13-3853, 7th circuit court, May 19, 2015.

Obergefell v. Hodges, 576 U.S. ___ (2015).

Roe v. Wade, 410 U.S. 113 (1973).

Wheaton College v. Burwell, No. 14-2396, 10th circuit court, July 1, 2015.

© The Editor(s) (if applicable) and The Author(s) 2016   237
A. Von Hagel, D. Mansbach, *Reproductive Rights in the Age of Human Rights,* DOI 10.1057/978-1-137-53952-6

FEDERAL LAW

Abortion-Related Discrimination in Governmental Activities regarding Training and Licensing of Physicians, 42 U.S.C. §238n(a)(1) (1996).

Consolidated Appropriations Act, 2005. P.L. 108-447, Division F, § 508(d) (2005).

Coverage of Preventative Healthcare Services, 42 U.S.C. § 300gg-13(a)(4) (2010).

Department of Health and Human Services Appropriations Act for Fiscal Year 1994, P. L. No. 103-112, § 509, 107 Stat. 1113 (1994).

Discrimination Based on Sex or Blindness, 20 U.S.C. § 1681 (1972).

Exemption and Accommodations in Connection with Coverage of Preventive Health Service, 45 C.F.R. § 147.131(a) (2014).

Free Exercise of Religion Protected, 42 U.S. Code § 2000bb–1 (2009).

Health Programs Extension Act, P. L. No. 93-45, 197 (1973).

Hyde Amendment, P. L. No. 95-205, § 101, 91 Stat. 1460 (1978).

Hyde Amendment, P. L. No. 95-480, § 210, 92 Stat. 1586 (1979).

The Patient Protection and Affordable Care Act, P.L. 111-148 (2010)

© The Editor(s) (if applicable) and The Author(s) 2016
A. Von Hagel, D. Mansbach, *Reproductive Rights in the Age of Human Rights*, DOI 10.1057/978-1-137-53952-6

Proposed Laws

Abortion Insurance Full Disclosure Act, H.R. 3279, (2013).
Abortion Insurance Full Disclosure Act, S. 1848 (2013).
Care for Life Act, H.R. 7091, (2008).
Departments of Labor, Health and Human Services, and Education, and Related Agencies Appropriations Act, H.R. 3020, (2015).
First Amendment Defense Act, H.R. 2802 (2015).
Health Care Conscience Rights Act, H.R. 940 (2015).
Health Care Conscience Rights Act, S. 1204 (2015).
Health Plan Notice Requirement Act, H.R. 3953 (2013).
No Taxpayer Funding of Abortion and Abortion Insurance Full Disclosure Act, H.R. 7 (2013).
Post Abortion Support and Services Act. S. 2271, (2002).
Proposing an Amendment to the Constitution of the United States Relating to Marriage, H.J. Res 51 (2013).
Protecting Life and Taxpayers Act, H.R. 3197 (2015).
State Marriage Defense Act, S. 435, (2015).
Taxpayer Conscience Protection Act, H.R. 489 (2015).
Taxpayer's Freedom of Conscience Act, H.R. 777 (2005).
Title X Family Planning Act, S. 85 (2009).
Title X Abortion Provider Prohibition Act, H.R. 4133 (2007).
H.R. 399 (2015).
H.J. Res 51 (2013).

© The Editor(s) (if applicable) and The Author(s) 2016
A. Von Hagel, D. Mansbach, *Reproductive Rights in the Age of Human Rights*, DOI 10.1057/978-1-137-53952-6

STATE LAWS

Ariz. Rev. Stat. Ann. § A 36-2907 (1988)
Kansas Stat. Ann. § 65-443, (2012)
N.D. Cent. Code § 14-02.3-01 (1979)
Miss. Code Ann. § 41-79-5, (1987)
R.I. Gen. Laws § 27-18-28 (1989)
18 PA. Cons. Stat. Ann. § 3215(e) (1993)
South Dakota Codified Law 28-6-4.5 (1978)

© The Editor(s) (if applicable) and The Author(s) 2016   243
A. Von Hagel, D. Mansbach, *Reproductive Rights in the Age of Human Rights*, DOI 10.1057/978-1-137-53952-6

Proposed State Laws

Arizona, S.B. 1062 (2014).
Arizona, S.B. 2625 (2012).
Indiana, S.B. 101 (2015).
South Dakota, S.B. 128 (2014).
Texas, H.J. Res. 55, (2015).

© The Editor(s) (if applicable) and The Author(s) 2016
A. Von Hagel, D. Mansbach, *Reproductive Rights in the Age
of Human Rights*, DOI 10.1057/978-1-137-53952-6

INDEX

© The Editor(s) (if applicable) and The Author(s) 2016
A. Von Hagel, D. Mansbach, *Reproductive Rights in the Age of Human Rights*, DOI 10.1057/978-1-137-53952-6